The New Revised General Electric Microwave Guide and Cookbook

Random House
New York

Published in the United States by Random House, Inc., New York, and simultaneously in Canada by Random House of Canada Limited, Toronto.

Library of Congress Cataloging in Publication Data
Main entry under title:
The New revised General Electric microwave guide and cookbook.
    Rev. ed. of: The General Electric microwave guide & cookbook. c1977.
    Includes index.
    1. Microwave cookery. I. General Electric Company. II. General Electric
Company. The General Electric microwave guide & cookbook.
TX832.N48   1983   641.5′882   82-42828
ISBN 0-394-53151-5

Manufactured in the United States of America

This Cookbook and the Innovative New DUAL WAVE™ Microwave System from GE

General Electric introduced its first countertop microwave oven, the JET 80, in 1972. Since that time, there have been extensive refinements in oven features. In 1974 GE introduced the Microthermometer™ temperature probe which monitors the internal temperature of foods, and also added touch control features to its product line. In 1977 GE introduced multiple power levels, and in 1980, Auto Cook and Auto Roast, features which literally take the guesswork out of microwaving many foods.

The latest innovation, however, is not another new feature. It is a new design of the oven's distribution system, the new DUAL WAVE™ Microwave System.

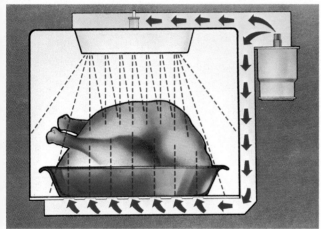

DUAL WAVE™ Microwave System distributes energy from both top and bottom, similar to regular conventional ovens for more even heat distribution. As a result the cook can pay less attention to the food — less stirring, turning or rotating — while it's in the oven.

Microwave ovens with the DUAL WAVE™ Microwave System deliver 625 watts of energy at high power, the same wattage that was available with earlier GE microwave ovens. Wattage determines how fast the food cooks. Since wattage has not changed from earlier models, microwaving time has not increased or decreased. With this new system, the only change is that generally less attention is necessary to make the food cook evenly.

When using earlier GE ovens, or brands other than GE, with this cookbook, you will find that your oven's cooking time will be similar to cooking times specified here. However, depending on your oven's microwave energy distribution system, you may find that you need to give the food more attention — more rotating, turning over or stirring. Also, you will want to read the introductory pages to the food chapters, especially the meat and baking sections, paying special attention to the size of foods recommended. The DUAL WAVE™ Microwave System has made it possible to cook some larger size foods which may not microwave well in some other ovens.

See Microwaving Adapting Guide, pages 17 to 35 for more information. Pages 30 and 31 may be especially helpful, if your oven does not have a DUAL WAVE™ Microwave System.

General Electric Microwaving products satisfy individual needs.

GE provides a variety of microwave ovens with the new DUAL WAVE™ Microwave System. Each oven provides a special variety of features so cooks can select the type of microwaving which suits their needs.

JET202 Features:
Variable Power Control, Time Cook, 25 Minute Timer, Recipe Guide and Double-Duty™ Two Position Shelf.

JET210 Features:
Electronic Digital Readout Panel, Time Cook, Temp Cook, Auto Roast Control, Defrost, 10 Power Levels, Hold/Timer, Three Stage Cooking, Clock, Double Duty™ Two Position Shelf.

JET230 Featues:
Electronic Digital Readout Panel, Time Cook, Temp Cook, Defrost, 10 Power Levels, Hold/Timer, Three Stage Cooking, Clock, Double Duty™ Two Position Shelf, Automatic Cooking Control, Including Auto Cook, Auto Roast with Temp Hold and Simmer Setting, and Auto Defrost.

2 How to use this book

This extraordinary new guide and cookbook is the result of over 20 years of microwave oven research and testing. It was written to help you adapt your favorite recipes and just as important, increase the use of your microwave oven.

Much of the comprehensive consumer oriented information you will find throughout this book is presented in clearly illustrated step-by-step photographs and helpful hints. We suggest you start with the introductory guide which will help teach you the principles and techniques of microwaving. In each chapter we show you what to do, what to expect, how the food should look, and how to tell when it's done. These adapting tips and how-to ideas will soon become your *basics* in fast, nutritious, everyday good cooking. You'll soon learn that using your microwave oven is not only faster, but often easier than conventional cooking.

This cookbook covers all the basic features of your microwave oven. However, some of our easy-to-use automatic features are covered in your oven's use and care book, so check both sources for complete information.

Paula Cooper Matthews

Consumer Information Testing Laboratory

Many thanks to home economists:

Diana Williams Hansen
Louise Meek
Beverly Sheldon Kastan
Judith Watson Brown
Rhonda Nahrwold DeVaux
Janet Walther Hamblen
and Terry Taylor Stacy

All foods pictured were microwaved in General Electric microwave oven models Jet 130, Jet 230 and JBV 42 according to recipes in this book and photographed exactly as they came from the oven.

Precautions to Avoid Possible Exposure to Excessive Microwave Energy

1. **Do Not Attempt** to operate the oven with the door open since open-door operation can result in harmful exposure to microwave energy. It is important not to defeat or tamper with the safety interlocks.
2. **Do Not Place** any object between the oven front face and the door or allow soil or cleaner residue to accumulate on sealing surfaces.
3. **Do Not Operate** the oven if it is damaged. It is particularly important that the oven door close properly and that there is no damage to the (1) door (bent), (2) hinges and latches (broken or loosened), (3) door seals and sealing surfaces.
4. **The Oven Should** not be adjusted or repaired by anyone except properly qualified service personnel.

Contents

4   Heating or Reheating Chart

1. Directions below are for reheating already-cooked foods at refrigerator or room temperature. Use microwave oven safe containers.

2. Cover most foods (see tips) for fastest heating. Exceptions are rare or medium meats, some sandwiches, griddle foods like pancakes and baked foods.

3. Where appropriate, use the automatic food temperature control for accurate heating. Place probe horizontally so tip is in center of food. Bubbling around edges of dish is normal, since center is last to heat. Suggested serving temperatures are given for most foods. Young children usually prefer cooler food, generally about 20° lower. Adjust temperatures to your personal taste. Stir foods before serving.

4. Be sure foods are heated through before serving. Steaming or bubbling around edges does not necessarily mean food is heated throughout. As a general rule, hot foods produce an area warm to the touch in center of underside of dish.

ITEM	Amount	Suggested Serving Temp.	Power Level	Approximate Time, Min.
Appetizers				
Saucy; such as meatballs, riblets, cocktail franks, etc.	1 to 2 servings	150°	HI (10)	1½-4
	3 to 4 servings	150°	HI (10)	4-6
½ cup/serving				
Dips; cream or process cheese	½ cup	130°	Med (5)	2½-3½
	1 cup	130°	Med (5)	3-5
Pastry bites; small pizzas, egg rolls, etc.	2 to 4 servings		HI (10)	1-2

Tip: Cover saucy appetizers with wax paper. Cover dips with plastic wrap. Do not cover pastry bites, they will not be crisp.

ITEM	Amount	Suggested Serving Temp.	Power Level	Approximate Time, Min.
Plate of Leftovers				
Meat plus 2 vegetables	1 plate	150°-160°	HI (10)	2-4

Tip: Probe works well in saucy dishes or vegetables (use in largest serving) but not in meat slices. Cover plate of food with waxed paper or plastic wrap.

ITEM	Amount	Suggested Serving Temp.	Power Level	Approximate Time, Min.
Meats and Main Dishes				
Saucy Main Dishes: chop suey, spaghetti, creamed chicken, chili, stew, macaroni and cheese, etc.	1 to 2 servings	150°-160°	HI (10)	3-7
	3 to 4 servings	150°-160°	HI (10)	8-14
¾-1 cup/serving	1 can 16-oz.	150°-160°	HI (10)	4½-6
Thinly sliced roasted meat:				
Rare beef roast, minimum time; Medium Rare, maximum time	1 to 2 servings		Med-HI (7)	1-2
	3 to 4 servings		Med-HI (7)	2-3½
3 to 4-oz./serving				
Well done; beef, pork, ham, poultry, etc.	1 to 2 servings		Med-HI (7)	1½-3
	3 to 4 servings		Med-HI (7)	3-5
Steaks, chops, ribs, other meat pieces:				
Rare beef steak	1 to 2 servings	130°	Med-HI (7)	2½-4
	3 to 4 servings	130°	Med-HI (7)	5-9
Well done beef, chops, ribs, etc.	1 to 2 servings	150°	Med-HI (7)	2-3
	3 to 4 servings	150°	Med-HI (7)	4-7
Hamburgers or meat loaf	1 to 2 servings		HI (10)	¾-2
4-oz./serving	3 to 4 servings		HI (10)	1½-3½
Chicken pieces	1 to 2 pieces		HI (10)	¾-2
	3 to 4 pieces		HI (10)	2-3½
Hot Dogs and sausages	1 to 2		HI (10)	1-2
	3 to 4		HI (10)	2½-3½
Rice and pasta	1 to 2 servings	150°	HI (10)	1-2
⅔-¾ cup/serving				
Topped or mixed with sauce	1 to 2 servings	150°-160°	HI (10)	3-6
⅔-¾ cup/serving	3 to 4 servings	150°-160°	HI (10)	8-12

Tip: Cover saucy main dishes with plastic wrap. Cover other main dishes and meats with waxed paper. Do not cover rare or medium rare meats.

ITEM	Amount	Suggested Serving Temp.	Power Level	Approximate Time, Min.
Sandwiches & Soups				
Moist filling: Sloppy joe, barbecue, ham salad, etc. in bun ⅓ cup/serving	1 to 2 servings		Med-HI (7)	1-2½
	3 to 4 servings		Med-HI (7)	2½-4
Thick meat-cheese filling; with firm bread	1 to 2 servings		Med-HI (7)	2-3
	3 to 4 servings		Med-HI (7)	4-5
Soup				
Water based	1 to 2 servings	150°-170°	HI (10)	2-6
1 cup/serving	3 to 4 servings	150°-170°	HI (10)	7-11
	1 can 10-oz.	150°-170°	HI (10)	6-7
Milk based	1 to 2 servings	140°	Med-HI (7)	3-8
1 cup/serving	3 to 4 servings	140°	Med-HI (7)	10-14
	1 can 10-oz. reconstituted	140°	Med-HI (7)	7-8

Tip: Use paper towel or napkin to cover sandwiches. Cover soups with waxed paper or plastic wrap.

ITEM	Amount	Suggested Serving Temp.	Power Level	Approximate Time, Min.
Vegetables				
Small pieces: peas, beans, corn, etc.	1 to 2 servings	150°-160°	HI (10)	1-3
½ cup/serving	3 to 4 servings	150°-160°	HI (10)	3-4½
	1 can 16-oz.	150°-160°	HI (10)	3½-4½
Large pieces or whole: asparagus spears, corn on the cob, etc.	1 to 2 servings		HI (10)	1½-3
	3 to 4 servings		HI (10)	3-4½
	1 can 16-oz.		HI (10)	4-4½
Mashed	1 to 2 servings	150°-160°	HI (10)	1-3
½ cup/serving	3 to 4 servings	150°-160°	HI (10)	4-7

Tip: Cover vegetables for most even heating.

ITEM	Amount	Suggested Serving Temp.	Power Level	Approximate Time, Min.
Sauces				
Dessert: chocolate, butterscotch	½ cup	125°	HI (10)	½-1½
	1 cup	125	HI (10)	1½-2½
Meat or main dish, chunky type; giblet gravy, spaghetti sauce, etc.	½ cup	150°-160°	HI (10)	1½-2½
	1 cup	150°-160°	HI (10)	2½-4
	1 can 16-oz.	150°-160°	HI (10)	4-6
Creamy type	½ cup	140°-150°	HI (10)	1-1½
	1 cup	140°-150°	HI (10)	2-2½

Tip: Cover food to prevent spatter.

ITEM	Amount	Suggested Serving Temp.	Power Level	Approximate Time, Min.
Bakery Foods				
Cake, coffee cake, doughnuts, sweet rolls, nut or fruit bread	1 piece		Low (3)	½-1
	2 pieces		Low (3)	1½-2
	4 pieces		Low (3)	1½-2½
	9-in. cake or 12 rolls or doughnuts		Low (3)	2-4
Dinner rolls, muffins	1		Med (5)	¼-½
	2		Med (5)	½-¾
	4		Med (5)	½-1
	6-8		Med (5)	¾-1½
Pie: fruit, nut or custard	1 slice		HI (10)	½-1
⅛ or 9-in. pie = 1 slice	2 slices		HI (10)	1-1½
(use minimum time for custard)	4 slices		Med-HI (7)	2½-3½
	9-in. pie		Med-HI (7)	5-7

ITEM	Amount	Suggested Serving Temp.	Power Level	Approximate Time, Min.
Griddle Foods				
Pancakes, French Toast or Waffles (3″ × 4″)				
Plain, no topping	2 or 3 pieces		HI (10)	½-1
Syrup & butter	2 or 3 pieces		HI (10)	1-1¼
With 2 sausage patties (cooked)	2 or 3 pieces		HI (10)	1¼-1½

ITEM	Amount	Suggested Serving Temp.	Power Level	Approximate Time, Min.
Beverages				
Coffee, tea, cider	1 to 2 cups	160°-170°	HI (10)	1½-3½
other water based	3 to 4 cups	160°-170°	HI (10)	6-7
Cocoa, other milk based	1 to 2 cups	140°	Med-HI (7)	2½-7
	3 to 4 cups	140°	Med-HI (7)	7-10

Tip: Do not cover bakery foods, griddle foods (pancakes, etc.) or beverages.

6 Defrosting Chart

1. Food packaged in all-paper or plastic packages may be defrosted without unwrapping. If food is foil wrapped, remove foil and place food in cooking dish for defrosting.
2. After first half of cooking time, unwrap package and check food. Turn food over, if necessary; break apart or separate food if possible. On very large foods like turkey, some shielding of thin wing or leg areas may be necessary.
3. Be sure large meats are completely defrosted (or, on roasts allow extra microwaving time). Turkeys may be placed under running water until giblets can be removed.
4. When defrosted, food should be cool but softened in all areas. If still slightly icy, return to microwave oven very briefly, or let stand a few minutes.

POWER LEVEL: Defrost (3)

FOOD	First Half Time, Min.	Second Half Time, Min.	Comments
Meat			
Bacon (1 pkg.)	3½-5	none	Place unopened package in oven. Microwave just until strips can be separated.
Franks (1-lb.)	4-5	none	Place unopened package in oven. Microwave just until franks can be separated.
Ground: beef & pork (1-lb.)	4	4-6	Turn over after first 4 minutes.
(2-lbs.)	6	6-8	Scrape off softened meat after second half of time. Set aside. Break up remaining block, microwave 5-6 minutes more.
(5-lbs.)	12	12-14	Scrape off softened meat after second half of time. Set aside. Break up remaining block, microwave 11-12 minutes more.
Roast: Beef	3-4 per lb.	3-4 per lb.	Place unwrapped roast in oven. After half of time turn roast over. Defrost for second half of time. Let stand for 30 minutes.
Roast: Pork	5-6 per lb.	5-6 per lb.	Place wrapped package in oven. Turn over after first half of time. After second half of time, separate pieces with table knife. Let stand to complete defrosting.
Spareribs, pork (1 pkg.)	2-4 per lb.	2-4 per lb.	
Steaks, chops & cutlets; beef, lamb, pork & Veal	2-4½ per lb.	2-4½ per lb.	Place wrapped package in oven. Turn over after first half of time. After second half of time, separate pieces with table knife, let stand to complete defrosting.
Sausage, bulk (1-lb. tray)	2½	2½-4½	Turn over after first 2½ minutes.
(1-lb. roll)	2	2-4	Turn over after first half of time.
Sausage, link (1½ to 1-lb.)	2	1½-2½	No turn needed.
Sausage, patties (12-oz. pkg.)	1	1-2	No turn needed.
Poultry			
Chicken, broiler-fryer, cut up (2½ to 3½-lb.)	7-8	7-8	Place wrapped chicken in oven. Unwrap and turn over after half of time. After second half of time, separate pieces and place in cooking dish. Microwave 2-4 minutes more, if necessary.
Whole (2½ to 3½-lb.)	9-11	9-11	Place wrapped chicken in oven. After half of time unwrap and turn over chicken. Shield warm areas with foil.
Cornish hen	4-6 per lb.	5-6 per lb.	Place wrapped package in oven breast side up. Turn package over after first half of time.
Duckling	2-3 per lb.	2-3 per lb.	Place wrapped duckling in oven. After first half of time, unwrap and turn over into cooking dish. Shield warm areas with foil.
Turkey	4½-5½ per lb.	4½-5½ per lb.	Place unwrapped turkey breast side down. After first half of time, remove wrapper and shield warm areas with foil. Turn turkey breast side up for second half of time. Run cool water into cavity until giblets and neck can be removed. Let soak in cool water for 1-2 hours or refrigerate overnight to complete defrosting.

POWER LEVEL: Defrost (3)

FOOD	First Half Time, Min.	Second Half Time, Min.	Comments
Fish & Seafood			
Fillets (1-lb.)	4	4-6	Place unopened package in oven. (If fish is frozen in water, place in cooking dish.) Rotate ½ turn after first half of time. After second half of time, hold under cold water to separate.
Steaks (6-oz.)	2-3	none	
Whole fish (8 to 10-oz.)	2	2-4	Place fish in cooking dish. Turn over after first half of time. After second half of time, rinse cavity with cold water to complete defrosting.
Shellfish, small pieces (1-lb.)	7-8	none	Spread shellfish in single layer in baking dish.
Shellfish, blocks Crab meat (6-oz. pkg.)	4-5	none	Place block in casserole.
Oysters (10-oz. can)	6½-8	none	Place block in casserole. Break up with fork after first half of time.
Scallops (1-lb. pkg.)	7-9	none	Place unopened package in oven.
Shellfish, large Crab legs—1 to 2 (8 to 10-oz.)	4-6	none	Arrange in cooking dish.
Lobster tails—1 to 2 (6 to 9-oz.)	6-8	none	Arrange in cooking dish.
Whole lobster or crab (1½-lb.)	8-9	8-9	Place in cooking dish with light underside up. Turn over after first half of time.
Breads, Cakes			
Bread or buns (1-lb.)	3-4	none	
Heat & serve rolls (7-oz. pkg.)	2-4	none	
Coffee Cake (11 to 14¾-oz.)	3½-5	none	
Coffee ring (10-oz. pkg.)	3½-4	none	
Sweet rolls (8¾ to 12-oz.)	2½-4	none	
Doughnuts (1 to 3)	1½-4½	none	
Doughnuts, glazed (1 box of 12)	2-3	none	
French Toast (2 slices)	5½-6½	none	
Cake, frosted 2 to 3 layer (17-oz.)	2-2½	none	
Cake, filled or topped 1 layer (12½ to 16-oz.)	2-3	none	
Pound cake (11¼-oz.)	2	none	
Cheesecake, plain or fruit top (17 to 19-oz.)	5-7	none	
Crunch cakes & cupcakes	½ to 1 each	none	
Fruit or nut pie (8-in.)	8-10	none	
Cream or custard pie (14-oz.)	2-3	none	
Fruit			
Fresh (10 to 16-oz.)	6-11	none	Place package in oven. Remove foil or metal. After minimum time, break up with fork. Repeat if necessary.
Plastic pouch—1 to 2 (10-oz. pkg.)	5-10	none	Place package in oven. Flex package once.

8 Convenience Food Chart

1. Most convenience foods can be reheated by microwave only, since they are already cooked. Always use microwave safe utensils (glass or plastic). For foods needing browning or crisping, conventional baking is recommended.
2. Remove food from foil containers over ¾-in. high.
3. See "Freezer to Table Convenience Foods," page 38 for additional tips on defrosting and heating.
4. Amounts can be increased. To cook multiple packages, add times together.

FOOD	Container	Cover	Power Level & Time (or Internal Temp.)		Comments
Appetizers & Snacks Pastry Bites	Microwave safe dish	No	HI (10)	½ to 2 min.	
Frozen prepared sandwiches	Paper towel	No	HI (10)	1-2 min. per sandwich	Remove from foil package and wrap in paper towel. Rotate dish ½ turn after half of time.
Eggs & Cheese					
Scrambled egg substitute (8-oz. carton)	Microwave safe dish	No	HI (10)	3½ to 4½ min.	Microwave about 1 minute per ¼ cup mixture. Stir after half of time.
Cheese souffle (12-oz.)	Microwave safe 8" pie plate and custard cups	No	Defrost (3) Med-HI (7)	9 to 13 min. 9 to 11 min.	To Defrost: Place in 8-in. pie plate. Stir twice. To Cook: Divide between 3 or 4 buttered custard cups, 6 or 7-oz. Rearrange after 5 minutes. Souffles are done when center is set.
Scrambled eggs breakfast (6¼-oz.) with sausage and hash brown potatoes	Package paper tray	Package cover	Med (5)	4 to 6 min.	Remove paper tray from carton, turn back oven film to expose potatoes.
Welsh rarebit (10-oz.)	Microwave safe dish	No	HI (10)	5 to 6 min.	Stir before serving.
Fish & Shellfish					
Crab or shrimp newburg (6½-oz.)	Package pouch	No	HI (10)	4 to 5 min.	Puncture pouch with fork to vent.
Fish & chips (5 to 14-oz.)	Package tray	No	HI (10)	3½ to 4½ min.	Remove foil cover. Return tray to carton or distribute evenly on microwave safe dish.
Deviled crab (6-oz.)	Microwave safe dish	No	HI (10)	3 to 4 min.	
Breaded fish (5 to 10-oz.) (14 to 16-oz.) (23 to 25-oz.)	Microwave safe dish	No	HI (10)	4 to 5 min. 7 to 9 min. 10 to 12 min.	Distribute evenly on microwave safe dish.
Meat					
Frozen meats (5 to 8-oz.) (10 to 16-oz.) (16 to 32-oz.)	Microwave safe dish or pouch	No	HI (10)	3½ to 6 min. 5 to 11 min. 12 to 20 min.	If pouch package is used puncture with fork to vent.
Dry mixes (hamburger added)	Microwave safe casserole		HI (10)	11 to 20 min.	Add cooked, drained hamburger.
T.V. dinners (6 to 11½-oz.) (12 to 20-oz.)	Package tray and carton	Carton	HI (10)	6 to 10 min. 7 to 10 min.	Remove foil cover, replace in carton. Can cook up to 4 dinners at once; see page 39.
Pasta, Rice					
Canned spaghetti, etc.	Microwave safe dish	Lid or plastic wrap	HI (10)	3 to 5 min.	Stir before serving.
Frozen rice in pouch (10-oz.)	Pouch		HI (10)	6 to 8 min.	Puncture pouch with fork to vent.
Frozen macaroni & cheese, spaghetti (8 to 14-oz.)	Microwave safe dish	Lid or plastic wrap	HI (10)	7 to 10 min.	Stir before serving.
Frozen Lasagna (21-oz.)	Microwave safe dish	Wax paper or plastic wrap	HI (10)	13 to 18 min.	

FOOD	Container	Cover	Power Level & Time (or Internal Temp.)		Comments
Poultry					
Canned (7½ to 10½-oz.)	Microwave safe dish	Lid or plastic wrap	HI (10)	2½-4 min.	Place in microwave safe dish. Cover; stir after half time.
(14 to 24-oz.)			HI (10)	4 to 6 min.	
Frozen Pouch (5 to 6½-oz.)			HI (10)	2½ to 3½ min.	Slit pouch before microwaving.
Main dish (12 to 17-oz. pkg.)	Microwave safe dish	No	HI (10)	7 to 14 min.	Stir after 5 minutes.
Fried chicken 2-pieces	Microwave safe dish	No	HI (10)	2 to 4 min.	If label does not state "fully cooked", check for doneness.
1-lb., 6 pieces			HI (10)	6 to 7 min.	
2-lbs., 8-10 pieces			HI (10)	8 to 10 min.	
Sauces, Gravies					
Canned (10 to 16-oz.)	Microwave safe dish	Lid or plastic wrap	HI (10)	3 to 6 min.	
(32-oz.)				6 to 9 min.	
Vegetables					
Frozen breaded (7-oz.)	Microwave safe dish	No	HI (10)	3 to 5 min.	Place on microwave trivet or dish.
Canned (8 to 9-oz.)	Microwave safe dish	Lid or plastic wrap	HI (10)	1½ to 2½ min.	Place vegetables in microwave safe dish. Add ½ cup liquid or liquid from can. Cover. (Or use temperature probe set to 150°.)
(15 to 17-oz.)			HI (10)	3 to 4 min.	
(28 to 32-oz.)			HI (10)	4 to 6 min.	
Instant mashed potatoes:	Microwave safe dish	Lid or plastic wrap			Use container size and amounts of water, milk, butter and salt on package. Cover. After heating, briskly stir in potatoes, adding extra 1 to 2 tablespoons dry mix.
2 to 6 servings			HI (10)	5 to 6 min.	
8 to 12 servings			HI (10)	8 to 14 min.	
Souffle frozen (12-oz. pkg.)	Microwave safe pie plate and custard cups	No	Defrost (3)	9 to 13 min.	To Defrost: Place souffle upside down in pie plate. To Cook: Divide between 4 custard cups. Souffles are done when centers are set.
			Med-HI (7)	9 to 11 min.	
Potatoes: baked, stuffed, frozen	Microwave safe dish	Wax paper			Check to see that potatoes are NOT IN FOIL. Place on microwave safe dish.
1 to 2			HI (10)	4 to 7 min.	
3 to 4			HI (10)	7 to 10 min.	

10 Meats

1. Always use microwave-safe dish, plastic or glass. See meat chapter introduction for information about microwave trivet.
2. Standing time: Allow about 10 mintues standing time for most roasts, before carving.
3. To microwave frozen roasts, see recipe chapters.

FOOD	Container	Cover	Power Level & Time (or Internal Temp.)		Comments
BEEF					
Ground Crumbled (for casseroles or soup)	Casserole	No	HI (10)	1 lb.: 4 to 6 min. 1½ ID.: 7 to 9 min.	Add sauce or casserole ingredients and finish. To cook frozen block, microwave 10 to 15 minutes breaking up and stirring every 5 minutes.
Meatballs	Pie plate or oblong dish	Wax paper	HI (10)	1 lb.: 9 to 12 min. 2 lb.: 10 to 13 min.	Round dish: arrange ¾ to 1-in. apart in circle around edge of dish. Oblong dish: arrange ¾ to 1-in. apart.
Patties	Oblong glass dish (with trivet if desired) ceramic dinner plate (For 1 or 2 patties use paper plate lined with double thickness paper towels.)	Wax paper	HI (10)	4 patties/lb. 1 to 2 patties: 2 to 4 min. 3 to 4 patties: 4 to 6 min.	Cover with wax paper or cook uncovered and turn patties over. If desired, add browning sauce or agent.
Meat loaf	Pie plate or loaf dish	Plastic wrap	HI (10) Med-HI (7) or cook to 170°	Round loaf: 15 to 20 min. Loaf shape: 17 to 19 min.	Let stand 10 minutes after cooking.
ROASTS					
Pot roasts	Oblong dish or casserole	Lid or plastic wrap	Med (5)	18 to 23 min./lb.	Brush with browning sauce and add ½ cup water to 3 to 5 lb. roast. Turn over after half of time. Add vegetables if desired after half of time. Recover and finish.
Simmered beef (corned beef or brisket)	Casserole	Lid or palstic wrap	Med (5)	90 to 120 min.	Add 1 cup water per lb. meat. Turn over after half of time. Let meat stand in broth at least 10 minutes after cooking. For boiled dinner, remove meat, cook vegetables in broth.
Tender roasts (rib, high quality rump, sirloin tip)	Oblong dish and trivet	Wax paper	Med (5)	Min. per lb. / Internal Temp. — Rare 11 to 13 / 120° to 125° — Medium 13 to 16 / 130° to 140° — Well 16 to 19 / 155° to 165°	Temperature probe cooking yields most accurate results. Let meat stand 10 to 15 minutes before carving. If desired, brush with browning sauce or agent before cooking.
PORK					
Bacon	Microwave safe plate	Paper towel	HI (10)	Per slice: ¾ to 1 min. per slice 1 lb.: 15 to 17 min. total	Arrange in single layer on paper towels or on trivet set in dish. Layer many slices between layers of paper towels.
Pork sausage (raw)	Microwave safe utensil	Wax paper	HI (10)	½ lb.: 4 patties 1½ to 2½ min.	Arrange in single layer.
Pork link sausage (raw)	Microwave safe utensil	Wax paper	HI (10)	½ to ¾ min. per link	Arrange in single layer.
Canadian bacon	Microwave safe utensil	Wax paper	HI (10)	2 slices ¾ to 1¼ min. 4 slices 1½ to 2 min. 6 slices 2 to 2½ min.	Arrange in single layer.
Pork chops	Microwave-type dinner plate, or 9-in. pie plate	Plastic wrap	Med (5)	2 — 14 to 18 min. 3 — 19 to 24 min. 4 — 26 to 32 min. 6 — 33 to 37 min.	Brush with barbecue sauce or browning agent, if desired. Let stand covered 5 to 10 minutes before serving.

FOOD	Container	Cover	Power Level & Time (or Internal Temp.)		Comments
Pork roast	Microwave dish 13×9×2-in.	Cooking bag method	Med (5)	15 to 19 min. per lb. Or microwave to 170° internal temp.	Add ½ cup of water to roast in bag. Tie end of bag securely. Do not use metal twist ties. Or place bone side up on trivet in dish. Add water to dish and cover with wax paper. Microwave at Med (5) 13 to 15 min. per lb.
Spare ribs	13×9×2-in. dish or 3-qt. casserole	Plastic wrap or cover	Med (5)	25 to 30 min. per lb.	Add ⅔ cup water per lb. spare ribs. Turn over or rearrange after half of minimum time. After minimum time, drain liquid and add barbecue sauce; microwave few minutes to finish.
Ham roast	12×8×2-in. or 13×9×2-in. dish	Plastic wrap	Med (5)		Shield top edge of ham with 1½-in. strip of foil. After cooking period let ham stand 10 minutes before carving.

				Min. per lb.	Internal Temp.	
			Precooked	11 to 13	115°	
			or Canned	12 to 15		
			Raw (Uncooked)	13 to 18	170°	

FOOD	Container	Cover	Power Level & Time (or Internal Temp.)		Comments
Ham loaf	10×6×2-in. dish	Plastic wrap	Med (5)	25 to 30 min. (or microwave to internal temp of 170°)	Shape into oval loaf with rounded corners. Remove loaf from oven, let stand 5 minutes before serving. If a glaze is desired, spoon pineapple or apricot preserves over cooked ham loaf a few minute before serving.
Ham slices & steaks	12×8×2-in. dish	Wax paper	HI (10)	18 to 27 min.	Turn over at half time.
LAMB					
Chops	Brown 'N Sear dish (preheated for 8 min.)	No	HI (10)	4 chops — 5 to 7 min.	Brush chops lightly with oil. Place in preheated dish. Turn meat at half of time.
Roast (Leg or shoulder)	Oblong dish and trivet	Wax paper	Med (5)	18 to 21 min. per lb. (Or cook to 180°)	Let roast stand 10 minutes before carving. When using temperature probe, insert so tip is not in bone or fat.
VEAL					
Chops	See lamb chops above.				
Roast (shoulder)	Oblong dish and trivet	Wax paper	Med (5)	19 to 21 min. per lb. (Or cook to 155°)	Let roast stand 10 minutes before carving. Slice thinly.

1. Use microwave trivet for chicken and other small poultry, but avoid trivet for cooking turkey.
2. Let chicken and other small poultry stand after microwaving for up to 10 minutes. Turkey should be allowed to stand 20 minutes.
3. For frozen-to-cooked chicken, see page 114.

FOOD	Container	Cover	Power Level & Time (or Internal Temp.)		Comments
CHICKEN					
Pieces	Plate or oblong dish	Wax paper	HI (10)	Per piece: 2½ to 3 min. per piece Whole chicken (8 pieces): 18 to 22 min. total	Brush with browning agent if desired. Arrange in single layer in cooking dish so thickest meaty pieces are to outside edges of dish.
Whole uncut (stuffed or unstuffed)	Oblong dish	Oven-proof cooking bag	Med-HI (7) (Or cook to 190° internal temp.)	7 to 9 min. per lb.	Brush with browning agent if desired. Add ⅓ cup water to cooking bag. Slit bag near closure to vent. Do not use metal tie on bag. Cook breast side up. Or, place chicken breast down on trivet in dish and cover with wax paper. Microwave at Med-HI (7) 9 to 10 minutes per lb., turning over and recovering after half of time.
Stewing	Large casserole	Lid or plastic wrap	HI (10) Med (5)	15 min. Then 25 to 30 min. per lb.	Add 1¼ cups water per lb. chicken, along with 1 to 2 cups onions, celery or carrots as desired. Turn chicken over after half of time.
CORNISH HENS					
Whole (Stuffed or unstuffed)	Square or oblong dish and trivet	Wax paper	HI (10)	6 to 8 min. per lb.	Place breast side down in dish. Turn over after half of time.
Halves	Square or oblong dish	Wax paper	HI (10)	9 to 10 min. per lb.	Arrange skin side up in dish, on bed of stuffing if desired.
DUCKLING	Oblong dish and trivet	Wax paper	HI (10)	7 to 9 min. per lb.	Shield bottom of legs. Microwave breast side up for first half of time. Brush with browning sauce. Baste with sauce. Or do not apply browning sauce and broil top surface of cooked bird until brown and crisp.
TURKEY	Large oblong dish — do not use trivet		Med (5)	11 to 13 min. per lb.	Brush with browning agent if desired. Add ½ cup water to cooking bag. Slit bag near closure to vent. Do not use metal tie on bag. Cook breast side up. Or, place turkey breast up in dish and cover with plastic wrap. Microwave at Med (5) 21 to 23 minutes per lb. Remove plastic wrap, baste and turn ½ turn after half of time.

Breads

1. Crust on breads will be soft, outside color of foods will be same as color of batter (outsides will not brown). If desired, sprinkle top of batter with cinnamon-sugar mixture, chopped nuts or other topping for brown color. Or, increase brown color on upside down breads by lining dish before microwaving with brown sugar caramel mixture, or savory topping like crushed canned french fried onion rings.

FOOD	Container	Cover	Power Level & Time (or Internal Temp.)		Comments
Coffee Cakes From refrigerated biscuits	8-in. tube dish*	No	Med (5)	6 to 8 min.	Arrange biscuits over brown sugar-butter topping before microwaving. Invert to serve.
Corn Bread	8 to 9-in. tube dish*	No	HI (10)		For flavorful browned topping sprinkle cooking dish with finely chopped canned French fried onions before microwaving. Turn out of pan upside down to serve.
Frozen Bread Dough	9×5×3-in. greased loaf dish	No	To Defrost: Warm (1) To Proof: Warm (2): To Microwave: Med (5)	30 min. 30 min. 10 to 12 min.	While defrosting, turn loaf over and rotate dish ¼ turn after half of time. While proofing, rotate ¼ turn after half of time. While microwaving, rotate.
Muffins	Paper-lined muffin cups (Do not use foil liners)	No	Med-HI (7) 1 Muffin: 2 to 4: 3 to 6:	½ to 1 min. 1 to 1½ min. 2½ to 4 min.	Use microwave muffin container or homemade muffin cups page 182.
Quick Breads, Loaf	Glass loaf dish	No	Med-HI (7)	9 to 12 min.	When done, toothpick inserted in center will come out clean. Let stand 15 min. before turning out of dish. Cool.

*If tube dish is unavailable, microwave in 8″ round dish with drinking glass placed open-side-up in center.

Eggs and Cheese

1. Prepare eggs many ways in the microwave oven, see below. Always pierce whole yolks before microwaving to prevent bursting.
2. Never hard cook eggs in the shell, and do not reheat in-shell hard cooked eggs. They could explode.
3. Cook eggs just until set, they are delicate and can toughen if overcooked.

FOOD	Container	Cover	Power Level & Time (or Internal Temp.)		Comments
EGGS					
Scrambled	Glass measuring cup or casserole	No	HI (10)	¾ to 1 min. per egg.	Place 1 teaspoon butter per egg in dish. Microwave at HI (10) until melted. Scramble the eggs with the butter and 1 tablespoon milk per egg. Place in oven and microwave for ½ of total time. Stir set portions from the outside to the center. Allow to stand 1 or 2 minutes to set eggs.
Basic eggs	Buttered custard cup	Plastic wrap	Med-HI (7)	1 to 1¼ min. per egg	Puncture membrane of yolk to prevent bursting.
Poached eggs	1½-qt. casserole	Casserole cover	HI (10)	5 to 6 min. Boil 2 cups water ¾ to 1 min. per egg	Heat 2 cups hot tap water 5 to 6 minutes on HI (10). Break eggs onto plate, puncture membrane. Swirl boiling water with spoon, slip in eggs gently. Cover. Let stand in water a few minutes.
Omelet	9″ pie plate	No	HI (10) Med (5)	Melt butter 1 min. 7 to 10 min.	Sprinkle cheese over omelet. Microwave ½ to 1 minute until cheese is slightly melted.
Quiche	Microwave safe 1-qt. measure and quiche dish	No	Med-HI (7)	Filling: 2 to 3 min. Quiche: 6 to 8 min.	Combine and microwave filling, stirring every 2 minutes. Pour filling into precooked shell. Microwave additional time shown at left.
CHEESE					
Fondue	Microwave safe 2-qt. dish	Cover or plastic wrap	HI (10) Med (5)	To heat wine 4 min. 3 to 4 min.	Use 1 cup wine and 3 tablespoons flour per lb. of shredded cheese. Add cheese, flour and seasonings to hot wine and microwave at Med (5) stirring twice.

Fish and Seafood

1. Fish is done when it flakes easily with a fork. Center may still be slightly transluscent, but will continue cooking as fish stands a few minutes after cooking.
2. Cook fish with or without sauce. A tight cover steams fish, or use a lighter cover of wax paper or paper towel for less steaming.
3. Do not overcook fish. Check at minimum time.

FOOD	Container	Cover	Power Level & Time (or Internal Temp.)		Comments
FISH					
Fillets or steaks 1 lb.	Oblong dish	Wax paper or plastic wrap	HI (10)	6 to 8 min.	Microwave until fish flakes easily.
Whole fish	Oblong dish	Plastic wrap	HI (10)	5 to 7 min. per lb. Temp. (150°)	Shield head and thin tail with aluminum foil.
Clams, 6	Pie plate or shallow dish	Plastic wrap	HI (10)	3 to 5 min.	
Shrimp — 1 lb. (peeled)	Pie plate or shallow dish	Plastic wrap	HI (10)	3 to 6 min.	
Shrimp (unpeeled) 2-lb.	2-qt. casserole	Lid or plastic wrap	HI (10)	6 to 10 min.	Stir after 5 minutes.

14 Vegetables

1. Always use microwave-safe utensils, glass or plastic. Cook most vegetables with tight cover to steam them. Exceptions are potatoes cooked in their skins and watery vegetables which need no water added for steam.

2. Do not salt tops of vegetables before microwaving. If desired, add salt to water in dish before adding vegetables. Salt can sometimes cause brown spots on vegetables during microwaving.

3. Cooking time for vegetables affects finished taste and texture. Minimum time on chart gives fresh taste and crisp-tender texture. For soft texture with well developed flavor, cook maximum time or longer.

4. Size of pieces affect cooking time. Large pieces generally take longer than small uniform pieces.

5. Just as when cooking conventionally, vegetable mixtures should have similar densities or degrees of firmness in order to cook together successfully. Firm, crisp vegetables like carrots, cauliflower, broccoli microwave together well. If microwaving a firm vegetable with a soft one (carrots and peas, for example) cut the carrots in julienne strips so they will cook as fast as the peas. Or, start cooking larger carrot pieces first, and add peas during last few minutes.

VEGETABLES	Container	Cover	Power Level & Time (or Temperature)		Comments
Slices, pieces	Casserole	Yes	1-lb.: HI (10) 2-lbs.: HI (10)	11 to 17 min. 15 to 20 min.	Add ¼ to ½ cup water. If frozen reduce time 3 to 5 minutes because vegetables are blanched.
Whole - Halves or large or starchy vegetables (Potatoes, winter squash, cauliflower, etc.)	Potatoes: Cook on oven shelf (no container) Other vegetables: Square or oblong dish or casserole	Potatoes: No Winter squash, cauliflower, etc.: Yes	1-lb. (3-4): HI (10) 2-lb. (6-8): HI (10)	12 to 20 min. 16 to 20 min.	Prick skin of potatoes before cooking.
Watery (Tomatoes, Summer Squash)		Yes	1-lb. (3-4): HI (10) 2-lb. (6-8): HI (10)	4 to 5 min. 6 to 8 min.	Cut in pieces or halves. No additional water needed.
Vegetable Casseroles		Yes	Casserole made with raw vegetables: HI (10) Precooked vegetables: HI (10)	18 to 20 min. 10 to 12 min.	Use large enough casserole to allow for boiling in dish.
Stir-Fry Vegetables		Yes	HI (10)	10 to 12 min. (6 to 8 servings)	To stir fry one type of vegetable, substitute 1 tablespoon oil for water and follow times in cooking chart p.168.
Blanching fresh vegetables for freezing	Glass casserole	Yes	HI (10)	3 to 5 min.	Blanch only 1-lb. or 1-qt. prepared vegetables at a time. Place in 1 to 2-qt. casserole with ¼ to ½ cup water. Blanched vegetables will have bright even color and will be slightly softened. Cool drained blanched vegetables immediately by plunging in container of ice water.

Gravies & Sauces

1. No cover is needed, except for thick chunky spaghetti sauce.

2. Because microwaved sauces evaporate less than on the range top, they are thinner than conventionally cooked sauces made with the same amount of thickening. Increase thickening by adding extra teaspoon to 1 tablespoon flour or cornstarch for each cup of liquid.

3. Microwaved sauces do not need to be stirred constantly but most should be whisked vigorously with wire whisk once or twice while microwaving.

4. Vary basic white sauce by adding cheese, egg yolks, cream or dry milk solids. Add flour with mayonnaise or wine.

FOOD	Container	Cover	Power Level and Microwave Time (or Temperature)		Comments
Gravies and sauces thickened with flour or cornstarch	Glass measure or bowl	No	1 cup: HI (10)	4 to 5 min.	Microwave fat, flour and salt together to melt and blend. Whisk in liquid and finish. Increase time 1 to 2 minutes per additional cup of sauce.
Thin, liquid sauces (Au jus, Clam, etc.)	Casserole	No	1 cup: HI (10)	2 to 3 min.	Add cornstarch-water mixture to heated ingredients. Stir well and microwave to finish.
Melted butter sauces, clarified butter	Glass measure	No	½ cup: HI (10)	½ to 1 min.	Microwave butter just to melt. For clarified butter, bring to boil then let stand until layers separate. Pour off and use clear top layer.
Thick spaghetti, barbecue or sweet/sour sauces	Casserole, large bowl	Yes (spaghetti)	2 cups: HI (10)	5 to 7 min.	Stir ingredients together then microwave, stirring after half of time. Let stand 5 to 10 minutes to develop flavor.

Pasta and Rice

1. Always use microwave-safe utensil, glass or plastic.
2. For pasta use about half the amount of water needed for conventional boiling; there is less evaporation in a microwave oven. Add regular amount salt and 1 teaspoon oil (optional, to prevent sticking).
3. For rice or minute rice use the same or slightly greater amount water as with conventional boiling. Add regular amount salt.
4. Cover pasta and rice tightly while microwaving. When using plastic wrap, turn back one corner to vent.
5. Stir or rearrange after half of cooking time. Drain pasta immediately after microwaving.
6. Microwaving time is about the same as conventional boiling.

PASTA and RICE	Container	Cover	Power Level and Microwave Time (or Temperature)		Comments
Macaroni (8-oz.)	2-qt. casserole	Lid or plastic wrap	HI (10)	15 to 18 min.	Add 3 cups water. Stir after 10 minutes. For rotini type, check for doneness after 10 minutes.
Spaghetti (16-oz.)	13×9×2-in. oblong dish	Plastic wrap	HI (10)	16 to 19 min.	Add 6 to 7 cups water. Rearrange after 10 minutes.
Egg Noodles (8-oz.)	3-qt. casserole	Lid or plastic wrap	HI (10)	23 to 25 min.	Add 8 cups water. Stir after 10 minutes. Time is the same for spinach or regular noodles.
Lasagna (8 to 16-oz.)	13×9×2-in. oblong dish	Plastic wrap	HI (10)	11 to 16 min.	Cover with water in dish. Rearrange after 7 minutes.
Manicotti (5-oz.)	12×8×2-in. oblong dish	Plastic wrap	HI (10)	22 to 25 min.	Brush with oil then cover with water in dish. Using fork, turn over every 5 minutes while microwaving.
Rice, regular long grain (1 cup)	3-qt. casserole	Lid or plastic wrap	HI (10)	18 to 21 min.	Add 2¼ cups water. Stir after 10 minutes.
Rice, minute (1½ cups)	2-qt. casserole	Lid or plastic wrap	HI (10)	4 to 6	Add 1½ cups water. Stir after 2 minutes.

Cereal

1. Always use microwave-safe utensils, glass or plastic. Use large enough container to avoid spillover.
2. Start with hottest tap water to shorten cooking time.
3. Do not cover (prevents spillover).
4. Stir half-way through cooking time.

FOOD	Container	Cover	Power Level and Microwave Time (or Temperature)		Comments
Oatmeal, Quick	China or pottery bowl, paper bowl	No	HI (10)	2 to 2½ min. per serving	Mix cereal, salt and hottest tap water before microwaving. Stir before serving. For 6 servings, use 3-qt. casserole.
NOTE: To microwave single-serving packet of instant oatmeal, follow package directions for amount of water and microwave at HI (10) for ½ to 1 minute.					
Oatmeal, long cooking	1-qt. casserole or bowl	No	HI (10)	3 to 5 min. for 1 serving	Increase casserole size for more than one serving. Increase time about 2 minutes for each additional serving you are cooking.
Grits, Quick	China or pottery bowl, paper bowl	No	HI (10)	3 to 4 min. for 1 serving	Mix cereal with hottest tap water. Increase casserole size and microwave time by 2 minutes per additional serving.
NOTE: To microwave single-serving packet of instant grits, follow package directions for amount of water and microwave at HI (10) for ½ to 1 minute.					
Cream of Wheat	1-qt. casserole or bowl	No	HI (10)	3 to 4 min. for 1 serving	Increase time 1 minute per additional serving.
Cream of Rice	China or pottery bowl, paper bowl	No	HI (10)	1½ to 2 min. for 1 serving	Increase time about 1 minute per additional serving.

16 Cakes and Desserts

1. Always use microwave-safe utensils, glass or plastic.
2. Before adding batter, grease dishes but do not flour. Or, for easy removal, line dish with wax paper or paper towel.
3. Crust on cakes will be soft. Refrigerate cake if firm exterior is desirable for frosting.
4. Fruit desserts will be fresh looking and tasting.

FOOD	Container	Cover	Power Level & Time (or Internal Temp.)		Comments
CAKES					
Commercial mix	oblong round square dishes		Med-HI (7)	12×8×2-in. dish. 14 to 16 min.	Grease dishes before adding batter. Remove an egg when preparing batter. Microwave according to pan size. Let stand 5 to 10 minutes before inverting to cool.
				8-in. round dish: 7½ to 10 min. 8-in. square dish: 7½ to 10½ min.	
	Fluted tube cake pan or 13×9×2-in. dish		HI (10)	11 to 14½ min.	Rotate 13×9×2-in. size cake after half of time. Let tube cake stand 5 to 10 minutes before inverting to cool.
Basic butter or chocolate cake	Greased 8-in. round dish		HI (10)	7 to 8 min.	Let stand on heat-proof counter or wooden board to cool 15 minutes.
Pineapple upside down cake	8-in. round dish		HI (10)	10 to 12 min.	When done, toothpick stuck in cakes comes out clean. Invert cake onto plate, let dish stand over cake a few minutes.
Cupcakes — 6	Paper lined cupcaker		HI (10)	2½ to 3½ min.	When cooking several cupcakes, you may notice some will be done before others. If so, remove cupcakes as they are done and continue cooking the rest a few seconds more.
Bar cookies	8-in. square dish		HI (10)	8-in. square dish: 6 to 8 min. 12×8×2-in. dish: 8 to 14 min.	Grease dish before adding batter. Rotate dish ½ turn after half of time. Cut when cool.
Baked apples or pears	Microwave safe dish or casserole	Lid or plastic wrap	HI (10)	2 to 4 min. per piece	Pierce fruit or peel to prevent bursting.
Custard (3 eggs)	Glass 1½-qt. casserole	Lid or plastic wrap	Low (3)	12 to 15 min.	Scald milk before combining with egg-sugar mixture.

Candies

1. Always use microwave-safe utensils, glass or plastic. For easy cleanup, melt chocolate in paper wrappers seam side up, or place chocolate in paper bowl to melt.
2. Candies which are boiled become very hot, be sure to handle cooking containers carefully.

FOOD	Container	Cover	Power Level & Microwave Time (or Temperature)		Comments
S'Mores	paper napkin or paper plate	No	HI (10)	15 to 20 seconds	Cover graham cracker with chocolate and marshmallow. Microwave.
Caramel Apples	1 pint (2 cup) measure	No	HI (10)	3 min.	Unwrap a 14-oz. package of caramels into measuring cup. Add 1 tablespoon water. Microwave and stir smooth before dipping 4 apples into mixture.
Marshmallow Crisp	12×8×2-in. dish	Yes	HI (10)	1 min. to melt butter 3 min. to melt marshmallows	In 12×8×2-in. container melt ¼ cup butter. Add 10-oz. package marshmallows. Cover with wax paper and microwave to melt. Stir in 5 cups crispy rice cereal.
Chocolate Bark	1½-qt. casserole or bowl	Yes	HI (10)	3 to 5 min.	Place 12-oz. semi-sweet chocolate pieces in container. Microwave to melt. Add 1 cup whole toasted almonds. Spread over wax paper on cookie sheet. Chill until firm.

Water Boils in a paper cup. One of the remarkable characteristics of microwave energy is that it heats the food, not the utensil. Utensils become warm when heat from food has transferred to them.

"Microwaving" means to cook, heat or defrost foods with microwave energy. Just like any other type of cooking it has its own characteristics. Throughout this book you will see how microwaving compares to the old familiar conventional cooking, and how you can adapt your favorite recipes to microwaving.

Microwave Adapting Guide

The microwave oven is called an "oven" because it looks more like an oven than any other conventional appliance, but it can take over many of your top-of-range jobs with less time, attention and clean-up. Foods which you used to bake in a conventional oven will taste the same, but may look different. For example, a casserole will heat through quickly, but will not crust over, because the air in a microwave oven is room temperature, not hot and dry. Since microwave energy penetrates foods from the top and bottom in this oven, most foods will not need the extra attention required by many other microwave oven models.

Like any new skill, microwaving takes a little practice. Until you are used to its speed, you may overcook. Some foods will be removed from the oven before they look done, because they finish cooking with internal heat. This book is designed to teach you what to expect, and how to achieve successful results with microwaving.

Television is radio waves converted to a picture on the screen. Microwave energy is very short radio waves converted to heat in food.

How This Oven Works

Microwaves are very short, high-frequency radio waves, and your microwave oven is similar to a miniature broadcasting system. Microwaves are the same type of energy as AM, FM or CB radio, but the wave length is much shorter.

Where other types of radio waves broadcast over a distance, the microwave broadcasting system is self-contained. When the door is closed and the oven is turned on, a transmitter, called a magnetron, sends a signal to a receiver within the oven. The moment you open the door, the microwave oven stops broadcasting, just as your radio will not play if the station has "signed off". No energy will be received from the oven while the door is open.

The receiver deflects the microwave energy into the metal-lined oven cavity, where it agitates food molecules. Since microwaves cannot penetrate metal, all the energy remains inside the oven, where it turns to heat in the food.

18 Photos Show How Microwaves Cook

Thermography, which makes images of heat, demonstrates the different ways in which foods cook. At the General Electric Applied Science and Technical Laboratory, potatoes were heated on a range top, in a conventional oven, and in a microwave oven, then cut in half and thermographed to show how heat is distributed in each cooking method. Blue stands for cool areas, red represents warmth and yellow indicates the hottest area.

Range Top

Cut Potato in skillet is placed on range surface unit set at medium heat. Potato was sliced so that a large flat surface could be exposed.

After 3 Minutes some heat from surface unit transferred through pan to cut side of potato. On range top, bottom part of food is always hottest.

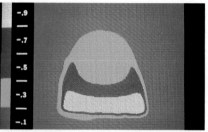

After 8 Minutes hot yellow area has increased and heat is being conducted into red, warm portions. The top of the potato is still cool.

Conventional Oven

Whole Potato is placed on shelf of a conventional oven preheated to 400°. Air inside oven is hot and dry.

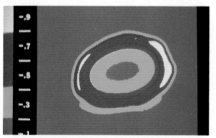

After 7 Minutes, thin yellow areas indicate air in oven has heated surface of potato. Prolonged exposure to hot, dry air will make outside dry and crusty.

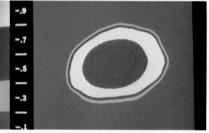

After 15 Minutes, heat is spreading to interior through conduction; center is still cool. It takes about 1 hour to bake a potato conventionally.

Microwave

Potato placed on oven floor with paper towel to absorb moisture, is microwaved at High Power. Air in oven is room temperature.

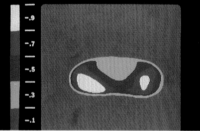

After 1½ Minutes, yellow areas of heat appear inside potato. Microwave energy penetrates ¾ to 1¼-in. through food surfaces. Heat is conducted inward and outward.

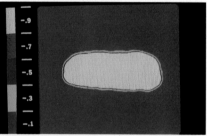

After 5 Minutes, potato is heated throughout although a brief standing time is needed to cook it thoroughly.

Multiple Foods in Oven

Two Potatoes are microwaved to show oven's increased capacity using special shelf. Time to cook will be doubled.

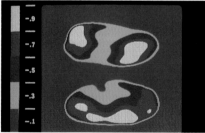

After 3 Minutes, about the same proportion of each potato is yellow, showing even microwave distribution from both top and bottom of oven.

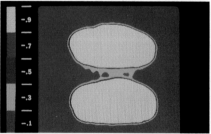

After 10 Minutes, both potatoes are heated through and ready to stand. Heat gathering between potatoes is shown as blue area.

Understanding the way in which food cooks by various methods helps you compare the benefits of each. It also helps indicate whether or not a food cooked by one method may be adapted to another method.

Saving energy seems to be more and more important today. The chart on this page tells you at a glance how microwaving compares with familiar range top and oven cooking methods.

Comparison of Microwave & Conventional Cooking

Range Top. On the range top, heat from the surface unit transfers through the pan to the bottom of the food. Stirring the food while it cooks brings heated portions to the top and prevents scorching Covering the pan holds in steam and speeds cooking. Rearranging or turning foods over helps them cook evenly. Because the bottom of the pan is hot, fried or griddled foods become crisp or crusty.

Conventional Oven. In a conventional oven, the heating units heat the air inside the oven. The oven may be preheated until the air reaches the proper cooking temperature. Heat from this hot dry air enters the food through its exterior surfaces, and gradually spreads to the interior through conduction. The process is usually slow, so by the time the center is done, the surfaces have become dry and crusty.

Microwave Oven. Microwaves penetrate ¾ to 1¼-in. through all food surfaces; top, bottom and sides. At this depth they are absorbed by moisture, sugar or fat molecules, which begin to cook. Heat is then conducted into the center and out to the surfaces. The food cooks by internal heat, not by contact with hot air or a hot pan. Because microwaves penetrate foods and cook them below the surface, cooking is faster for most foods, but the surface remains moist, not dry and crusty. Occasionally, the surface is the last place to cook.

Comparison of Microwave & Conventional Energy Consumption

Microwaving can save energy and reduce electric bills, but savings depend on what, and how much, you cook. Many foods make efficient use of microwave energy, as shown in chart below.

The amount of food cooked, and whether you are comparing microwaving to range top or a conventional oven affect energy consumption also. Four baked potatoes require about 70% less energy when microwaved, but about 12 baked potatoes bake more efficiently in a conventional oven. Greater savings result when you use a microwave oven instead of a conventional oven and when microwaving foods from the frozen state.

Summary-Energy Consumption — Conventional ▢ Microwave ■

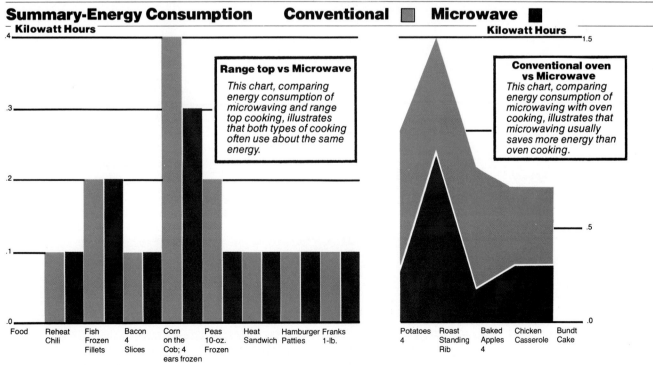

Range top vs Microwave
This chart, comparing energy consumption of microwaving and range top cooking, illustrates that both types of cooking often use about the same energy.

Conventional oven vs Microwave
This chart, comparing energy consumption of microwaving with oven cooking, illustrates that microwaving usually saves more energy than oven cooking.

Some Foods Microwave with Exceptional Quality

Some foods microwave so well that you may never want to cook them any other way. Many can be measured, mixed and cooked in the same utensil for easy clean-up.

The excellent flavor and texture of microwaved fish, vegetables and fruits makes superior flavor the principle reason for cooking them by microwaves. In addition, there are some things unique to microwaving which cannot be done any other way.

Vegetables retain their fresh, crisp texture and bright color when microwaved according to chart, page 168.

Baked Potato microwaves fluffy, moist and tender. A potato microwaves in about 5 minutes.

Puddings and custards cook smooth and creamy with no more than an occasional stirring. Cook and serve them from one dish.

Defrost foods rapidly. 1 pound of ground beef is ready to cook in 8 to 9 minutes. "I forgot to defrost", is never an emergency.

Melt Chocolate right in its paper wrapper. You have nothing to clean up and there is no danger of scorching or overcooking.

Eggs scramble fluffy, with greater volume. Compare 1 egg, cooked conventionally, left, with 1 microwave scrambled egg.

Reheat a meal right on the serving plate. If family members eat at different times, cook once and serve everyone a hot meal.

Fish steam tender and moist in their own natural juices, without additional water, for delicate flavor and pleasing texture.

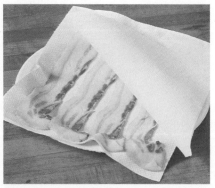

Bacon microwaves crisp, brown and flat on paper towels. You don't have to turn it over, drain it, or scour a crusty pan.

These Microwaved Foods Save Time and Results Compare to Conventional Cooking

A Hamburger microwaves in 2 to 3 minutes, right on a paper or microwave ovenproof plate. It won't stick to the dish, so you save clean-up time.

Chicken pieces are tender, juicy and ready to serve quickly. A cut up broiler-fryer microwaves in about 20 minutes. Skin will not be crispy.

Meatloaf takes about 15 to 20 minutes to microwave. Add another 8 to 9 minutes if you must defrost the meat first.

Upside-down Cake becomes a last-minute dessert or afternoon snack when it takes only about 10 minutes.

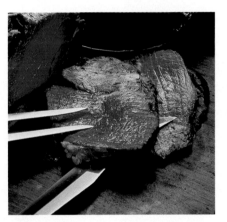

Sirloin Tip roast will be tender and medium-rare when microwaved at Medium Power for 1¼ hours.

Popcorn microwaves in 3 to 5 minutes, using a special microwave popper or bags labeled "microwave popcorn".

Some Foods Do Not Microwave Well

No single appliance does everything well, and your microwave oven is no exception. Some things should not be done, either because results are not satisfactory, or because conventional cooking is more efficient.

Large size foods, such as a 25-lb. turkey or a dozen potatoes cook more efficiently in a conventional oven.

Eggs in Shells and shelled boiled eggs can burst.

Pancakes do not crust, but they reheat well. Fully-prepared, frozen pancakes are available for microwaving.

Popcorn is too dry to attract microwave energy unless you use a special popcorn accessory or use popcorn labeled "microwave popcorn".

Canning requires prolonged high temperatures.

Deep Fat Frying can cause burns.

Bottles with narrow necks may shatter if heated.

You can use your microwave oven in preparing the recipes in this book and in general food preparation.

Often the microwave can save you time and extra effort, as well as clean-up.

Microwaving Can Make Food Preparation Easier

Melt or clarify butter. To melt, microwave at High (10) for 1 minute in glass measure. You can also melt chocolate in its paper wrapper and marshmallows. To clarify butter, place ½ cup (¼-lb.) butter in 1 pint measure. Microwave at High (10) for 2 minutes, until boiling. The clear layer that floats to top is clarified and may be poured off into a serving container.

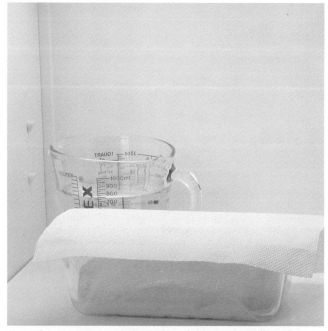

Proof yeast bread dough quickly and easily using microwave energy. Place 3 cups of steaming hot tap water in 1-qt. measure. Place in oven next to bowl of dough that has been lightly covered with towel. Microwave at Warm (1) for 20 to 24 minutes (see pages 188, 189).

Heat milk or water to dissolve or reconstitute convenience foods. To prevent boil-over of milk, use microwave food temperature control; set to 180°.

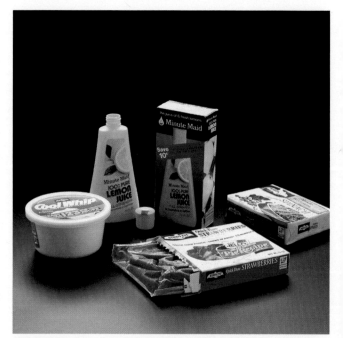

To defrost packaged foods quickly and easily, set at Defrost (3) for 1 to 5 minutes. Be sure packages are not foil or metal.

Boil water for instant coffee or tea. Microwave 1 cup water in glass measure or microwave oven safe cup at High (10) for 3¼ to 3¾ minutes. (Single cup of instant coffee, heated just to hot but not boiling, takes about 1½ minutes. Heat in drinking cup.)

Toast nuts or seeds. In 9-in. pie plate place ¼ cup slivered almond and 1 teaspoon butter. Microwave at High (10) for 5 to 6 minutes, stirring every 2 minutes until toasted. Stir in ½ teaspoon seasoned salt for flavor.

Soften processed cheese, cheese dips, cream cheese, or cheese spreads by microwaving at Low (3) for 1 to 2 minutes. Remove cheese from jar or wrapper before microwaving. To melt processed cheese, microwave at Low (3) for 1 to 2 minutes. Add liquid to natural cheeses, or they may become stringy and toughen.

Saute chopped vegetables. In 2-qt. casserole place 1 tablespoon butter and 1 cup chopped vegetables (onions, green pepper or celery, etc.). Cover. Microwave at High (10) for 3 to 4 minutes, until softened.

How to Adapt Your Favorite Recipes

Once you begin to use your microwave oven you will soon be able to adapt most of your conventional cooking quite easily to microwave cooking techniques. The more you use your microwave oven, the more you will enjoy using it. Not only will you save the time, trouble and energy necessary in conventional cooking, you will have more flavorful food and fewer dishes to wash. Simply cook, or reheat and serve foods in the same dish.

Before using your microwave oven, we suggest you carefully read through this guide book, then practice with a few of our suggested recipes.

This entire guide book has been designed to help you **adapt** your favorite recipes for microwaving. You will find a wealth of information on converting recipes and adapting techniques in every chapter.

Recipes in this cookbook have been written for an oven which has microwave energy from both top and bottom for more even or attention-free microwaving. If you have this oven system, you can often eliminate some of the stirring, shielding or rotating which is called for in other microwave recipe books by referring to the adapting charts in each recipe chapter.

If you are using this book with another type of microwave system, follow the recipes and cooking charts, but watch closely the first time you microwave to determine whether additional attention is needed.

Cook foods to minimum time recommended by microwave recipe books and check for doneness.

Below we have listed some general rules and comments about adapting your own recipes to microwaving. We have also presented a specific example of how easy adapting can be.

With microwaving, neither the ground beef nor the peppers in the recipe need be precooked as they do conventionally because the penetrating nature of microwaves allows them to cook throughout very quickly. In the conventional oven, the fresh raw foods would need approximately twice the cooking time if they were not precooked.

How to Adapt Conventional Recipes for Microwaving

Before converting your recipe, study it in terms of microwaving. Is it one of the many foods which microwave well? Look for cooking techniques which are similar to microwaving techniques, such as covering, steaming or cooking in sauce or liquid. If the food requires a crisp, fried crust or very dry surface, you may prefer to cook it conventionally. Some recipes may not be exactly the same when microwaved, but you will be pleased with the results.

Many recipes will not need changing. Moist, rich cakes, candies and meatloaves are examples.

Since liquids do not evaporate when microwaved, reduce the amount in saucy casseroles. Add more thickening to sauces and gravies. Reduce some seasonings also; they will not lose intensity in short microwaving times. Salt meats and vegetables **after** cooking. If an ingredient takes longer to microwave than others in the same dish, precook that ingredient before adding to the others as we have done with the rice in the following example.

Favorite Stuffed Peppers

6 medium green peppers
1½ lb. ground chuck beef
1 small onion, chopped (½ cup)
1 cup cooked rice
1½ teaspoons salt
¼ teaspoon pepper
1 clove garlic, minced
1 can (10¾ oz.) condensed tomato soup
½ cup water
2 cups grated cheese

Makes 6 servings.

Conventional Method

Cut off tops of green peppers; remove seeds and membrane. Cook peppers in enough boiling water to cover 5 minutes; drain. In medium skillet on range top, cook and stir ground beef and onion until onion is tender. Drain off fat. Stir in rice, salt, pepper and garlic. Divide evenly into peppers. Arrange peppers upright in 8-in. square dish.

Blend soup and water until smooth; pour over peppers. Cover. **Bake at 350° for 45 minutes to 1 hour.** Sprinkle with cheese, recover and let stand 5 to 10 minutes to melt cheese.

Microwave Method

Cut off tops of green peppers; remove seeds and membrane. Mix raw beef with onion, rice, salt, pepper and garlic. Divide evenly into peppers. Arrange peppers upright snugly in 3-qt. casserole, so one pepper fits into center of dish.

Blend soup and water until smooth; Pour over peppers. Cover. **Microwave at High (10) for 28 to 32 minutes.** Sprinkle with cheese, recover and let stand 5 to 10 minutes before serving.

Many of the techniques used in microwaving are the same ones you use in conventional cooking. Most of them either speed cooking or promote even heating.

While the techniques may be familiar, their application may be somewhat different because of the unique way in which microwave energy cooks.

Adapting Conventional Cooking Techniques to Microwaving

Covering. In both conventional and microwave cooking, covers hold in moisture and speed heating. Conventionally, partial covering allows excess steam to escape. Venting plastic wrap or covering with wax paper serves the same purpose when microwaving.

Standing Time. In conventional cooking, foods such as roasts or cakes are allowed to stand to finish cooking or set. Standing time is especially important in microwave cooking. Note that the microwaved cake is not placed on a cooling rack.

Arranging on Oven Shelf. In conventional baking, you position foods, such as tomatoes or potatoes, so that hot air can flow around them. When microwaving, you arrange foods in a ring, so that all sides are exposed to microwave energy.

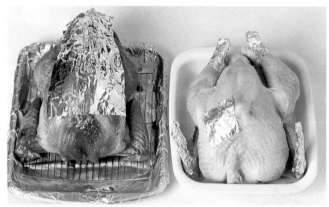

Shielding. In a conventional oven you shield turkey breasts or baked foods to prevent over-browning. When defrosting, you use small strips of foil to shield thin parts, such as the tips of wings and legs on poultry, which would cook before larger parts were defrosted.

Stirring. In range-top cooking, you stir foods up from the bottom to help them heat evenly. When microwaving you stir cooked portions from the outside to the center. Foods which require constant stirring conventionally will need only occasional stirring.

Boiling. Microwaves exaggerate boiling in milk-based foods. A temperature probe turns off the oven before foods boil over. Use a lower power setting and watch carefully when not using a probe.

Bury Vulnerable Foods. Foods which attract microwave energy, such as cheese or meat, should, when possible, be buried in sauce or other ingredients. In conventional stewing or pot roasting, meat not covered with liquid dries out.

Prick Foods to Release Pressure. Steam builds up pressure in foods which are tightly covered by a skin or membrane. Prick potatoes (as you do conventionally), egg yolks and chicken livers to prevent bursting.

A Technique Unique to Microwaving

Turning Over. In range top cooking you turn over foods such as hamburgers, so both sides can directly contact hot pan. When microwaving, turning is often needed during defrosting, or when cooking foods such as hamburgers from the frozen state.

Rotating. Occasionally, repositioning a dish in the oven helps food cook evenly. To rotate ½ turn, turn the dish until the side which was to the back of the oven is to the front. To rotate ¼ turn, turn the dish until the side which was to the back of the oven is to the side.

28 Microwave Adapting

Several factors which influence timing and results in conventional cooking are exaggerated by microwave speed. From conventional cooking you are familiar with the idea that more food takes more time. Two cups of water take longer to boil than one. Size and shape of foods are important, too. Cut-up potatoes cook faster than whole ones, and round shapes microwave more evenly than angular ones. The delicacy of food is another factor. Lower temperature and longer cooking time keep these foods from toughening.

Understanding Effects of Food Characteristics When Conventional Cooking or Microwaving

In the pictures below you will notice that differences in food size, shape or density effect microwaving time and cooking results more greatly than in conventional cooking. This is because energy penetrates and turns to heat directly in the food. Knowing what affects speed and evenness of cooking will help you enjoy all the advantages of microwaving.

Piece Size. Small pieces cook faster than large ones. Pieces which are similar in size and shape cook more evenly. With large pieces of food, reduce the power setting for even cooking.

Natural moisture of food affects how it cooks. Very moist foods cook evenly because microwave energy is attracted to water molecules. Food uneven in moisture should be covered or allowed to stand so heat can disperse evenly.

Density of Food. In both conventional and microwave cooking, dense foods, such as a potato, take longer to cook or heat than light, porous foods, such as a piece of cake, bread or a roll.

Quantity of Food. In both types of cooking, small amounts usually take less time than large ones. This is most apparent in microwave cooking, where time is directly related to the number of servings.

Shape of Food. In both types of cooking, thin areas cook faster than thick ones. This can be controlled in microwaving by placing thick pieces to the outside edge with thin pieces to the center.

Height in Oven. In both types of cooking, areas which are closest to the source of heat or energy cook faster. Vulnerable foods which are higher than 3 inches may need to be shielded if microwaved for long periods.

Delicacy. Foods with a delicate texture are best cooked at lower power settings to avoid toughening. Custard on the left was cooked at Low Power and custard on the right at High.

Starting Temperature. Foods taken from the freezer or refrigerator take longer to cook than foods at room temperature. Timings in our recipes are based on the temperatures at which you normally store the foods.

Round Shapes. Since microwaves penetrate foods to about 1-in. from top, bottom and sides, round shapes and rings cook more evenly. Corners receive more energy and may overcook. This may also happen when cooking conventionally.

Oven shelf may be used to microwave foods with similar cooking times, moisture content and fat.
See page 50.

In adapting recipes to your microwave oven, often the cooking energy is expressed in more than one way. This is because the microwave industry has not yet determined exactly how microwave power will be expressed in all recipes. The chart below gives you equivalent cooking power for the several ways you may see this in recipes from other sources.

Understanding Power Levels

POWER LEVEL	APPROXIMATE WATTAGE	PERCENT OF POWER	FRACTION OF POWER	GENERAL USES
HIGH (10)	625	100%	1	Boiling candy, puddings, sauces, vegetables, cooking chicken pieces, fish, hamburgers, baked apples, beverages, cakes, bar cookies.
MEDIUM HIGH (7)	435	70%	about ¾	Whole vegetables and chicken, loaf-shaped meatloafs, omelets, bread puddings, drying homemade noodles, muffins.
MEDIUM (5)	310	50%	about ½	Roasting meats by time or temperature cooking, pot roasting, poached eggs, bread loaves, coffee cakes from refrigerated biscuits.
LOW/DEFROST (3)	185	30%	about ⅓	Most defrosting. Custards, stewing and braising, delicate sour cream dips.
WARM (2)	120	20%	about ⅕	Proofing bread. Slow gentle reheating.

Understanding Cooking Patterns

Cooking pattern or how evenly a microwave oven cooks is another consideration when adapting recipes from one microwave oven to another. Tips such as the ones below help food cook evenly in all microwave ovens, but are more important in some ovens than in others. This cookbook is designed to be used with an oven requiring infrequent use of these techniques. Therefore they will be called for in recipes less often than some other microwave ovens need. When using other ovens, if you see some areas of the food cooking faster than others, the tips below can help you.

Rotate foods ¼ to ½ turn during cooking time for more even cooking from side to side.

Turning over may be necessary more often than is mentioned in this cookbook, if your oven only has microwave energy coming from the top.

Stirring food once or twice may be necessary if edges become dry, or boil-over.

While this cookbook is designed for specific ovens, much of the information is generic to microwaving. In order to understand how to adjust our recipes to other microwave ovens it is important to know your oven's wattage because wattage influences cooking time. More discussion about wattage is presented below.

Adapting Our Recipes to a Different Oven

Our recipes were developed for microwave ovens of 625 watts. However, house power varies from one part of the country to another, or during periods of peak consumption, such as early evening or extremely hot or cold weather. To prevent overcooking, recipes which are cooked by time direct you to check for doneness after the minimum cooking time, then add more time if needed. Fluctuations in power do not affect cooking with the temperature probe.

If you are uncertain about your house power, or have purchased this book for use with a different microwave oven, you can determine wattage with the following test. You will need a 1-qt. measure, a 1 cup measure and a watch or clock with a second hand.

Bring tap water from cold to boil as shown in pictures below. Time how long it takes. If your oven has 625 watts, timing will be approximately 3½ minutes, and recipe times in this cookbook should be correct for you. If your timing is significantly longer, expect recipe times to be about maximum or more. If your time is shorter, use minimum or less time.

Combine 1 cup cold tap water with 8 ice cubes. Stir together one minute.

Pour off 1 cup water without ice cubes. Temperature of water will be about 38°.

Microwave water at High (10) power, timing carefully, until many bubbles break on the surface (212°). *Immediately* open oven door and carefully look at water. Look for bubbles breaking at the surface rather than vigorous rolling boil.

Understanding Wattage

If your oven is between 600 and 700 watts, you can use the recipes in this book, making only minor time adjustments. If your oven has a higher or lower wattage and has variable power levels, you can change power levels to correspond to information in this book.

Use the chart below to help you determine how your power levels correspond to the ones in this book. For example, if the boiling water test described above takes 5¼ to 6 minutes, at your high power setting, you can see that it is the same as the Medium-High (7) setting on the oven used in this book. Adjust the power level in our recipes accordingly—using High instead of Medium-High, for example. You can use the same boiling water test and the chart below to test other power level settings on your oven.

If your oven does not have variable power, use the boiling water test to determine which power level your setting corresponds to. Then, you can adjust cooking time to compensate. You may find differences in food results, however, since different foods cook best at specific power levels (see facing page).

TIME TO BOIL IN MINUTES	APPROXIMATE WATTAGE	POWER LEVEL TESTED RECIPES IN THIS BOOK
3¼ - 3¾	625	High (10)
5¼ - 6	435	Medium-High (7)
7¼ - 8¼	310	Medium (5)
13½ - 15	185	Low or Defrost (3)

Utensils you already have may be suitable for microwaving. Oven glass casseroles, cooking dishes, measuring cups and custard cups are common household utensils. Pottery or china dinner ware which does not have gold or silver trim or glaze with a metallic sheen can be used.

How to Test Your Dishes at Home for Microwaving

Most glass ceramic oven-to-table ware is labeled "suitable for microwave." If you are uncertain about a dish or container, test by measuring 1 cup of water in a glass cup. Place in oven on or beside dish. Microwave 1 minute at High (10). If water becomes hot, dish is microwave safe. If dish heats, it should not be used for microwaving.

What to Look for When Buying Utensils for Microwaving

Casserole Dishes come in varied sizes and materials including individual serving dishes. They go directly from freezer or refrigerator to microwave. Non-stick finishes or smooth surfaces make cleaning easier.

Trivet fits in its own dish or in microwave oven-safe dishes you already have. It holds meat out of juices to prevent stewing. If you don't have a trivet, cook meat on a microwave ovenproof plate or saucer inverted in the baking dish.

Domes are even more convenient than wax paper or plastic wrap when covering foods. They prevent spatters and retain moisture during microwaving. Circular styles cover plates, while rectangular styles are ideal for microwave roasting. Microwave popcorn poppers have dome tops. Domes without venting holes on the top can double as casserole dishes.

Ring Molds (fluted and straight sided) and cupcakers are ideal for cakes, quick bread and meatloaf. All provide the ring shape preferred for microwaving as well as an attractive appearance. Some plastic dishes are available with non-stick coating.

Microwave Utensil Guide

Use this guide to help you evaluate and select utensils for microwaving. Some items can only be used for heating. Others are suitable for cooking. Many microwave utensils are designed both for cooking and attractive serving. Brands listed are among those recommended by their manufacturers for microwaving.

TYPE OF UTENSIL	**Paper Towels and Napkins, Wax Paper**	**Paper or Styrofoam Plates and Cups such as:** Chinet, Diamond International, Dixie, St. Regis, Sweetheart
MICROWAVE USES	Cooking Bacon. Absorbing moisture and preventing spatters. Heating and serving sandwiches or appetizers. Light covering to hold in steam.	Heating and serving foods and beverages. Styrofoam should be used for short-term heating to low temperatures and for serving.
COMMENTS	Recycled paper products can contain metal flecks which may cause arcing or ignite. Paper products containing nylon or nylon filaments should be avoided, as they may also ignite. Dye from some colored paper products may bleed onto food.	Be sure paper plates are plastic coated if heating saucy foods. Also see column on left about recycled paper and dyes. "Hot drink" cups may be used for soups and beverages. Styrofoam distorts when bacon and other high-fat foods are microwaved on it.

Glass jars, such as for baby foods, vegetables, entrees, syrups, salad dressing.	**Plastic Wrap, Cooking Bags, Boil-in-bags, Storage Bags, such as:** Glad Wrap, Handi-Wrap, Saran Wrap, Cooking Magic, Reynolds, Baggies, Ziploc.	**Boilable Hard and Soft Plastics, such as:** Rubbermaid
Avoid heating baby food in jars, especially meat and egg mixtures. Remove metal caps to warm syrup or soften salad dressing from refrigerator.	Covering to hold in steam (wrap). Cooking (cooking and boil-in-bags). Heating (storage bags).	Cooking ground beef (colander). Defrosting. Heating.
Jars which aren't heat tempered should not be used to heat food to very hot temperatures. Most vegetables and entrees are best removed to glass or plastic microwave-proof container.	Storage bags can melt at high temperatures.	May discolor from fat. May distort when used with foods with high fat content (except colander).

TYPE OF UTENSIL	**Microwave Plastics such as:** Anchor Hocking Microware, Bangor Plastics, Mister Microwave, NordicWare, Republic, Tara, Wearever Nupac.	**Oven Glass such as:** Anchor Hocking, Fire King, Glassbake, Heller, Jena, Pyrex	**Glass-Ceramic (Pyroceram), such as:** Corning Ware, Progression G. by Noritake
MICROWAVE USES	Cooking.	Cooking and heating.	Cooking and heating.
COMMENTS	Never microwave these utensils without food or liquid in them.	Inexpensive and readily available in supermarkets, hardware and department stores.	Attractive for serving. Plastic storage lids, available with individual casseroles, should not be used for microwaving.

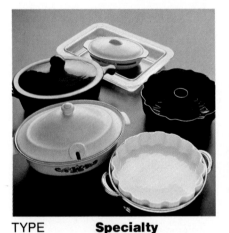

TYPE OF UTENSIL	**Specialty Glass-Ceramic and Porcelain, such as:** El Camino, F. B. Rogers, Heller, Marsh Industries, Pfaltzgraff, Shafford	**Straw and Wood**	**Boxes lined with paper or plastic, Paper or plastic packages, Styrofoam base, Shallow frozen dinner tray.**
MICROWAVE USES	Recommended for microwave oven-to-table cooking of special foods.	Short term heating (baskets and boards). Cooking (spoons, whisks, picks and skewers).	Refresh foods, defrost meat and baked goods. Cook vegetables. Heat frozen foods.
COMMENTS	Microwave ovenproof ceramics may be sold with metal holders. Ceramic part, but not holders, may be used in microwave oven.	Spoons and whisks may be left in foods while microwaving.	Do not use foil trays higher than ¾-in.

Handmade Pottery, Porcelain, Stoneware

Cooking and heating.

Avoid glazes with metallic sheen. Use the dish test, page 32, to determine if hand-made pottery is microwavable.

Regular Dinnerware, such as: Corelle by Corning, Dansk Generation, Denby, El Camino, Franciscan, International Stoneware, Lenox Temperware, Marsh, Mikasa, Pfaltzgraff

Heating and some cooking.

Check for "Recommended for microwave" seal, or use dish test. Avoid metal trim.

Unsuitable Dinnerware, such as: Corning Centura, Fitz and Floyd Oven-to-table Ware, Malamine, Dishes with metal trim.

None.

Warranty for Centura and Fitz and Floyd dishes states unsuitability for microwave.

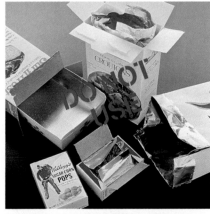

Foil-lined Paper Bags, Boxes and Baking Trays

Avoid. Use only foil trays ¾-in. or less. Foil or metal will reflect microwaves, thus preventing even heating. Arcing can occur if foil is closer than 1-in. to oven walls.

Check for foil lining before attempting to microwave food in original packages.

Metal or part metal pots, Pans, Thermometers, Skewers and Foil Trays

Avoid. See explanation left.

Glass, pottery, pyroceram, wood or straw with metal fittings (screws, handles, clamps, etc.)

Avoid or remove metal parts.

NOTE: *Electrical sparks (arcing) can occur in a microwave oven when two pieces of metal are placed within 1 inch of each other. Metal walls, wires, utensils or foil strips can cause arcing which can pit oven walls or cause fire within the utensil or the food. To prevent arcing, avoid utensils as listed above and carefully follow the recommendations for other uses of metal foil in recipes in this book.*

The automatic temperature probe takes the guesswork out of timing. Factors which influence time cooking, such as the amount, type and starting temperature of food are automatically adjusted in temperature cooking. Foods cook to a pre-set internal temperature, then the oven signals you and turns off.

Probe placement is important for accurate results. Throughout this book you will find pictures and instructions for positioning the probe in different types of food. If food has been frozen, make sure it is completely defrosted before inserting the probe. Do not use the probe with TV dinner trays or with the Brown 'N Sear Dish.

Casseroles and leftovers heat just to serving temperature when probe is set for 150°.

Scald milk without boiling it by setting temperature probe to 180°.

Cook Meatloaves without special attention. Insert probe into center of loaf or ring.

Using the Probe with the Auto Roast Feature

The Auto Roast feature, available on some touch control models, now makes meat roasting easier and more accurate then ever.

Unlike regular temperature cooking, which uses a single power level Auto Roast uses up to 3 power levels that switch automatically during microwaving for even cooking. And it can hold automatically for up to an hour without overcooking. To compare microwave roast cooked with temperature probe and Auto Roast with conventional roasting, see page 92.

Auto Roast Code 6 is for automatic simmering.
On some ovens with Auto Roast, a special automatic simmer feature is available, using Auto Roast Code 6. Using the automatic temperature probe allows you to hold food at a near-constant 180° for slow cooking to a tender consistency and well developed flavor. Automatic simmering will not shut itself off automatically. Time the food using the chart below as a guide.

Roast beef cooks to rare, medium or well done, depending on which Roast Code is set. Codes are on oven's control panel.

For automatic simmering, place temperature probe in dish halfway between center and edge of dish. Time foods for several hours.

Automatic Simmer Chart (Auto Roast Code 6)

FOOD	APPROX. TIME/HRS.
Beef	
Pot Roast*	6-8
Stew	6-8
Chili	11-13
Chicken*	
Stewing	11-12
Broiler/Fryer	4-6
Ham or Pork	
Roast	4-6
Soup	
Stock/Vegetable	3-6
Split Pea	13-15

*For Frozen, add 2 to 3 hours.

Ice absorbs microwave energy slowly, while water and moisture respond rapidly. Where microwaves penetrate frozen foods and moisture appears, melting is exaggerated. Defrosting techniques which redistribute microwave energy help foods defrost evenly and speed defrosting as well.

Techniques for Even Defrosting

If you try to defrost food without any attention, vulnerable spots, such as edges and thin areas, will start to cook before centers or thick areas are defrosted. Step-by-step instructions for defrosting specific foods are included throughout the recipe sections. Be sure to observe standing time where directed. Some microwave ovens allow you to program standing time.

Flex pouches of fruit, vegetables or convenience foods.

Break up large amounts of hamburger after defrosting.

Thin meaty areas like poultry legs or wings may be shielded during second half of defrost.

Use blunt knife to separate steaks, chops or beef patties.

Use trivet or paper towel to prevent soggy rolls.

Foods which do not freeze well include custard, and some smoked meats.

How to Convert Defrost (Power 3) Times to Higher Power Levels

For most defrosting, you will want to use techniques for the defrost setting, power level 3, in this book. However, defrosting at higher power levels can be done, especially with small porous foods like breads and rolls, and small portions of frozen foods. Large foods do not defrost well at high power levels because their size and density prevents rapid heat conduction.

MINUTES AT DEFROST SETTING (POWER 3)	TRANSLATES TO MINUTES AT THESE HIGHER POWER SETTINGS		
	POWER LEVEL		
	Med (5)	Med High (7)	High (10)
15	12	10	5½
10	8	6	3
8	6½	5	2½
6	4¾	3½	2
4	3½	3	1½
2	1½	1	½

Many touch control model ovens have a step by step programming feature which allows you to set your microwave oven to Defrost, Hold (no heat), then Time Cook all at one time. The oven will automatically switch power levels for you as cooking progresses. Because of adding the hold time, this process takes longer but heating is more even, and stirring is often eliminated.

Tips for Using Step by Step Oven Setting Feature for Frozen Foods

This 3-step cooking process is especially ideal for foods which are uneven in moisture content or composition. Foods with moist or juicy filling and meats with thin bony areas may be defrosted and microwaved this way, as can dense casseroles and meat dishes which tend to cook on the outside edges before the center finishes if not enough holding time is allowed.

Place dry food like pizza, egg rolls, sandwiches and rolls on trivet for dry or crisp texture.

Arrange saucy casserole frosty-side-up in microwave safe casserole to prevent drying.

Warm pie wedges or whole pies. Fruit, nut, pumpkin and custard work well.

FROZEN CONVENIENCE FOODS CHART

AMOUNT	DEFROST TIME	HOLD TIME	COOK TIME (MED. HIGH)
8-oz.	10	5	4-5
9½-12-oz.	10	5	8-9
14-16-oz.	15	5	9-10
21-oz.	15	10	8-10
2-lb.	15	10	20-25

FROZEN BAKED GOODS CHART

FOOD	DEFROST TIME	HOLD TIME	COOK TIME (MED. HIGH)
Coffeecake (10- to 20-oz.)	3-4	10	3-4
Sweet rolls (7- to 10-oz.)	2	5	2
Pies			
Whole (20- to 22-oz.)	6	15	6
Individual (8-oz.)	3	10	3½

How to Cook Many Convenience Foods at Once Using the Oven Shelf

Check empty containers for fit in oven, then add frozen foods.

Arrange entrees and meats on top shelf, vegetables or desserts on oven floor.

To determine microwave time, add together times for each food. Check and stir after half of time. Because of extended cooking time, step by step setting is not needed for even cooking.

TV Dinners

You can microwave TV dinners at either High (10) or Medium High (7) Power. Medium High results in a more evenly microwaved dinner.

TV Dinner Chart

Size	Cook Time at HIGH (10)	Alternate Cook Time at MED-HIGH (7)
8-oz. (entree-type or breakfast)	4 to 6	6 to 8
10 to 12-oz. (regular-type)*	6 to 8	8 to 12
16 to 20-oz. (hearty or man-size type)*	7 to 10	9 to 13

*See tip below about avoiding crisp or baked-type foods.

How to Heat Frozen Foods in a Foil Tray

Most TV dinners come in foil trays. These trays can be used in the microwave oven if the precautions stated below are followed. The foil cover must be removed as explained below. Foods in metal trays cook only from the top; trays should be no more than ¾-in. deep. To avoid electrical sparks: "arcing", place trays at least 1 inch from oven walls. Foods in deeper trays should be removed to microwave oven-proof containers.

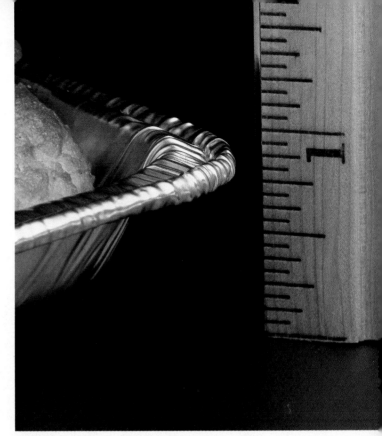

Height of TV foil tray should be ¾-in. or less.

Peel Off foil lid from shallow tray to allow microwaves to enter and heat the food. Return tray to box.

Place box in oven. To prevent arching, allow at least 1 inch between tray and sides of oven.

Remove box and pull out tray to serve. Stir loose or juicy foods if desired.

Tips for Microwaving Frozen Dinners

Cover dinner plate of food removed from foil tray with wax paper or vented plastic wrap. Follow minimum cooking times on chart, above.

Avoid French fries, batter foods and foods which do not microwave well or remove them from the tray and cook conventionally.

Microwave up to four TV dinners at once by inserting oven shelf at high position. Add together cooking times and reverse positions (top to bottom) of dinners after half of time.

Certain techniques should be used in preparing foods for freezing to assure even defrosting and cooking in the microwave oven later.

Be sure containers are appropriate for the freezer. Some paper containers, for example, are recommended only for short term freezing. Cover the container well. Unless your freezing container is microwave-safe, pop the food out of the container before defrosting and heating. Freeze food in individual serving containers for faster defrosting and reheating.

Tips for Freezer to Table Foods

Undercook pasta and rice for casseroles, as they will complete cooking when defrosted and heated. Add crumb or cheese toppings after removing from the freezer for defrosting and heating. Saucy foods work well for freezing and microwave cooking. Anything without a sauce should have moisture added (e.g., oil on chicken) to prevent drying out. If cornstarch is used as a thickener, substitute flour because cornstarch breaks down when frozen, and the resulting sauce may be too thin.

How to Prepare Foods for Freezer to Table Microwaving

Cut wings and drumsticks from breasts and thighs. Wash and spread separately on cookie sheet to freeze, package in freezer bags.

Shape meatloaf in a ring, using a 2-qt. casserole with a paper cup in the center. Freeze slices or wedges of cooked meatloaf individually.

Freeze stuffed peppers, mushrooms, cabbage rolls and meatballs on cookie sheet, with space between. Package in plastic bags.

Spread foods evenly in shallow dishes, (pie plates, 8-in. round, square or 12×8×2-in. dishes), up to 1 inch from top. Keep casseroles half full.

Omit potatoes from stews and soups. After defrosting and heating food, add canned or microwaved potatoes and reheat briefly, if needed.

Submerge pieces of meat and vegetables in broth when freezing soups and stews. Freeze pouches in dishes so they will be bowl shaped.

Foods prepared from recipes in this book may be defrosted and cooked or heated, according to this chart. Start by defrosting the food; let it stand and then cook as specified. Allowing frozen foods to stand between defrosting and cooking periods helps to finish defrosting evenly. If you choose to reconstitute these frozen foods completely at High Power (10), you may wish to check these foods occasionally while cooking. Directions here are for full or half recipes or for individual servings.

Tips for Even Defrosting and Heating

Defrost (3) 1 lb. of fish fillets 4 minutes. Quarter, place in 8-in. dish; coat with 1 can undiluted soup; cover with plastic wrap. Defrost 10 minutes. Let stand 5 minutes. Cook 10 to 12 minutes at Medium (5).

Add ½ cup water, bouillon or tomato juice to top of whole cooked meatloaf before defrosting and heating. Top slices or wedges of meatloaf with sauce.

Save metal containers from purchased frozen foods to freeze leftovers. If container is over ¾ inch deep, pop out food for microwaving.

Freezer to Table Home Frozen Foods Chart

FROZEN ITEM	AMOUNT	DEFROST TIME	HOLD TIME	COOK TIME & POWER LEVEL	COMMENTS
Meatballs, raw	1 recipe (12)	5	5	7-9 High (10)	Arrange in circle, cover with plastic wrap. For precooked meatballs reduce each time period by 2 minutes.
Meatloaf, raw	1 recipe (round ring or loaf)	30	15	25-30 High (10)	Cover with plastic wrap. If precooked, add ½ cup water and reduce cook time period by 10 minutes.
Saucy Casseroles (Chicken a la King, chili, spaghetti sauce, beef stew)	1 recipe (1½-qts.)	30	none	25-30 High (10)	Cover with plastic wrap. For 3 cups food, reduce each time period by half. Freeze food in flat oblong casseroles for fastest heating.
	1 cup (8-oz.)	8	5	4-5 Med-High (7)	
Soup	2-qt.	20	none	15-20 Med-High (7)	Cover. Break up and stir while defrosting and cooking, to speed heating.
	1-qt.	20	15	10-15 Med-High (7)	

Use microwave safe-plastic, ceramic or paperboard containers for microwave reheating.

One of the big advantages of microwaving is that foods can be heated or reheated without changing their quality. Foods can be prepared in advance, when cooking may be more convenient, and reheated at serving time.

Types of Food for Heating

Plates of food can be set aside and heated to give late comers a hot meal. Leftovers will taste freshly cooked when reheated.

Many types of fruit dishes, desserts and breads can be heated to enhance their flavor. See the appropriate sections in this book for tips on heating.

The microwave also can help you speed certain recipe steps and meal preparation. Ice cream can be softened, butter can be softened or melted and chocolate can be melted quickly in the microwave.

Consult the chart on the inside front cover for times and power levels recommended for various types and quantities of food.

Factors Which Affect Microwave Heating Time

Starting Temperature. Foods taken from the refrigerator take longer than foods stored on your pantry shelf.

Quantity. One serving heats faster than several. Heat large amounts at Medium (5).

Automatic Temperature Probe. Heat foods by temperature for accuracy. Moist casseroles heat well. Serve at 150° to 160°.

Tips for Multi-Food Heating

Food Temperature. Frozen vegetables in small amounts heat in same time as larger, more dense canned entrees at room temperature. Add roll during last minute of cooking time.

Multiple Single Servings. Microwave these in about 1 minute per serving if at room temperature and about 2 minutes per serving if at refrigerator temperature. Check and continue cooking if necessary.

Up to 4 dinner plates may be microwaved at once. Allow 2 to 3 minutes per plate at High (10). Check and rotate food, if necessary.

Freshening

Arrange plates with hardest to heat foods on the outside of dish. Make a depression in dense foods like mashed potatoes, to give them a ring shape. Where possible, spread foods to keep a low, even profile.

Reheating Tips

When assembling plates from leftovers, start with foods of the same temperature; all refrigerated or all room temperature. Fast heating items can be added at the end.

Cover most foods with wax paper, tucking it under the plate before placing in microwave oven, to hold in heat and prevent spatters without steaming. When more moisture is desired, cover with plastic wrap. Be careful of steam when removing wrap.

When heating by time at High (10), you may want to rotate the plate after ½ the time. Heat for 3 to 5 minutes and test by feeling the bottom of the plate.

Oven Shelf, featured with many microwave oven models, increases cooking capacity for full meal cooking or twice as many single foods.

How to Heat Single Plates of Food

Arrange thick areas and dense foods to the outside of dish, with easy-to-heat foods on the inside.

Delicate foods which can overheat, such as macaroni and cheese or seafood, may be microwaved at Medium to keep them tender.

Cover foods with plastic wrap to keep them moist and saucy.

How to Use Your Microwave Oven to Freshen Foods

Freshen Snacks, chips, pretzels, etc., by microwaving them, uncovered, for a few seconds. Let stand a minute or two to crisp. Dry a quart of bread crumbs or croutons at High (10) 6 to 8 minutes.

Soften lumpy brown sugar by placing in a microwave ovenproof container with a slice of apple. Cover or seal tightly and microwave ¼ minute or more, until moisture from the apple has softened the sugar.

Sprinkle a little fruit juice or water over dried fruits, cover with plastic wrap and microwave ½ to 1 minute at High (10) to moisten and plump.

For those who like to freeze fresh vegetables while they are in season, highest in quality and lowest in price, the microwave oven is a great help. It's especially useful to home gardeners, since vegetable crops do not ripen uniformly. You can pick vegetables as they reach the peak of flavor, even if you have only a few servings. Minutes after the vegetables are picked, you'll have them blanched and ready-to-freeze.

Prepare vegetables (wash, peel, slice or dice) as you would for regular cooking: Measure 1 quart or 1 pound of vegetables into the recommended casserole. Add water, as given in the chart. DO NOT ADD SALT. Cover.

Set Power at High. Microwave for ½ the minimum time and stir. Recover the casserole and microwave for second ½ of minimum time. Stir again.

Check for doneness. Vegetables should have an evenly bright color throughout. If all the vegetables are not evenly bright, recover the casserole and microwave for maximum time. Drain vegetables.

How to Blanch and Freeze Vegetables

	POWER LEVEL: **High (10)**			
VEGETABLE	AMOUNT	CASSEROLE SIZE	WATER	TIME MIN.
Asparagus	1-lb. cut into 1 to 2-in. pieces	2-qt.	¼ cup	3-4
Beans, Green or Wax	1-lb.	1½-qt.	½ cup	4-6
Broccoli (1-in. cuts)	1 bunch 1¼ to 1½ lb.	2-qt.	½ cup	4-5½
Cauliflower	1 head, cut into flowerets	2-qt.	½ cup	4-5½
Corn on the Cob	corn cut from 4 ears (Cool by setting casserole in ice water.)	1-qt.	¼ cup	4-5
Onions	4 medium quartered	1-qt.	½ cup	3-4½
Parsnips	1-lb. cubed	1½-qt.	¼ cup	2½-4
Peas	2-lb. shelled	1-qt.	¼ cup	3½-5
Spinach	1-lb. washed	2-qt.	None	2½-3½
Squash, Summer, Yellow	1-lb. sliced or cubed	1½-qt.	¼ cup	3-4½
Turnips	1-lb. cubed	1½-qt.	¼ cup	3-4½
Zucchini	1-lb. sliced or cubed	1½-qt.	¼ cup	3-4½

Blanching Vegetables

For vegetables not given in the cooking chart below right, refer to Vegetable Cooking Charts starting on page 168. Follow directions for fresh vegetables, but do not add salt.

Blanching time will be ¼ to ⅓ of the regular cooking time. Stir, test and cool, as directed in blanching steps.

Plunge vegetables into ice water immediately, to prevent further cooking. Spread them on paper towels and blot with additional towels to absorb excess moisture.

Package in freezing containers or boil-in-bag pouches. Label packages with type of vegetable, amount and date. Freeze.

To loose-pack vegetables in larger containers or bags, spread individual pieces on cookie sheet. Place in freezer until vegetables are frozen, then place loose pieces in containers. Seal, label and freeze.

Microwaving Frozen Blanched Vegetables

A one pint container holds about the same amount of vegetables as a 10-ounce package of commercially frozen vegetables.

To microwave this amount, follow directions on the Vegetable Microwaving Chart, beginning on page 168. If you package vegetables in smaller or larger amounts, adjust the casserole size, amount of water and microwaving time proportionately. DO NOT OVER-COOK.

Home frozen vegetables taste best when cooked to crisp-tender. Cook for minimum time, then let stand, covered, an additional 5 to 10 minutes to finish softening and develop flavor.

Timesaving "No Mess" Blanching Tip

This tip won a $1,000 award in a microwave recipe contest for being the most innovative cooking tip.

In a 1-qt. heat-seal or zip-seal plastic freezer bag place 2 cups vegetables (about ½ lb., prepared for blanching as above) and ¼ cup water. Microwave at High (10) for 2 to 2½ minutes, until vegetables take an evenly bright color, as pictured above. Immediately plunge sealed bag into bowl of ice water to cool. Freeze.

To cook, remove vegetables to microwave-safe 1-qt. casserole. (No additional water is needed. If you wish to salt vegetables place salt in bottom of dish before adding vegetables.) Cover and microwave at High (10) 5 to 10 minutes, until tender. Let stand a few minutes before serving.

Proper procedures should be taken in sealing jars of relishes, pickles and preserves to assure their wholesomeness after storage. If relishes and pickles are to be stored on the shelf at room temperature, they must be vacuum sealed in glass jars with 2-piece metal lids available for that purpose. Be sure to use canning-type jars.

Sealing and Storing Relishes, Pickles and Preserves

Sterilize the jars and lids in a kettle of boiling water and keep in hot water until just before filling. Ladling the boiling hot relish, pickle or preserve mixture into hot jars and sealing with hot lids is the best way to assure a good vacuum seal. Be sure rim of jar is clean before adding lid; wipe with damp cloth just before sealing. To completely assure proper seal, the U.S. Department of Agriculture recommends processing all relishes and pickles in water bath canner 10 to 15 minutes (see below).

If you do not use the type of jars which may be vacuum sealed, store relishes and pickles in the refrigerator after they have cooled. Glass jars saved from purchased foodstuffs may be used as refrigerator storage jars, but do not use them for on-the-shelf storage at room temperature. Or, for gift giving, ladle relishes or pickles into attractive re-usable serving containers or glasses such as brandy snifters, unusual serving bowls, champagne glasses, etc. Cover with plastic wrap and store in refrigerator until giving.

General Recommendations for Microwaving Jelly and Jam

1. Use High (10) Power on all recipes.

2. Always use pectin in recipes because of less evaporation in microwaving. Check pectin for additional recipes. Add gradually, stirring very well.

3. Use pot holders because sugar mixtures get very hot.

4. Avoid steam burns by lifting lid away from you when removing.

5. Pour jelly into hot sterilized jars or glasses; wipe off rim well, then seal with hot sterilized lids or paraffin. Sterilizing should be done in pot of boiling water on surface unit. Paraffin manufacturers recommend melting paraffin in a double boiler.

6. If the weather is warm or humid, the U.S. Department of Agriculture recommends that you water-bath process the filled and sealed jars of chunky preserves and jams for about 5 minutes.

Why Home Canning Is Not Recommended for Microwaving

Canning should still be done on the range top and is not recommended for either the conventional or the microwave oven.

Special range top canning utensils rapidly bring the water and jars to a boil, and maintain consistent heat to each jar during the canning process. When pressure canners are used, temperatures above boiling are developed to preserve low acid or non-acid foods.

While it is an excellent appliance to use for cooking jelly and preserve mixtures, the microwave oven is not efficient in processing the canning jars.

To sterilize jars and lids for canning and preserving, use the range top for efficiency. After filling and sealing, the U.S. Department of Agriculture recommends processing of high-acid foods like relishes, pickles and preserves in a water bath canner 10 to 15 minutes. Or use pressure canner for low-acid foods, set to 10-lb. pressure.

Colorful Corn Relish

POWER LEVEL: High (10)
MICROWAVE TIME: 20 to 22 min., total

1 cup sugar **2 tablespoons cornstarch** **1 tablespoon instant minced onion** **1 tablespoon mustard seed** **1 teaspoon celery seed** **¼ teaspoon turmeric** **1 cup vinegar** **¾ cup hot tap water**	In 3-qt. casserole stir together sugar, cornstarch, minced onion, mustard seed, celery seed and turmeric. Gradually add vinegar and water, blending well. Cover. **Microwave at High (10) 5 Minutes.** Stir well.
3 cans (12-oz. each) whole kernel corn with chopped peppers, drained (about 5 cups)*	Add corn to sauce. Cover. **Microwave at High (10) 15 to 17 Minutes,** stirring well after 7 minutes, until mixture boils. Stir well. Ladle into prepared glasses. Seal. Makes about 5½ cups

*Sold as Mexicorn or Corn 'n' Peppers.

Fresh Strawberry Jam

POWER LEVEL: High (10)
MICROWAVE TIME: 17 to 21 min., total

4½ cups crushed fresh strawberries (wash and stem before crushing) **1 box (1¾-oz.) powdered fruit pectin**	In 3-qt. casserole place berries and pectin. Stir well. Cover. **Microwave at High (10) 8 to 10 Minutes,** until mixture is at a full rolling boil.
7 cups sugar	Add sugar to boiling mixture and stir well.

Microwave at High (10) 8 to 10 Minutes, uncovered, stirring after 5 minutes, until mixture reaches a full rolling boil. **Then, time for 1 minute of boiling.** Skim off foam with metal spoon, stirring jam about 5 minutes before ladling into prepared glasses. Seal.

Makes about 8 cups

Fresh Apple Jelly

Use basic proportions of fruit juice, sugar and pectin to make crabapple jelly. Crush fruit for flavorful, but less clear jelly. Straining the juice helps to clarify jelly, but is optional.

POWER LEVEL: High (10)
MICROWAVE TIME: 36 to 40 min., total

3 lb. apples (about 14), peeled, cored and cut into fourths (about 10 cups prepared) **4 cups water**	In 3-qt. casserole place apples and water. Cover and **Microwave at High (10) 20 Minutes,** stirring after 10 minutes, until apples are fork tender. Strain, saving juice, but do not press apples through strainer. Strain juice again through 2 thicknesses of cheesecloth. Measure 2 cups juice.
3½ cups sugar	In same 3-qt. casserole, stir together strained 2 cups juice and sugar. Cover. **Microwave at High (10) for 12 to 14 Minutes,** stirring after 6 minutes, until boiling.
½ bottle (6-oz.) liquid fruit pectin	Stir in pectin, mixing thoroughly. Cover. Return to oven and continue cooking 4 to 6 minutes more until mixture returns to boil. **Then time for 1 minute of boiling.** Skim off foam if necessary. Ladle into prepared glasses. Seal. Makes about 3 cups

Dry herbs between paper napkin or towel approximately ½ to 1 minute until they can be crumbled. Watch small amounts carefully after half minute, since they could overheat and catch fire easily.

48   Meal Timing

When planning any meal, it is important to consider your cooking equipment as well as the foods you plan to serve. Your microwave is a helpful supplement to regular cooking, or it can be used alone for meals, as shown below.

Range top/microwave oven meals are probably the most common type. You are no doubt aware that you can cook several things on the range top at the same time that you are using the microwave oven for something else. If you analyze the foods you plan to serve, especially after seeing the food comparisons throughout this book, you can quickly determine which ones are best for range top cooking and which are best for the oven.

The combination oven meal is an easy and practical plan, especially now that you can prepare foods so quickly with microwave cooking. Within this book, we have presented several ways to make complete microwave oven meals.

Complete oven meals are a good idea when you are cooking foods that require only a few preparation steps before cooking, when you have a short amount of time to prepare a meal, and when the foods you are combining cook at the same power level and oven temperature and for approximately the same amount of time.

For step-by-step meals, you cook the various foods when it is most convenient for you. Generally, this meal plan is best for recipes that require many preparation steps and/or attention during cooking. It is also preferred when you want to cook most foods in the oven, but prefer to do most of the cooking before mealtime. You can cook a cheese cake or other chilled foods early in the day, then put it in the refrigerator to chill for supper. Or, before a party, you can prepare and cook the appetizers, then reheat them by microwave when your guests arrive. Step-by-step cooking is best for foods that cook at different power levels, temperatures, and times. In these and earlier pages, we have given several examples of step-by-step meals that explain how to "count down" to serving time so that everything is ready at the same time.

Plan These Foods First

Casseroles improve in flavor and consistency as they stand after microwaving. While standing, heat accompaniments and rolls.

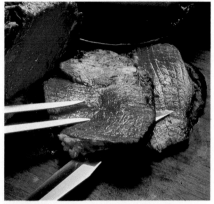

Meat Roasts take longer than other foods, also require standing. Plan to microwave potatoes and other vegetables during meat's standing time.

Vegetables are short cooking items. They are best served fresh after brief standing. Cook these just before the meal.

Then Add These Accompaniments

Appetizers may be prepared well ahead of a meal and reheated fresh. If necessary you can remove other food from microwave to reheat.

Rolls are heated in mere seconds. They may be popped in and out of the microwave oven as other foods are being served.

Desserts from scratch can be microwaved ahead of mealtime. Frozen convenience desserts are easy to defrost while clearing plates from main course.

Timetable for Two Step-By-Step Meals

Crumb Coated Chicken, p. 118
Beans, p. 168   Tossed Salad
Warm Rolls
Fruit Topped Cake, p. 203

Time
5:00 Assemble ingredients for all foods.
5:15 Microwave Fruit Topped Cake.
5:25 Remove cake to cool. Microwave chicken.
5:45 Remove chicken and let stand. Microwave beans.
5:55 Remove beans and let stand. Microwave rolls just before eating.
6:00 Serve dinner.

Basic Meatloaf, p. 75
Baked Potatoes, p. 170   Peas, p. 170
French Bread
Apple Graham Pie, p. 198

Time
12:00 noon. Make Apple Graham Pie.
5:10 Assemble ingredients for all other foods in meal. Prepare meatloaf.
5:20 Place meatloaf and 4 potatoes in microwave oven. Microwave at High (10) 28 to 32 minutes, until all foods are done.
5:50 Remove meatloaf and potatoes. Cook peas.
5:57 Warm bread.
6:00 Serve dinner.

If your microwave oven is equipped with a shelf, use it to double the capacity of your oven. Several ideas for meals using shelf cooking are presented here.

Shelf cooking is a natural when you want to reheat a number of leftovers. Just fit them on the shelf and oven floor, use High power and remove the smallest amounts (which will be done fastest) before the rest.

Tips for Foods and Utensils for Complete Oven Meals

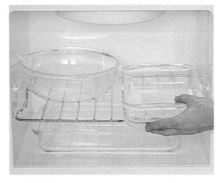

Place empty utensils in oven. Check for fit.

Place main dish, or longest cooking food, on top shelf.

Arrange other foods around main dish or on oven floor.

Techniques for Shelf Cooking

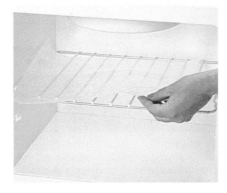

Cover shelf with wax paper or paper towel to prevent top shelf foods from dripping onto foods below.

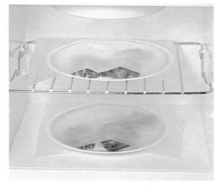

Add total time for all foods, using your cookbook heating guide. Microwave for ½ of time. Reverse (top to bottom) position of plates. Heat for ½ of time.

Check areas of foods which are close to oven walls. Energy reflected off walls can cook these areas faster than center.

Do not use the Brown 'N Sear dish on oven shelf. Best cooking results are obtained with this dish on glass ceramic oven floor.

Whether you use the microwave shelf to cook several foods or microwave them one at a time, depends on the type of food and amount of attention you wish to give it. Shelf cooking requires more care than regular microwaving.

Two foods which microwave well at high power may save time when cooked on the shelf with a third food on the oven floor. Microwave timing depends on quantity, two plates of food take twice as long as one; however, both are ready to serve together when you use the shelf.

Two Shelf Positions for Versatility

Low shelf position is ideal for most complete oven meals. This position allows plenty of room for tall meats on the oven shelf while still providing space for low dishes on the oven floor.

High shelf position works best for 2 equal size casseroles, 2 cake layers or batches of muffins or cookies.

High shelf position is recommended for heating many small quantities of foods at one time. Arrange largest amount of food on top, remove foods when done.

Techniques for Arranging Foods for Complete Meal Microwaving

The open arrangement acts like a sieve. Part of the energy is absorbed by foods on both shelf and the floor of the oven, but the spaces between them allow complete circulation of microwave energy around all foods. With this arrangement it is possible to cook raw foods even on both oven shelves.

The closed arrangement fills an oven shelf closely with food so there is little space for circulation of microwaves. This arrangement requires a more careful selection of foods. Check food after partial cooking and rotate or rearrange if necessary. This meal of Crumb Coated Chicken (page 118), Squash Combo (bottom of chart page 171) and 4 ears of corn in husk (page 170) was cooked with vegetables on shelf and chicken on floor for 20 minutes, then reversed to finish cooking 20 more minutes. Cover with wax paper.

The staggered or stacked arrangement allows you to microwave two like foods together at the same time. Small foods have complete access to microwaves by placing one food to the rear of the shelf and one to the front of the oven floor. Larger foods, especially baked items may be stacked with a food on the oven shelf placed directly over the food on the oven floor. Usually food cooked in the stacked position must be reversed after half the cooking time.

Timing Two Oven Meal Foods with Different Power Levels and Cooking times

Select foods compatible in flavor and texture. Casseroles, meats, vegetables, fruit desserts and muffins cook together well.

Prepare all foods up to point of final cooking step.

Arrange foods on shelf and floor as described on page 50-51. To determine total cook time, add together cook times of each food. Check foods after about ¾ of time, remove foods as they are done.

Timing Two Oven Meal Foods with Different Power Levels and Cooking times

Check recommended power levels of foods for a complete meal. There should be a difference of only one power level in all foods. Plan to microwave the meal at highest power level of any of the foods, but use minimum recommended time for foods with lower power levels.

Step. 1. Start cooking the longest cooking food. Time for the difference between this food and the next longest cooking food.

Step 2. Add the second food. To determine time, add remaining time for the first food plus total time for the second food.

Step 3. Check food for doneness after ¾ of time given in Step 2. Stir, rearrange or continue to microwave as necessary.

When planning meals for either conventional or microwave cooking, the problem of how to time the foods seems to be greater than the problem of planning which foods may be served together. Timing in this section may be used as a guide for typical microwave meals.

Quick Breakfast
Bacon, Page 103
Scrambled Eggs, Page 150
Convenience Roll or Coffee Cake, Page 187

7:00 AM Arrange slices of bacon on trivet in microwave-safe dish or paper towel-lined plate. Place on oven shelf.

7:05 AM In 1 pint measuring cup, beat 4 eggs with other ingredients for scrambling. Place on oven shelf beside bacon.

7:08 AM **Microwave at High (10) for 5 to 8 minutes,** stirring eggs after half the time. Remove eggs and continue cooking bacon 1-2 minutes, if needed. If desired, after stirring eggs, add 2 rolls or 2 slices of frozen baked coffee cake to oven floor last minute of total time.

7:15 AM Serve breakfast.

Chicken 'n Dressing Meal
Chicken 'n Dressing, Page 118
   (Use chicken breasts variation, see note in recipe)
Broccoli, Frozen Chopped
   2 pkg. (10-oz. ea.), Page 169
Easy Fruit Pudding, Page 190

5:10 PM **Assemble ingredients.** Prepare chicken and dressing in 8 × 8 × 2-in. dish, cover with wax paper. Place broccoli in 9 × 5 × 3-in. loaf dish, cover with wax paper. Make Easy Fruit Pudding to the point of final cooking step.

5:25 PM Place chicken and dressing to left side of oven shelf and broccoli to right side of oven shelf. Place fruit pudding on oven floor. **Microwave at High (10) 40-42 minutes.** Rearrange and rotate foods after 20 minutes.

6:05 PM Remove foods and let stand 5 minutes.
6:10 PM Serve dinner.

Turkey Meal

Whole Turkey (9 lb.), Page 130
Peas, Frozen, 2 pkg. (10-oz. ea.), Page 170
Apple Graham Pie, Page 198

4:00 PM   Prepare defrosted turkey by brushing with browning sauce, if desired, and placing in cooking bag with ½ cup water in 13×9×2-in. dish. Close and tie bag as directed in recipe.

4:15 PM   **Microwave turkey on oven shelf at Medium (5) for 60 minutes.** Meanwhile prepare pie according to recipe.

5:15 PM   Add pie to right side on oven floor. **Continue microwaving 30 minutes more,** give pie half turn and add peas with ¼ cup water in covered 9 × 5 × 3-in. loaf dish to left on floor. **Continue microwaving 45 minutes,** stirring peas after 15 minutes.

6:40 PM   Remove turkey and pie. Let stand 15 minutes while continuing to cook peas 5 to 7 more minutes. Serve foods with tossed salad or warm rolls, as desired.

6:45 PM   Serve dinner.

Note: Be sure turkey is no more than 9½ lbs. to follow this plan. Turkey up to 10½ lb. will require 90 minutes for initial cooking.

Fish Fillet Meal

Fish Fillets, Page 138
Green Rice Casserole, Page 163
Streuseled Apples, Page 192
   (Use 2-qt. casserole instead of 8-inch square dish as noted in recipe.)

5:20 PM   Assemble ingredients for all recipes. Prepare all recipes to the point of final cooking.

5:40 PM   Place fish and green rice in microwave oven on shelf, and add streuseled apples to oven floor. **Microwave at High (10) for 25 to 30 minutes,** checking fish and rotating if necessary after 15 minutes.

6:10 PM   Remove all foods from oven. Serve meal.

Ground Beef Meal

Hamburger (4 patties, 1½-lb. meat)
Potatoes, 4, Page 170
Green Beans, Frozen, 2 pkg. (10-oz. ea.),
   Page 168

5:00 PM   Place frozen vegetables with ¼ cup water in 1½-qt. casserole. Cover with plastic wrap and place on oven floor. Place potatoes along the left side of the shelf. **Microwave at High (10) for 20 minutes.** Meanwhile, form hamburger into 4 patties and place on bacon tray or in an 8-in. square dish. Cover with wax paper.

5:30 PM   Turn over and rearrange potatoes by switching the two in front with two in back. Stir vegetables. Add hamburger patties to shelf. **Continue to microwave all foods 13 to 15 minutes.**

5:45 PM   Remove foods and let stand 4 to 5 minutes.

5:50 PM   Serve meal.

Casserole Meal

Scalloped Tuna and Chips, Page 140
Frozen Peas, 2 pkg. (10-oz. ea.), Page 170
Baked Apples, Page 190

5:15 PM   Assemble ingredients. Prepare Scalloped Tuna Casserole. Place 10-oz. pkg. of frozen peas with 4 tablespoons water in 1½-qt. casserole; cover with plastic wrap. Prepare apples and place in 2-qt. casserole. Cover with plastic wrap.

5:45 PM   Place casserole on oven shelf. Add peas to shelf and apples on oven floor. **Microwave at High (10) for 30 to 32 Minutes,** stirring peas after 15 minutes.

6:15 PM   Serve meal.

Microwaving makes exciting hot appetizers and snacks as easy to serve as the more ordinary cold ones.
A minute or two after your guests arrive, you can offer them hot and tempting nibbles to stimulate appetites and conversation. Since all the preparation is done ahead, you can serve an unusual variety without last minute fuss.
Use the microwave directions provided on fully prepared packaged and frozen appetizers and check the following pages for additional convenience ideas.

How to Adapt Your Favorite Appetizer Recipes

For defrosting and warming precooked appetizers, follow directions for convenience foods on page 67.

ITEM	POWER LEVEL	TIME, MINUTES BY QUANTITY		COMMENTS
		12	24	
Meatballs (1-lb., 48-balls)	High (10)	1-2	3-4	
Hot Dogs, (1-lb.) or Precooked Sausage	High (10)	5-6	6-7	Add ½ cup water to dish before cooking.
Small Seafood (1-lb.)	High (10)	3-4	5-6	
Vegetables, stuffed	High (10)	2-3	4-5	
Spreads on Pastry Base or Crackers	High (10)	½-1	1-2	Delicate mayonnaise base should be microwaved at Low (3) adding ½ minute to times.
Pastry Appetizers	High (10)	3-4	7-8	
Pizza		1	2	For crisper crust, use pyroceram Pizza Crisper, or Brown 'N Sear dish.
Individual	High (10)	3-4	4-5	
Whole, 12-in.	High (10)	7-9	10-12	
Dips and Spreads, (8-oz.) (Warming and softening)				
Cheese	Medium (5)	3-4	—	
Sour Cream	Low (3)	1½-2½	4-5	

Soup and Beverage Heating Chart

If heating soup with sandwich, start soup then microwave half time recommended in last column. Add sandwich, finish microwaving. Use paper towel or napkin to cover sandwiches. Use Temp. Control Setting with soup to prevent boil-over or scalding.

TYPE	AMOUNT	TEMP. SETTING	POWER LEVEL	APPROX. TIME/MIN.	TOTAL TIME, MIN. IF SANDWICH ADDED
Water based	1-2 cups	160°	High (10)	2-4	4-7
	4 cups	160°	High (10)	8-10	12-14
Milk based	1-2 cups	140°	Med High (7)	5-7	5-8
	4 cups	140°	Med High (7)	12-14	15-17
Liquor based	1-2 cups	160°	High (10)	2-4	6-8
	4 cups	160°	High (10)	6-8	12-14

Note: These times are based on 8-oz. (1 cup) servings.

*Pictured top to bottom: Hoagie Sandwich (page 66), Bacon Poles (page 61),
Vegetable Platter (page 64) and Stuffed Mushrooms (page 63).*

Appetizers and snacks are among the easiest food to microwave. On these pages you'll find the basic principles of microwaving which assure success, some possibilities unique to microwave, and helpful ideas for using your microwave oven to make entertaining easier and more varied.

Adapting Tips:

For best results follow these techniques and recipe directions carefully. Apply the principles for successful microwaving, as described earlier in this book, when preparing appetizers and hot snacks.

Arrange pieces, such as meatballs, mushrooms or canapes in a circle for even heating. To serve, place a bowl of sauce or another snack, such as pretzels, in center.

The Temperature Probe turns the oven off when dips such as Chili Con Queso, page 60, reach correct serving temperature. Stir dip well before serving.

Dry Mixtures, such as Party Mix, must be stirred, as in conventional cooking, but they cook much faster in the microwave oven.

Wooden or Plastic Picks, even those with frills, may be used in the microwave oven. Use bamboo skewers instead of metal, when making kabobs.

Cover foods according to the amount of moisture needed. Paper towels absorb it, waxed paper holds in a little, plastic wrap and lids seal it in.

Soften Cream Cheese for spreads or dips by removing foil and microwaving at Medium 1 to 1½ minutes.

Dry Croutons, page 61, for snacks, using leftover bread, herbs and butter. Also great for salads and soups.

Sloppy Joe Filling, canned or deli, spooned on buttered bun, makes an easy snack in ½ minute at High.

Warm Cheese from refrigerator ½ to 1 minute at Medium High which makes it easier to slice.

Use Paper Plates for heating and serving. Let guests microwave their own hors d'oeuvres.

Shell Nuts easily. Microwave 2 cups pecan or Brazil nuts in 1 cup water 4 to 5 minutes at High.

Soften Tortillas and crepes in their package or by wrapping them in a damp towel and warming at High ½ to 1 minute.

Refresh Salty Snacks, by microwaving a few seconds at High. Let stand to crisp.

For Fast Canapes, spread ham salad or cheese spread on crackers. Microwave at High a few seconds.

Soft Smokey Cheese Ball

Soft Smokey Cheese Ball

POWER LEVEL: High (10)
MICROWAVE TIME: 2 to 2¼ min., total

1 roll-shaped pkg.	Unwrap cheeses. In 1½-qt.
(6-oz.) smokey	casserole place smokey
cheese spread	cheese. **Microwave at**
2 pkgs. (3-oz. each)	**High (10) 1 Minute.** Add
cream cheese	cream cheese.
1 teaspoon	**Microwave at High**
Worcestershire	**(10) 1 to 1¼ Minutes**
sauce	more, until cheeses can
1 cup (4-oz.)	be mixed together. Add
shredded sharp	Worcestershire sauce
cheddar cheese	and blend mixture well.
	Stir in shredded cheese.
	Mixture should remain
	gold-flecked.
½ cup chopped fresh . . .	Chill cheese mixture about
parsley	15 to 30 minutes in freezer
½ cup chopped	or about 1 hour in
pecans	refrigerator, until it can
	be formed into a ball with
	the hands. Roll cheese
	ball in parsley, then
	pecans. Chill to set. Serve
	with crackers.

Makes 1 cheese ball, about 1-lb.

Sour Cream Dips with Variations

POWER LEVEL: Low (3)　　　　　　TEMP: 90°
MICROWAVE TIME: 4 to 5 min.

1. Use **1 cup (8-oz.) dairy sour cream** as a basis for the following variations. In 1-qt. casserole or microwave ovenproof bowl, stir sour cream together with ingredients of one of the variations. Insert temperature probe so tip is in center of dip. Cover with plastic wrap, arranging loosely around probe to vent.

2. Attach cable end at receptacle. **Microwave at Low (3). Set Temp, Set 90°.** Stir before serving.

NOTE: Due to the delicate nature of sour cream, it is best microwaved **at Low (3).**

VARIATIONS:

Onion Dip

1 packet (½ of 2⅞-oz. box) onion soup mix
1 teaspoon lemon juice
1 tablespoon sherry wine (optional)

Makes about 1 cup

Zippy Dip

2 tablespoons chili sauce
1 tablespoon minced green pepper

Makes about 1 cup

Deviled Ham Dip

1 can (4½-oz.) deviled ham
2 tablespoons chopped green olives
2 teaspoons instant minced onion
⅛ teaspoon pepper

Makes about 1½ cups

Chili Con Queso Dip

Served fondue style, and accompanied by a salad, Chili Con Queso makes a nice informal luncheon. Dip is very thick and should be served with sturdy dippers such as large tortilla chips.

POWER LEVEL: Medium High (7)　　　TEMP: 140°
MICROWAVE TIME: 8 to 11 min.

1 lb. block	In 1½-qt. casserole stir
pasteurized	together diced cheese
processed cheese,	and chili.
diced in 1½-in.	
pieces	
1 can (1-lb.) chili	
with beans	

Insert temperature probe so tip is in center of dip. Attach cable end at receptacle. **Microwave at Medium High (7). Set Temp, Set 140°.**

When oven signals, stir well. Let stand a few minutes before serving. Serve with tortilla chips.

Makes about 3 cups

Cheese Pastry Snacks

POWER LEVEL: High (10)
MICROWAVE TIME: 2¾ to 3¼ min., per plate

1 cup (4-oz.) . . . . **shredded cheddar cheese** **¾ cup unsifted all-purpose flour** **¾ cup coarsely crushed crisp rice cereal** **½ cup chopped walnuts** **½ teaspoon garlic salt** **⅓ cup butter, softened** **6 strips crisp cooked bacon, crumbled** **2 tablespoons cold water**	In large mixing bowl mix together cheese, flour, cereal, walnuts, garlic salt, butter, bacon and water with a fork until a dough forms. Drop 7 level tablespoonfuls in a circle onto each of 3 lightly buttered plates suitable for microwave. (Butter plates only around edges, where dough will be placed.)
Paprika	Sprinkle with paprika. Microwave one plate at a time.

Microwave at High (10) 2¾ to 3¼ Minutes, rotating dish ¼ turn after 1½ minutes. Dough will be slightly puffed when done and will crisp on drying. Remove immediately from plate. Serve hot or cold. Repeat with remaining mixture.

Makes 21 snacks

Nachos

To make Nachos "restaurant style", spread corn chips on pottery or paper plate, cover evenly with chopped green chilies, then with shredded cheese. Microwave until melted. Or use the recipe below to make neat individual appetizers.

POWER LEVEL: High (10)
MICROWAVE TIME: ¼ to ½ min., per plate

Large corn chips . . . . . **(plain or taco flavored)** **Jalapeno bean dip or refried beans** **Hot pepper cheese**	Mound about 1 teaspoon bean dip or refried bean mixture on each tortilla corn chip. Top with ⅛-in. thick slice of cheese, to cover bean dip. Place 8 to 12 pieces in circle on paper plate or small pottery plate, leaving center space open. **Microwave at High (10) ¼ to ½ Minute,** until cheese is melted.

Bacon Poles

POWER LEVEL: High (10)
MICROWAVE TIME: See Recipe

10 strips bacon . . . . **20 long, thin garlic bread sticks or sesame bread sticks**	With scissors, cut bacon strips in half lengthwise, making 2 long, thin strips from each slice. Wrap one strip in a spiral "barber pole fashion" around each bread stick.

TO MICROWAVE ENTIRE RECIPE: Place 2 paper towels in bottom of 13×9×2-in. dish. Distribute wrapped bread sticks so they don't touch each other. Cover with paper towel. **Microwave at High (10) 9 to 12 Minutes,** rotating dish ½ turn after 5 minutes, until bacon is cooked.

TO MICROWAVE 7 ON A PAPER PLATE: Makes 3 plates. Place 2 paper towels on a paper plate. Arrange wrapped bread sticks on top. Cover with paper towel. **Microwave at High (10) 2½ to 4 Minutes,** until bacon is cooked.

Total recipe makes 20

Croutons Italiano

POWER LEVEL: High (10)
MICROWAVE TIME: 10 to 12 min., total

1½ qts. bread cubes . . . . . **(6 cups)**	In 12×8×2-in. dish place cubes. **Microwave at High (10) 6 Minutes,** stirring every 2 minutes, until cubes begin to dry.
2 tablespoons . . . . **Italian herb seasoning** **½ teaspoon garlic salt** **½ cup (¼-lb.) melted butter**	Sprinkle herb seasoning and garlic salt evenly over bread cubes. Drizzle with butter, tossing to coat cubes.

Microwave at High (10) 4 to 6 Minutes, stirring every minute, until crisp and dry.

Makes 1½ quarts

Toasted Butter Pecans

POWER LEVEL: High (10)
MICROWAVE TIME: 5 to 6 min., total

1 lb. pecan halves . . . . . . **(about 4 cups)** **1 tablespoon seasoned salt** **¼ cup butter**	In 1½-qt. casserole place pecan halves. Sprinkle with seasoned salt. Cut butter into 4 pieces and arrange evenly over top.

Microwave at High (10) 5 to 6 Minutes. Mix to evenly distribute butter. Serve warm or cold.

Makes 1 pound

Tacos

Tacos

POWER LEVEL: High (10)
MICROWAVE TIME: 11 to 13 min., total

1 lb. ground chuck beef **½ cup chopped onion** **½ cup chopped green pepper** **1 clove garlic, minced**	In 2-qt. casserole break up ground beef in very small chunks. Add onion, green pepper and garlic. Cover. **Microwave at High (10) 6 to 7 Minutes,** stirring after 3 minutes. Drain well.
1 can (8-oz.) tomato sauce **1 teaspoon Worcestershire sauce** **⅛ to ¼ teaspoon cayenne pepper** **½ teaspoon chili powder** **½ teaspoon salt**	Add tomato sauce, Worcestershire sauce, pepper, chili powder and salt. Cover. **Microwave at High (10) 5 to 6 Minutes,** stirring after 3 minutes.

Use meat to fill prebaked, **packaged taco shells,** filling about half full. Finish tacos by topping with 2 or more of the following: shredded lettuce, shredded cheese, chopped tomatoes and chopped onions. Add hot sauce if desired.

Makes 12 tacos

Wrap bacon around liver and water chestnut and secure with a toothpick. Arrange in a ring for cooking.

Curried Beef Balls

POWER LEVEL: High (10)
MICROWAVE TIME: See Recipe

½ cup buttery flavored cracker crumbs or slightly crushed herb seasoned stuffing mix **⅓ cup evaporated milk** **¼ teaspoon salt** **1½ to 2 teaspoons curry powder** **1 lb. ground chuck beef**	In large mixing bowl thoroughly combine crumbs, milk, salt and curry powder. Add beef and blend well. Shape meat mixture into 48 (1-in.) balls.

In 8-in. square dish place about 24 balls. Cover with wax paper. **Microwave at High (10) 4 to 5 Minutes.** Repeat with other half of beef balls.

Makes 4 dozen hors d'oeuvres

Bacon-Wrapped Chicken Livers

This is often known by its Polynesian name of Rumaki. The picture at the lower left shows the traditional way to wrap them. For convenience, you can prepare ahead of time and store in the refrigerator until time to microwave. Because the chicken livers cook more quickly than the bacon, it is important to precook the bacon before using it to wrap the livers.

POWER LEVEL: High (10)
MICROWAVE TIME: 6½ to 7¾ min., per plate

1 lb. thinly sliced bacon	**Microwave at High (10) 1 Minute,** in the package, until slices easily separate. Divide bacon slices between 4 paper towel lined paper plates. Cover with paper towel. Microwave one plate at a time. **Microwave at High (10) 2½ Minutes.**
1 can (8-oz.) water chestnuts	Drain and cut each chestnut in half.
½ lb. chicken livers (about 20)	Rinse and drain livers. Cut in half.

Sprinkle bacon strips lightly with ground cloves and brown sugar. Place one piece of chicken liver and one piece of water chestnut at the end of each bacon strip. Roll up, securing with a toothpick. Arrange 10 in a circle on each of 4 paper towel lined (1 sheet) paper plates. Cover with paper towel. **Microwave at High (10) 3 to 4 Minutes,** rotating dish ¼ turn after 1½ minutes. When microwaving from refrigerator temperature, increase time for each plate ½ to 1 minute.

Makes 40 hors d'oeuvres

Stuffed Mushrooms

Choose large or medium-sized firm, fresh mushrooms. When fresh, mushrooms are pale grey or white and the gills (the accordian-like vents on the underside of the cap) should be tightly closed and firmly attached.

POWER LEVEL: See Recipe
MICROWAVE TIME: 3½ to 4½ min., per plate

1. For each of the following stuffings, use **12 large, fresh mushrooms,** 2-in. in diameter.

2. Wash mushrooms well, removing stems. Dry.

3. Prepare one of the following stuffing recipes. Divide evenly among caps and mound slightly. Arrange caps in a circle on plate suitable for microwave oven.

4. **Microwave at High (10) 3 to 4 Minutes.** If mushroom size is not uniform, smaller caps may cook in a shorter time.

Stuffed Mushrooms

Mushroom Stuffings:
Ham or Bacon-Onion Stuffing

Stems from mushrooms, finely chopped	In 1½-qt. casserole place chopped stems and onion. Cover. **Microwave at High (10) 4 Minutes,** stirring after 2 minutes.
½ cup finely chopped onion	
1 pkg. (3-oz.) cream cheese	To hot mixture above, add cream cheese, mashing and mixing well. Stir in crumbs and ham or bacon.
¼ cup fine dry bread crumbs	
½ cup chopped, cooked ham or bacon (8 slices)	
	Stuffs 12 large mushrooms

Spinach Stuffing

1 pkg. (12-oz.) frozen spinach souffle	Remove from foil container. With sharp knife cut in half. Return half to freezer; place other half in 1-qt. casserole. **Microwave at Medium (5) 1 to 1½ Minutes,** until partially defrosted. Mash with fork.
½ cup soft bread crumbs (about 1 slice)	Mix in crumbs, lemon juice, onion and salt.
1 teasoon lemon juice	
½ teaspoon instant minced onion	
¼ teaspoon salt	
	Stuffs 12 large mushrooms

Sweet-Tart Franks for a Crowd

Sauce is great with many types of meat.

POWER LEVEL: High (10)
MICROWAVE TIME: 7 to 10 min., total

In 3-qt. casserole, stir together 2-lbs. frankfurters, cut in 1-in. pieces, and Sweet-Tart Sauce, below. **Microwave at High (10) 6 to 8 Minutes.** Serve immediately or transfer to chafing dish, if desired.

Makes about 80 hors d'oeuvres

Sweet-Tart Sauce
Stir together in small bowl 1 jar (10-oz.) currant jelly and 1 jar (6-oz.) prepared mustard. **Microwave at High (10) 1 to 2 Minutes,** until mixture can be stirred smooth.

Appetizer Franks

If desired, 2 cans (4-oz. each) Vienna sausages, drained and halved, may be substituted for frankfurters.

POWER LEVEL: High (10)
MICROWAVE TIME: 2 to 3 min., per plate

3 frankfurters	Cut frankfurters into eighths and arrange in circle on plastic coated paper plate. Mix together preserves and mustard and spread over pieces. Stick each piece with wooden pick. **Microwave at High (10) 2 to 3 Minutes,** until hot.
¼ cup apricot preserves or apple jelly	
1 tablespoon prepared mustard	

Chili Franks: Substitute chili sauce for preserves and mustard.

Makes 24 hors d'oeuvres

Pizza-On-A-Plate is quick and tasty but may be slightly irregular in shape since it starts with triangles of dough.

Pizza-On-A-Plate

Pizza may be microwaved in rectangular shape on microwave proof trivet.

POWER LEVEL: Medium High (7)
MICROWAVE TIME: 10 to 14 min., per plate

1 can (8-oz.) refrigerated crescent roll dough **2 teaspoons cooking oil**	On each of two 12-in. pieces of wax paper, press ½ of dough to form a 9-in. circle. Press perforations together to seal. Brush each lightly with cooking oil. Place wax paper on microwave oven-proof plates. Microwave one pizza at a time. **Microwave at Medium High (7) 4 Minutes.** Holding wax paper, flip dough over onto plate and carefully peel off wax paper. **Microwave at Medium High (7) 3 to 3½ Minutes** more, until set and crisp. There will be some brown spots.
1 can (8-oz.) tomato sauce **1 pkg. (4-oz.) pepperoni** **1 cup (4-oz.) shredded mozzarella cheese**	Divide tomato sauce evenly between crusts, spreading to edges. Top each with half of pepperoni and sprinkle with half of cheese.

Microwave at Medium High (7) 3 to 4 Minutes.
Remove immediately to cooling rack for crisper crust.

Makes 2 (9-in.) pizzas

Vegetable Platter   (Pictured page 57.)

POWER LEVEL: High (10)
MICROWAVE TIME: 5 to 7 min., total

2 cups broccoli flowerets **1 cup cauliflower flowerets** **¼ cup sliced zucchini** **1 sliced carrot** **1 sliced green pepper** **1 sliced yellow squash** **¼ cup butter, sliced**	Select a 10-inch glass platter. Arrange broccoli pieces around outside edge, then cauliflower, carrots and pepper in concentric circles, with squash in the center. Dot with butter slices. Cover with plastic wrap. **Microwave at High (10) for 5 to 7 Minutes.**
1 teaspoon seasoned salt **1 teaspoon white pepper**	Season with salt and pepper before serving.

Curry Mayonnaise makes a perfect dip to serve with fresh vegetables. Mix 1 cup of mayonnaise with 1 to 2 teaspoons of curry powder.

Soups and Sandwiches

Soups are a natural for microwaving. Because they are moist they heat evenly. And even the thickest ones do not stick to the bottom of the dish.

French Onion Soup

POWER LEVEL: High (10)
MICROWAVE TIME: 18¾ to 21 min.

3 medium onions, sliced thinly **3 tablespoons butter**	In 3-qt. casserole, place onions and butter. Cover. **Microwave at High (10) 10 Minutes,** stirring after 5 minutes.
2 cans (10-oz. each) beef broth **1½ cups water** **1 teaspoon salt** **⅛ teaspoon pepper**	Add broth, water, salt and pepper. Cover and **Microwave at High (10) 8 to 10 Minutes.**
6 slices toasted French bread **1½ cups shredded Swiss cheese**	Spoon soup into 6 individual bowls and top each serving with 1 slice toasted bread. Divide cheese evenly among servings (¼ cup per serving). **Microwave** up to 3 bowls at a time, allowing ¾ **to 1 Minute** per serving.

Makes 6 servings

French Onion Soup

Adapting Tips: Heating Soups and Sandwiches in the Microwave

Water-Based Soups can be heated at High (10). A can of condensed soup, diluted with water in a 1-qt. glass measure or a 1½-qt. casserole takes 5 to 7 minutes. One cup (⅔ to ¾ full) takes 2½ to 3½ minutes; or use temperature probe. Set Temp, Set 150° to 170°.

Cream Soups should be heated at Medium High (7) because milk boils over rapidly so times will be slightly longer. For care-free heating, use the temperature probe. Set Temp, Set 140°.

For soup and sandwich lunch, start soup first. Microwave for recommended time in chart on page 56. Add sandwich and continue microwaving. Soups can be heated in serving dish or cup, sandwiches on paper napkin or bowl.

Tips for Microwaving Hot Sandwiches

Layer filling with cheese in the center. Cheese attracts microwaves and by hiding it in the middle of the sandwich you promote rapid heating and avoid overcooking the cheese.

Wrap the sandwich in a paper towel or napkin, to absorb moisture from the bread. For an attractive presentation, microwave the sandwich on a wooden board. (Wood is not affected by short heating times.)

Hot Hoagie Sandwich

POWER LEVEL: Medium High (7)   TEMP: 110°
MICROWAVE TIME: 5 to 7 min.

½ **loaf of unsliced** **Italian or French** **bread (10 to 12-in.** **in length)** **Mayonnaise** **Mustard** ½ **lb. meat**** 3 **to 4-oz. sliced** **cheese*****	Cut bread lengthwise to make two long, thin layers. Spread both cut sides evenly with mayonnaise and mustard, spreading completely to edges. Cover both sides with meat slices, then cover bottom of loaf with cheese.

Place meat covered top half of bread over bottom half. This arrangement results in cheese in center of sandwich with meat on either side. Place on board or platter with piece of paper towel over sandwich and tucked under edges. Insert temperature probe about ⅓ the length of bread loaf so tip is "sandwiched" into center of filling. Attach cable end at receptacle. **Microwave at Medium High (7). Set Temp, Set 110°.** Let stand a few minutes before slicing.

Makes 3 to 4 servings

****Meat Fillings:** Choose thin sliced hard salami, pastrami, pepperoni, corned beef, boiled ham, or a combination of these.

*****Cheese Fillings:** Choose sharp or milk cheddar, brick, Monterey Jack, Swiss, or a combination of these.

Corn Chowder Soup

POWER LEVEL: High (10)
MICROWAVE TIME: 17 to 19 min., total

1 **can (10¾-oz.)** **cream of potato** **soup** 2 **cans (1-lb. each)** **cream-style corn** 1 **can (13-oz.)** **evaporated milk** 1½ **cups milk** ¼ **cup finely chopped** **green pepper** **(optional)** 1 **tablespoon instant** **minced onion** 1 **teaspoon salt** ¼ **teaspoon pepper**	In 3-qt. casserole combine soup, corn, milks, green pepper, onion, salt and pepper. Cover. **Microwave at High (10) 17 to 19 Minutes,** stirring after 10 minutes, until hot.
Fresh frozen or **freeze dried chives**	Add chives and serve.

Makes 8 one-cup servings

Clam Chowder variation: Substitute 3 cans (6½-oz. each) drained minced clams for corn.

Appetizers

Appetizer and Hot Snack Helpful Hints

"When I microwave sandwiches the bread gets tough and soggy on the bottom. How can I avoid this problem?"

You should wrap sandwiches in a paper towel or napkin which will absorb excess moisture. Overcooking will toughen bread, so microwave just long enough to warm sandwich filling.

"How should large quantities of soup be heated in the microwave?"

More than 4 individual cups of soup can be heated in a large microwave oven safe casserole. Cover with plastic wrap, vented to insert the temperature probe. Set temperature at 160°.

"When I tried reheating pizza in my microwave the crust did not crisp. What do you recommend?"

Our tests show that a pyro-ceramic Pizza Crisper (preheated in the microwave for 5 min.) or Brown 'N Sear dish will produce a crisper, dryer crust. Also, a round, flat plate will provide better results than a plate with sloped sides.

Appetizer and Hot Snack Convenience Chart

POWER LEVEL: **High (10)**

ITEM	TIME, MIN.	COMMENTS
Frozen Egg or Pizza Rolls, 6½-oz. pkg.	2-3	
Frozen prepared sandwiches (4-oz.)	1-1½ per sandwich	Remove any foil packaging and wrap sandwich in paper towel.
Canned Sausage, 5-oz. can	1½-2½	Drain and cut into bite size pieces. Add ½ cup chili or cocktail sauce. Cover with wax paper.
Fish Sticks, (9-oz. pkg.)	4-5	
Pizza, frozen 12-in. 16-in.	10-12 (includes 5 min. preheat time for special dishes.)	Preheat Pizza Crisper or Brown 'n Sear Dish for 5 minutes, if used. Otherwise, heat pizza on glass or ceramic plate for only 5 to 6 minutes.

Pictured below, Microwaved Precooked Ham (page 110) with Sweet Mustard Sauce (page 159)
Pictured at right, top to bottom Layered Beef Taco Salad (page 76) Teriyaki Spareribs (page 97) and New England Boiled Dinner (page 91).

70 Ground Beef

Ground beef is still a mainstay of the American diet. With the microwave oven, it is now possible to defrost frozen blocks of hamburger and make fresh hamburger patties in minutes.

You can also microwave other forms of frozen ground beef easily. Frozen blocks go from freezer to cooked crumbled meat in a 1-step process, as can preformed frozen meat balls and loaves. See the adapting chart below.

Defrosting Ground Beef

Packaging affects defrosting time and amount of attention required. Flat, circular packages are easiest to defrost. Tubes should be rotated frequently and broken up as soon as possible. The ends defrost rapidly and may cook before center is defrosted.

Defrost wrapped package for first side time according to chart below. Turn end-over-end and microwave second side. Packages weighing over 1 pound need to be broken up, with cold center parts being defrosted additional time; break up and turn over these parts often.

When defrosted, beef should be cool, soft and glossy. Meat is red and fat is still white (if fat is transparent, meat has begun to cook). Some moisture may be visible. It will make patties that hold together during cooking.

Ground Beef Defrosting Chart POWER LEVEL: **Defrost (3)**

AMOUNT	FIRST SIDE	Defrosting Time, Minutes	
		SECOND SIDE	BREAK UP & FINISH
1-lb.	4	4-6	not necessary
2-lbs.	6	6-8	5-6
5-lbs.	12	12-14	11-12

Freezer to Table Ground Beef *(Also see chart page 71.)*

Unwrap packaged ground beef and place in cooking container called for in recipe. Microwave at High (10) for 10 to 12 minutes, breaking up and stirring meat every 5 minutes. Some areas will still be pink. Let meat stand 1 to 2 minutes until pink color disappears.

For patties or meat balls, place frozen meat in cooking container called for in recipe. Cook as directed, extending time as directed in adapting chart at right.

For meat loaf, cook as directed in adapting chart for frozen meat loaf (page 70). Use pie-shaped or ring-shaped containers which cook more evenly and quickly than the traditional loaf pan.

Grinding tenderizes meat by breaking down fibers. Since ground beef is naturally tender, it microwaves well at High Power. The short cooking time preserves its juiciness, but does not allow time for browning to develop, as shown with the first hamburger below.

Toppings and brown sauces may be used to add color if desired. Other than those shown below you may use teriyaki sauce, barbecue sauce, Worcestershire or steak sauce, or diluted liquid smoke. Commercial shake-on browners are also available, or make the recipe on page 95.

Plain Hamburger Immediately After Microwaving

Onion Soup Mix

Brown Bouquet Sauce With Butter

Brown 'N Sear Dish

Adapting Tips for Ground Beef

Cover ground beef and microwave as recommended in recipe or as directed in chart in page 70.

Ring-shaped and circular containers designed for microwave ovens will speed cooking, and give most even results.

Lower calories by microwaving ground beef in plastic colander set over a glass casserole or bowl. After microwaving, discard fat and place meat in cooking dish.

How to Adapt Your Ground Beef Recipes for Microwaving

POWER LEVEL: **High (10)**

ITEM	CONTAINER	TIME, MINUTES REFRIGERATED	FROZEN	COMMENTS
4 Patties (¼-lb. each)	8×8×2-in. glass	6-7	11-12	Cover meat while microwaving. If patties or meatballs are frozen, turn over after half of time. Let stand about 5 minutes before serving.
12 Meatballs (1-lb. beef)	12×8×2-in. glass	9-11	16-18	
Meat Loaf (1½-lbs. beef)	Pie plate, or loaf dish	18-22	25-30	
Casserole (1-lb. beef)	Glass, or ceramic	25-30	35-45	

Remember that the amount of fat in hamburger may vary as much as fifteen percent or more. Because fat displaces meat and microwaves quickly, hamburgers with high fat content will be done faster than lean ones.

You may wish to microwave fatty hamburgers on trivet as suggested below, so fat drips away from meat into cooking dish.

Tips for Microwaving Ground Beef Patties

Thickness and type of ground beef determine cooking time. Chart below is for medium-lean ground chuck. Fattier hamburgers might take less time, very lean ones, more.

A paper plate lined with a double thickness of paper towel gives you no-clean-up convenience. Cover patties with a single paper towel. (Without cover turn patties over after half of time.)

Place hamburger patties on a trivet set over a plate or dish. Cover with wax paper. Fat drains into dish.

Ideas for Hamburgers

Top plain hamburger with relish. Use Fresh Tomato Garnish (page 175) shown here and page 73, or your favorite toppings.

Stuffed Hamburger Patties: Make 8 thin patties from 1 pound hamburger. Place 4 each thin ham and cheese slices between 2 patties; seal by pinching firmly around edges. Place on microwave safe dish and cover with wax paper. Microwave at High (10) 6 to 7 minutes, turning after half the time.

Easy Salisbury Steaks: Mix 1 small chopped onion and salt and pepper with 1 pound ground beef. Shape 2 patties. Microwave at High (10) for 5 to 6 minutes. Pour over 1 can (10½-oz.) beef mushroom gravy. Microwave at High (10) for 1 to 2 minutes.

Hamburger Cooking Chart

POWER LEVEL: **High (10)**

Patty Size	No. of Patties	Fresh Time/Minutes	Frozen Time/Minutes		Brown 'N Sear Dish	
6 per pound (about ½-in. thick)	1	1 to 1¼	2		4	Use 9 or 10-inch dish.
	2	1½ to 2	4 to 4¼	Turn over after ½ of time	4	
	3	2 to 2½	5 to 5½		6	
	4	2½ to 3	6 to 6½		6	
	5	3 to 4	7½ to 8	Turn over every ⅓ of time.		
	6	4 to 5	9 to 10		8	Use 10-inch dish.
4 per pound (about ¾-in. thick	1	2 to 3	3 to 3½	Turn over after ½ of time	4	Use 9 to 10-inch dish.
	2	3 to 4	4½ to 5½		6	
	3	4 to 5	7 to 8	Turn over every ⅓	6	
	4	5 to 6	10 to 11	of time.	8	Use 10-inch dish.

*Preheat Brown 'N Sear dish or browning griddle for 8 min. uncovered. Follow timings on chart, but turn fresh hamburgers over after ⅔ cooking time. For frozen patties, turn as directed on chart.

Although ground beef patties are best loved in their plain unadulterated state, you can vary them with stuffings, seasonings and sauces to make a variety of recipes. Try the suggestions below, then adapt some of your own favorites to microwaving.

Hamburger Patty Stew

When arranging this casserole, be sure that the top layer of beef patties is well covered with vegetables or it will overcook. Be sure to set Medium Power.

POWER LEVEL: Medium (7)
MICROWAVE TIME: 25 to 28 min., total

2 medium potatoes **2 medium carrots** **2 medium onions**	Peel vegetables and slice into ¼-in. slices.
1 lb. ground chuck beef **1½ teaspoons salt** **⅛ teaspoon pepper** **¼ cup water** **Paprika**	Form beef into 12 small flat patties. In 2-qt. casserole layer half of beef patties then half of vegetables, sprinkling layers with salt and pepper. Repeat. Add water. Press down into casserole. Sprinkle with paprika. Cover. **Microwave at Medium (7) 25 to 28 Minutes.** Let stand 5 minutes before serving.

Makes 4 servings

Bacon Burgers

POWER LEVEL: High (10)
MICROWAVE TIME: 11 to 14 min., total

8 strips bacon	On paper or microwave ovenproof plate place double thickness of paper towel. Layer bacon (4 strips per layer) and separate layers by single paper towel. Cover. **Microwave at High (10) 3 to 4 Minutes,** just until partially cooked.
1 lb. ground chuck beef **1 teaspoon salt** **⅛ teaspoon pepper**	Meanwhile, divide ground beef into 8 equal parts; shape into thin patties. Sprinkle patties with salt and pepper.
4 thin slices onion **4 thin slices tomato**	Place one onion and one tomato slice over each of 4 patties; cover with remaining 4 patties and press together edges to seal well.

Wrap 2 partially-cooked bacon slices around to encircle the edges of each hamburger patty. Fasten with toothpicks. Place patties in 8-in. square dish. Cover with wax paper. **Microwave at High (10) 8 to 10 Minutes.** Serve on buttered hamburger buns if desired.

Makes 4 servings

Hamburger with Fresh Tomato Garnish

Meatballs microwave exceptionally well and turn brown after a short standing time, so they need no special browning. These recipes are good examples of favorite ways to cook meatballs. However, it is not at all difficult to adapt your own favorite recipes; just be sure to plan for the standing time.

Basic Meatballs

POWER LEVEL: High (10)
MICROWAVE TIME: 9 to 12 min., total

1 lb. ground chuck beef **1 egg** **½ cup fine bread crumbs** **1 teaspoon salt** **¼ teaspoon paprika** **⅛ teaspoon pepper**	Mix together beef, egg, crumbs, salt, paprika and pepper. Shape into 12 balls and arrange in a circle in 9 or 10-in. pie plate. Cover with wax paper. **Microwave at High (10) 9 to 12 Minutes** until done. If desired, serve with Italian Sauce, page 158. Makes 12 meatballs

VARIATIONS:
Add one of the following flavor combinations:
1 tablespoon Worcestershire sauce and ¼ cup chopped onion
1 tablespoon steak sauce and 1 clove crushed garlic (or ½ teaspoon garlic powder)
1 tablespoon chili sauce and ¼ cup finely chopped green pepper
2 tablespoons red wine and 1 teaspoon oregano

Swedish Meatballs

POWER LEVEL: High (10)
MICROWAVE TIME: 16 to 22 min., total

2 lbs. ground chuck beef **2 cups soft bread crumbs** **½ cup milk** **1 egg** **1 pkg. (½ of 2¾-oz. box) onion soup mix** **½ teaspoon salt** **½ teaspoon nutmeg**	Mix together beef, crumbs, milk, egg, soup mix, salt and nutmeg. Shape meat mixture into 40 balls. Cook 20 at a time in 13×9×2-in. dish. Cover with wax paper. **Microwave at High (10) 6 to 8 Minutes.** Remove meatballs from dish and keep warm, reserving meat drippings. Repeat.
2 tablespoons unsifted all-purpose flour **1 cup milk** **2 tablespoons brown bouquet sauce** **1 cup dairy sour cream (8-oz.)**	To ¼ cup drippings in dish, add flour, stirring until smooth. Gradually stir in milk and brown bouquet sauce. **Microwave at High (10) 3 to 4 Minutes,** stirring every minute, until thickened. Add sour cream. Stir well. Return meatballs to dish, mixing to coat evenly. **Microwave at High (10) 1 to 2 Minutes,** until hot. Serve over noodles or rice. Makes 40 meatballs (1-in.)

Arrange meatballs in a ring around the edge of a 9 or 10-in. pie plate. Small meatballs form a double row.

Meatballs in Onion Broth

If your oven has the Automatic Simmer feature you can slow cook these meatballs (Auto Roast Code 6) for 6 to 8 hours. Flavor will be well developed. See page 36 for temperature probe placement.

POWER LEVEL: High (10)
MICROWAVE TIME: 50 to 55 min., total

2 pounds very lean ground veal, pork and beef mixture **1 medium onion, finely chopped** **2 eggs** **2 tablespoons flour** **2 tablespoons dry onion soup mix** **1 teaspoon salt** **¼ teaspoon pepper**	In medium bowl mix together ground meat, onion, eggs, flour, soup mix, salt and pepper. Form into medium-sized balls (up to ¼ cup per ball). Set aside.
Boiling water **2 bay leaves** **2 tablespoons dry onion soup mix** **1 teaspoon salt** **1 teaspoon brown bouquet sauce (optional)**	Into 3-qt. casserole pour 4 cups boiling water. Add bay leaves, soup mix, salt and brown bouquet sauce. Carefully add meatballs. Add more boiling water if needed to cover. **Microwave at High (10) 50 to 55 Minutes,** stirring after ½ of time. Thicken broth if desired.

To Thicken Broth: Remove meatballs from broth and keep warm. Into hot broth in dish, stir mixture of ¼ cup cornstarch and ¼ cup water. Add additional dry onion soup mix for onion gravy. **Microwave at High (10) 4 to 6 Minutes,** stirring every 2 minutes.

Makes 16 to 18 meatballs

Round flat meatloaves cook fastest at High power (10). Loaf shaped meatloaves need Medium High power (7) to evenly cook the center without burning the corners.

Cheese Stuffed Meatloaf

This meatloaf tastes like a cheeseburger and will be popular with your family.

POWER LEVEL: High (10)   TEMP. 170°
MICROWAVE TIME: 25 to 30 min.

1½ lbs. ground chuck beef **3 slices fresh bread, cubed** **1 cup milk** **2 teaspoons salt** **½ teaspoon pepper**	Make meatloaf mixture: In large mixing bowl, mix together beef, bread, milk, salt and pepper.
½ cup chopped onion **¼ cup chopped green pepper** **¼ cup chopped celery** **2 tablespoons lemon juice** **1 egg, slightly beaten** **1 cup (4-oz.) shredded cheddar cheese** **3 slices fresh bread, finely crumbled**	Make cheese stuffing: In 1½-qt. casserole place onion, pepper, celery and lemon juice. **Microwave at High (10) 3 Minutes,** until lightly sauteed. Add egg to hot vegetables and stir to blend well. Stir in cheese and fine bread crumbs.

To assemble meatloaf: Pat half of meat mixture in bottom of 9-in. pie plate. Mound filling over meat leaving about 1-in. uncovered at edges. Spread remaining meat mixture over filling. (Meat mixture is soft and spreads easily.) Seal around edges. Brush assembled meatloaf with 1 tablespoon Worcestershire sauce

Insert temperature probe so tip is in center of stuffing. Cover tightly with plastic wrap, arranging loosely around probe to vent. Attach cable end at receptacle. **Microwave at High (10). Set Temp, Set 170°.**

When oven signals, remove meatloaf and let stand about 10 minutes to firm before serving. Serve in wedges.

Makes 4 to 6 servings

A 1½-lb. Loaf Shaped Meatloaf can be microwaved at Medium High (7) to 170°, in about 25 to 30 minutes.

Plain meatloaf looks grey. It needs a topping, sauce or browning agent for attractive color. For this picture we brushed the left side of the meatloaf with browning sauce, leaving the right side plain. Because microwave energy is attracted to sweet mixtures, toppings which contain sugar, syrup or preserves can increase over-browning if they come in contact with the bottom edges. When applied before microwaving, they should be brushed only on the top.

Insert temperature probe as horizontally as possible, so that tip is in the center of the loaf. Make sure disc does not touch the food. Cover tightly with plastic wrap, arranging loosely around probe to vent.

Basic Meatloaf

Add ¼ teaspoon herbs or dry mustard to vary flavor.
You can make this recipe in a loaf shape by following the tip under the picture at left. Time will be extended by about 5 minutes, but some people prefer the loaf shape in order to make neat slices of leftover meatloaf for sandwiches.

POWER LEVEL: High (10)   TEMP: 170°
MICROWAVE TIME: 15 to 20 min.

1½ lbs. ground chuck beef **¾ cup chopped onion** **½ cup fine dry bread crumbs** **1 egg** **2 tablespoons ketchup** **1 cup milk** **1 teaspoon salt** **¼ teaspoon pepper** **⅛ teaspoon paprika**	Mix together beef, onion, crumbs, egg, ketchup, milk and seasonings. Mold into a rounded, flat loaf in 9-in. pie plate.
2 tablespoon ketchup	Spread ketchup evenly over top of loaf.

Insert temperature probe and cover as shown in picture on preceding page. Attach cable end at receptacle. **Microwave at High (10). Set Temp, Set 170°.**

When oven signals, remove meatloaf and let stand about 10 minutes to firm before serving. Serve in wedges.

Makes 6 servings

Chili

If your oven has the Automatic Simmer feature (Auto Roast Code 6), use it to slow cook this recipe for up to 4 hours for more richly developed flavor. Place temperature probe halfway between center and edge of dish and set Auto Roast Code 6.

POWER LEVEL: High (10)   TEMP: 190°
MICROWAVE TIME: 40 to 45 min.

1½ lb. ground chuck beef	Into 2½ to 3-qt. casserole crumble beef.
1 can (28-oz.) tomatoes, undrained 1 can (6-oz.) tomato paste 2 cans (1-lb.) kidney beans, undrained 1 medium green pepper, finely chopped 3 teaspoons instant minced onion 1 to 2 tablespoons chili powder 2 teaspoons salt	Mix in tomatoes, tomato paste, beans, green pepper, onion, chili powder and salt. Insert temperature probe so tip rests on center bottom of dish. Cover tightly with plastic wrap, arranging loosely around probe to vent. Attach cable end at receptacle. **Microwave at High (10). Set Temp, Set 190°.** When oven signals, stir and let chili stand about 10 mintues to blend flavors before serving.

Makes 6 to 8 servings

Cabbage Rolls Italian Style

POWER LEVEL: High (10)
MICROWAVE TIME: 22 to 26 min., total

8 large cabbage leaves (from outer layers of cabbage)	In 3-qt. casserole place cabbage and water. Cover. **Microwave at High (10) 7 to 9 Minutes,** until leaves are pliable.
1 lb. ground chuck beef 1 egg 1 cup packaged pre-cooked (minute) rice 3 tablespoons chopped onion 1 teaspoon salt	While cabbage is cooking, mix together ground beef, egg, rice, onion and salt. Divide meat mixture into 8 equal portions. Place one portion on each partially-cooked cabbage leaf and roll meat into leaf, securing with toothpick if necessary. Return to 3-qt. casserole, placing rolls seam-side-down.
2 cans (8-oz. each) tomato sauce 1 tablespoon sugar 1 teaspoon oregano	Blend tomato sauce, sugar and oregano. Pour over cabbage rolls. Cover casserole.

Microwave at High (10) 15 to 17 Minutes, rotating dish ½ turn and basting with sauce after 9 minutes.

Makes 8 cabbage rolls

Layered Taco Salad

POWER LEVEL: High (10)
MICROWAVE TIME: 14 to 18 minutes   total

1½ pounds ground beef ½ cup chopped onions (1 small onion) 1 cup chopped green pepper (about 1 pepper) 1 can (16-oz.) hot chili beans in chili gravy (not drained)	In 1½ qt. casserole crumble beef. Add onion and green pepper. Cover. **Microwave at High (10) for 5 to 6 Minutes,** stirring after 3 minutes. Drain well. Add chili beans. Recover and **Microwave at High (10) for 5 to 6 Minutes,** until hot. Keep warm.
1 can (10-oz.) enchilada sauce, mild 1 can (8-oz.) tomato sauce 1 can (8-oz.) taco sauce, mild	In 2-qt. casserole combine sauces. **Microwave at High (10) for 4 to 6 Minutes,** stirring after 3 minutes.
6 to 10 ounce package of corn chips or tortilla chips 1 cup (8-oz.) shredded mozzarella cheese 4 cups shredded lettuce (about ½ head) 2 cups chopped tomatoes	Into 2-qt. salad bowl or casserole layer corn chips, meat mixture, one half of cheese, lettuce and tomatoes. Pour sauce over entire casserole and sprinkle with remaining cheese. Serve immediately, tossing just before serving if desired.

Serves 6 to 8

SLOPPY JOES

POWER LEVEL: High (10)
MICROWAVE TIME: 11 to 12 min., total

1½ lb. ground chuck beef ⅔ cup finely chopped onion ½ cup diced celery ¼ cup diced green pepper	In 1½-qt. casserole crumble beef. Add onion, celery and green pepper. Cover. **Microwave at High 6 Minutes.** Drain meat well.
½ cup ketchup 1 tablespoon Worcestershire sauce ½ teaspoon salt ⅛ teaspoon pepper	To cooked meat mixture, add ketchup, Worcestershire sauce, salt and pepper. Cover. **Microwave at High 5 to 6 Minutes,** until hot. To serve, stir, then spoon onto buns or crusty French rolls.

Makes 6 to 8 sandwiches

Sloppy Joes With Cheese: Add 1 cup (4-oz.) shredded cheddar cheese to meat mixture along with ketchup.

Sloppy Joes With Beans: Add 1 can (16-oz.) pork and beans to meat mixture along with ketchup.

Ground Beef Microwaving Helpful Hints

"I would like to microwave cabbage rolls, but I'm not sure how to form the rolls."

Shape meat mixture into rolls about 3-in. long. Place each meat roll on the base of a precooked cabbage leaf. Fold sides of leaf over meat and roll up securing with a toothpick. See recipe suggestion on page 76.

"Should ground beef used in chili and casseroles be pre-cooked?"

Lean, quality ground beef can be used raw in chili and casseroles. However, the meat's texture will be softer with this 1-step method.

See page 25 for recipe "Favorite Stuffed Peppers."

"When using my temperature probe to reheat left-over ground beef casseroles and stews, what is the proper temperature setting?"

For up to 2 quarts of leftover casseroles and stews set the temperature probe for 150°.

Convenience Ground Beef Cooking Chart

POWER LEVEL: HIGH (10)

Main Dishes such as canned or frozen barbecue beef, chili, hash, meatballs, patties or pieces with gravy, stew, meatloaf, salisbury steak, stuffed cabbage rolls and stuffed peppers can be microwaved following directions below.

CANNED AMOUNT	TIME MIN.	COMMENTS
Up to 16-oz.	3-5	May use temperature probe set for 150°.
FROZEN AMOUNT		
8 to 16-oz.	5-11	May use temperature probe only if completely defrosted. Set for 150°.

Dry Casserole Mixes: Always use hottest tap water and 3-qt. casserole for dishes containing pasta or rice. Stir once or twice during cooking. Let stand, covered, 5 minutes after cooking.

CASSEROLE MIXES	TIME MIN.	COMMENTS
Add Hamburger	18-22	Microwave crumbled ground beef 5 minutes, stirring after 3 minutes. Drain before adding remaining ingredients.
Add Cooked Beef	18-22	If milk is used for part of liquid, add 2 to 3 minutes cooking time.
One-pot Main Dish (freeze dried beef)	11-13	Add crumb topping just before serving.

78 Beef Strips and Chunks

Less tender beef, such as round or chuck, microwaves best when cut in small pieces and simmered gently at Low or sometimes Medium power setting. The temperature probe is not appropriate for small pieces of less tender meat. Recipes which call for Low power (3) setting will not be as tender if cooked at Medium (5).

Slower cooking allows the meat to simmer in its sauce until it is fork tender. When defrosting strips or chunks, place them in the cooking dish, separate and spread them out as soon as possible. Any juices which appear during defrosting can be added to the liquid in the recipe.

How to Defrost Strips & Chunks

1. Place plastic or paper wrapped package in oven. **Microwave at Defrost** ½ the minimum total time.
2. Turn package over and defrost second ½ of time.
3. Separate pieces with a table knife and let stand to complete defrosting, or microwave 1 to 2 minutes more.

Defrosting Time: 4 to 8 Minutes per pound

Tips for Microwaving Beef Strips & Chunks

Browning Agents eliminate the pre-browning step associated with conventional cooking. These may be soy or teriyaki sauce, brown bouquet or steak sauce. Brown gravy mix, dry onion soup mix or bouillon may also be used.

A Tight Cover not only speeds cooking but holds in steam which helps tenderize meat. If your casserole does not have a tight cover, seal the top with plastic wrap, turning back about 2-in. at one edge to vent. Be careful when removing the cover to avoid scalding hot steam.

Low Power Setting cooks meat gently in liquid and steam until it becomes fork tender. Microwave time will be slightly shorter than conventional cooking. Some recipes may call for Medium power.

How to Cook and Reheat Less Tender Beef Cuts by Time and Automatic Simmering

If your model has the Automatic Simmer (Code 6) Auto Roast feature, consider using it for less tender meat. Automatic Simmer uses the temperature probe to keep the food at a steady below-boiling temperature for many hours to tenderize and develop flavors. Cooking time for beef chunks and strips is longer than at medium or low power, but meat will be extra tender.

| TYPE | TIME COOK | | AUTOMATIC SIMMER | REHEATING FROM FROZEN- |
	POWER LEVEL	TIME/MIN.	TIME/HOURS	POWER LEVEL MEDIUM HIGH (7)
Beef Chunks, Short Ribs* (1½ to 2-lbs.)	High (10) Low (3)	20 and 60 to 70	6 to 8	18 to 22
Swiss Steak, Round Steak (1½ to 2-lbs.)	Medium (5)	70 to 80	6 to 8	18 to 22
Pepper Steak, other Beef Strips (1-lb.)	Medium (5)	30 to 40	3 to 4	15 to 20

*Beef Chunks or Short Ribs: Bring to boil at High (10) then switch to Low (3) for continued cooking until done.

How to Microwave Beef Stew with Automatic Simmering

Combine 1 can undiluted beef broth, 1½ cups liquid, ½ cup minute tapioca and 2 tablespoons brown bouquet sauce in casserole.

Bury stew meat and vegetables under liquid. Gently pour water over surface. Insert the temperature probe and cover with plastic wrap.

Vary the recipe with different meats and vegetables. Special seasonings such as curry give stews international flavor.

Basic Beef Stew

To lengthen automatic cooking of all beef stews by 1 to 2 hours, add one more can of beef broth and increase tapioca to ½ cup.

POWER LEVEL: Automatic Simmer (Auto Roast Code 6)
MICROWAVE TIME: 6 to 8 hrs.

2 lb. beef stew meat, cut in 1-in. cubes	In 4-qt. casserole place beef, potatoes, carrots,
2 large potatoes, peeled, cut into chunks	onions, celery, broth, water, tapioca, brown bouquet sauce, salt,
5 medium carrots, peeled, sliced	pepper and garlic powder. Mix together very
2 medium onions, sliced	thoroughly. Press chunks of meat to submerge
2 stalks celery, sliced	under liquid. Insert temperature probe so tip
1 can (10½-oz.) beef broth	rests on bottom of dish, halfway between center
1½ cups water	and side. Cover tightly with
½ cup minute tapioca	plastic wrap, arranging loosely around probe to
2 tablespoons brown bouquet sauce	vent. Attach cable end at receptacle. **Microwave**
2 teaspoons salt	**at Automatic Simmer**
¼ teaspoon pepper	**6 to 8 Hours.** Stir before
¼ teaspoon garlic powder	serving.

Makes about 6 servings

How to Cook Basic Beef Stew by Time Cooking

In casserole microwave stew meat with beef broth and water at Low (3) for 60 minutes. Mix in vegetables and other ingredients and continue cooking 20 to 30 minutes, stirring gently after 15 minutes until meat and vegetables are tender.

Short Ribs and Homemade Noodles

POWER LEVEL: High (10) and Low (3)
MICROWAVE TIME: 1½ hr. to 1 hr. 42 min., total

2 lb. short ribs, cut into 2 or 3 rib pieces	In 3-qt. casserole place short ribs, onion, celery, salt and water. Cover.
1 small onion, sliced	**Microwave at High**
1 stalk celery with leaves, cut in half	**(10) 20 Minutes.** Stir. Cover. **Microwave at**
2 teaspoons salt	**Low (3) 60 to 70**
3 cups water	**Minutes,** stirring after 30 minutes, until tender.
Homemade Noodles or 1½ cups (½ of 6-oz. pkg.) narrow egg noodles	Remove ribs and keep warm. Add dry noodles to broth. Cover. **Microwave at High (10) 10 to 12 Minutes,** until tender.

Makes 2 to 3 servings

Homemade Noodles

Beat together 1 egg, 2 tablespoons milk and ½ teaspoon salt. Add 1 cup unsifted all-purpose flour and mix to make a stiff dough. Roll out very thin on floured surface; let stand 20 minutes. Roll up loosely; slice ¼-in. wide. Spread loosely in 13×9×2-in. dish. **Microwave at Low (3) 10 to 12 Minutes,** stirring after 5 minutes, until noodles are dry.

Makes 3 cups cooked noodles

To speed drying spread noodles loosely in glass dish and microwave at Low Power.

80 Beef Strips and Chunks

Many of our touch control models have the step-by-step cooking feature described on page 38. If you have this feature, use it for soups like those below. This method allows you to set the oven to bring the soup to a boil, then automatically lower the power for continued simmering. Notice that the Defrost setting, which always comes first in step-by-step cooking, can be switched to High (10), before setting Time Cook at Medium (5) for the final simmering step.

How to Microwave Vegetable-Beef Soup

Combine 1 cup chopped onion, 2 cups each diced celery and carrot, ½ cup barley, 2 teaspoons salt, 1 teaspoon each celery salt and parsley flakes, ½ teaspoon each pepper and marjoram in a 5-quart casserole. Add 1 meaty soup bone.

Add 1 can (6-oz.) tomato paste, 8 cups water; stir and cover. Set the oven to Defrost at High (10) for 60 minutes, then Time Cook at Medium (5) for 99 minutes.

Dice meat from soup bone and return to soup. Stir in 4 cups water and 2 teaspoons salt. If desired, skim fat from soup before serving. Freeze left-overs in single servings for freezer-to-table microwaving.

How to Microwave Basic Beef Stock

(For ovens without Automatic Simmer feature or, for Time Cooking, use same oven settings as Vegetable Beef Soup above.)

Combine 2-3 lbs. soup bones or beef shortribs in 5-qt. casserole with 1 teaspoon salt, 1 teaspoon celery salt, 1 small chopped onion, 1 cup diced carrots, ½ cup diced celery and water to cover. **Insert** temperature probe so tip rests on bottom of dish, halfway between center and side. **Cover** tightly with plastic wrap, arranging loosely around probe to vent. Attach cable end at receptacle. **Microwave at Automatic Simmer (Auto Roast Code 6) 4 to 6 Hours.**

Strip meat from bones after microwaving and return to stock when making soup. Or, strain stock and freeze for broth.

Skim fat if using immediately, or refrigerate stock until fat solidifies and can be lifted off.

Tip: Make Soup or Basic Stock ahead and freeze in one cup containers. Defrost rapidly by microwaving when ready to use.

Any main dishes which call for water will taste richer if you substitute stock.

Less tender steaks, such as round, flank or cubed should be microwaved in liquid at Low (3) or Medium (5). Steam produced by the liquid softens the meat during its longer, slower cooking at the lower power settings.

Tenderizing Tips

In some of our recipes, we recommend the traditional technique of pounding the meat, or having it processed through the butcher's tenderizing machine, before cooking.

Frequently, less tender steaks are cooked with a slightly acid liquid, such as tomato juice or wine, which helps tenderize them. Marinating both tenderizes and imparts a delicious flavor to steaks. Try one of the marinades on page 82, and use some of the marinade as the cooking liquid. To save time you can substitute bottled oil and vinegar salad dressing for prepared marinade. Large less tender roasts may be marinated too. Microwave as on page 88.

How to Defrost Steaks

POWER LEVEL: **Defrost (3)**

4 to 8 Minutes Per Pound

1. Place plastic or paper wrapped package in oven. Microwave at Defrost ½ the minimum total time.
2. Turn package over and defrost second ½ of time.
3. Separate pieces with a table knife and let stand to complete defrosting, or microwave 1 to 2 minutes more.

Swiss Steak

Separate steaks as soon as possible and let stand until ice is no longer apparent. If meat is to be cut into strips, do this while it is still partially frozen. It will slice neatly and easily. Any juices which appear during defrosting can be added to the liquid in the recipe.

Swiss Steak

POWER LEVEL: Medium (5)
MICROWAVE TIME: 70 to 80 min., total

1½ lb. round steak, ½-in. thick, tenderized or pounded with meat mallet **¼ cup flour** **1½ teaspoons salt** **⅛ teaspoon pepper** **1 medium onion, sliced thin** **1 can (1-lb.) tomatoes**	Cut meat in 6 pieces, then coat with mixture of flour, salt and pepper. Place in 3-qt. casserole. Cover with onion. Break up tomatoes with fork and pour over top. Cover. **Microwave at Medium (5) 70 to 80 Minutes,** rearranging meat after 40 minutes, until tender.

Makes 6 servings

Swiss Style Cube Steak: Substitute ½-lb. cube steaks, ½-in. thick (about 6), for round steak. Cut in half, if desired.

NOTE: If thicker gravy is desired, stir in 2 tablespoons of flour per cup of juices. Microwave 2 to 3 minutes.

Select 2 to 3-lb. steak, chuck steak, flank steak and cube steak for marinating. The smaller the cut of meat, the more marinade flavor it will absorb because more surface is exposed.

Marinate in glass dish covered with plastic, turning steaks over once. Refrigerate 4 to 24 hours in marinade, turning meat over after half the time.

Lemon or Vinegar Marinade

½ **cup lemon juice or** **white vinegar** ½ **cup oil** 1 **sprig parsley or** 1 **tablespoon** **chopped parsley** 2 **bay leaves** 1 **garlic clove,** **crushed** 2 **slices onion** 1 **tablespoon sugar** **Pinch of nutmeg** 2 **drops liquid pepper** **seasoning** **(tabasco)**	In cooking container or 1-qt. glass measure mix together lemon juice, oil, parsley, bay leaves, garlic, onion, sugar, nutmeg, liquid pepper. Use as suggested.

Makes 1 cup

Tomato Marinade

1 **can (8-oz.) tomato** **sauce** 1 **teaspon bottled** **brown bouquet** **sauce** 1 **cup chopped onion** 1 **teaspoon basil** 1 **teaspoon sugar** 1 **teaspoon garlic** **powder**	In cooking container or 1-qt. glass measure mix together tomato sauce, brown bouquet sauce, onion, basil, sugar and garlic powder. Use as suggested.

Makes 1½ cups

Teriyaki Marinade

½ **cup soy sauce** ½ **cup brown sugar** **(packed)** 1 **clove garlic,** **minced** 2 **teaspoons ground** **ginger** 1 **teaspoon** **monosodium** **glutamate** **(Accent)** ½ **teaspoon pepper**	In cooking container or 1-qt. glass measure mix together soy sauce, brown sugar, garlic, ginger, monosodium glutamate and pepper. Use as suggested.

Makes ¾ cup

Wine Marinade

⅔ **cup sherry** ⅓ **cup cooking oil** 1 **medium onion,** **finely chopped** 1 **clove garlic,** **minced** ½ **teaspoon pepper** ¼ **teaspoon dried** **thyme**	In cooking container or 1-qt. glass measure mix together wine, oil, onion, garlic, pepper and thyme. Use as suggested.

Makes 1 cup

Turn Over steaks just before microwaving and, if desired, drain off some of marinade. Recover with plastic wrap to microwave.

Microwave at Medium 25 to 30 Minutes per Pound, turning steaks over, rearranging and recovering after half the cooking time.

Less Tender Beef Cuts Microwaving Helpful Hints

"Besides marinating, how else can I tenderize tough meat cuts?"

Place meat on a butcher block or cutting board and pound with a meat mallet, or edge of a foil covered saucer before microwaving. Be sure to remove, or avoid any bones.

"I like to cut steaks into strips before marinating or stir-frying, but I have trouble cutting the slices neatly."

Freeze the steak slightly before slicing. It will become firmer and easier to slice into neat strips. Marinate and cook as above; use cooked beef strips in Stir Fry Vegetable recipe page 174.

84 Tender Steaks

Steaks microwaved in the Brown 'N Sear dish are juicy and tender. Your microwave oven can also be useful when cooking steaks conventionally. See tips below.

How to Defrost Steaks

POWER LEVEL: **Defrost (3)**

4 to 8 Minutes Per Pound

1. Place plastic or paper wrapped package in oven. **Microwave at Defrost** ½ the minimum total time.
2. Turn package over and defrost second ½ of time.
3. Separate pieces with a table knife; let stand to complete defrosting, or **Microwave 1 to 2 Minutes** more.

Broil extra 1-in. steaks or hamburgers while preparing a batch for dinner in the conventional broiler; undercook the extras slightly. Cool, wrap and freeze for later reheating in the microwave. Directions below have been developed especially for this use.

Sear extra 1-in. steaks or hamburgers while charcoal grill is hot, but undercook them slightly. Cool, wrap and freeze as suggested at left. You'll have charcoal flavor without re-lighting the grill.

Frozen Precooked Steak	Step 1: DEFROST AT POWER LEVEL 3 MINUTES/LB.	COMMENTS	Step 2: After defrosting, or for reheating refrigerated precooked steaks MICROWAVE AT MEDIUM (5) MINUTES/LB.	COMMENTS
Rare	5-7	Turn over after half of time. Let stand covered a few minutes before serving.	5-7	Turn over after half of time. Let stand covered a few minutes before serving.
Medium	5-7		6-8	
Well	5-7		7-9	
Turn over after half of time. Let stand covered.				

The step-by-step information below may be used with most types of steaks and chops you cook in the Brown 'N Sear dish. This dish has a special undercoating which absorbs heat and allows the bottom of the dish to become as hot as a griddle. Uncoated raw cuts like steak and chops need no extra fat added to dish; however to develop more brown color, we recommend adding 1 tablespoon butter to heated dish just before adding meat. Crumb or flour coated chicken or fish pieces need about 1 tablespoon oil added to dish before frying, as do batter foods like pancakes.

Microwaving Steaks in Brown 'N Sear Dish

Times are given for ¾ to 1-in. thick steaks cooked to medium (pink center). To test for doneness, cut with knife tip from edge toward center of steak. Area closest to bone is last to cook. Ground beef patties up to 1-in. thick may also be microwaved this way. **Preheat empty and uncovered browning utensil 8 minutes,** or until the bottom turns yellow. For subsequent batches, preheat time will be half the original time.

POWER LEVEL: **High (10)**

TYPE	NO. OF STEAKS	1st SIDE MINUTES	2nd SIDE MINUTES
Cube Steak or Minute Steak (4-oz. each)	1 or 2	1	1 to 1½
Rib Eye or Strip	1 or 2	2	2 to 2½
T-Bone	1	3	2 to 3
Filet Mignon	1, 2 or 4	2	2 to 2½

Fit foods to the dish before cooking. Wipe the dish clean after fitting food; traces of fat and meat will scorch.

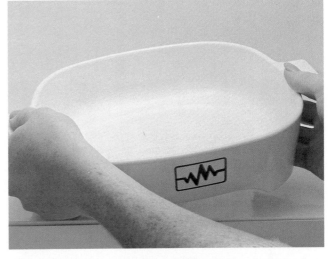

Preheat Uncovered Dish 8 Minutes or until the bottom turns yellow. For subsequent batches, preheat time will be half the original time.

Remove juices with a spoon after browning the first side of steaks.

Turn Over steaks and continue cooking according to time chart on this page.

Defrosting is one of the major benefits of the microwave oven, but it is not miraculous. Roasts need attention during defrosting or they will start to cook. Follow directions carefully for successful defrosting of these expensive cuts of meat.

The procedure demonstrated here applies to pork, lamb and veal roasts as well as beef. Warm areas after defrosting indicate that the meat has started to cook and should be roasted immediately. If you are defrosting a

How to Defrost Roasts
POWER LEVEL: **Defrost (3)**

10 to 12 Minutes Per Pound

Place unopened paper or plastic wrapped package in oven. Microwave at Defrost (3) for ½ the time.

Remove wrappings, which will come off easily.

Turn roast over onto a trivet set over a cooking dish.

Defrosting Roasts Over 6 Pounds

1. Place wrapped roast in oven and defrost for first ½ of time. Unwrap roast and shield any warm areas.

2. Turn roast over into baking dish. If roast is over 5-in. high, do not use trivet.

3. Defrost for second ½ of time. Let stand 30 minutes.

4. Roast cooking chart is on page 92.

roast for later cooking, be especially careful. We recommend that you defrost for ¾ the time and allow the roast to finish defrosting in the refrigerator.

Freezer to Table Roasts:

Cooking roasts from freezer to table depends on what kind of microwave system you have. This cookbook was written for ovens which have microwave energy from both top and bottom of the oven; with this system you can cook frozen beef roasts to table-ready. Follow the cooking times and power level on the chart page 92,

turning over the meat after half of total time. At this point meat should be thawed enough to insert the temperature probe. Check again after about ¾ of time and add bits of foil to shield if necessary.

If your oven does not have energy from both top and bottom, it is best to defrost roast thoroughly, then cook it using the temperature probe if you have one.

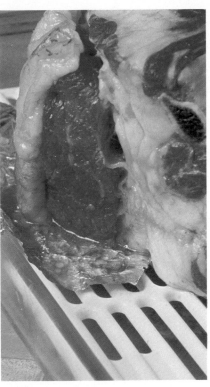

Feel roast for warm spots, especially on edges and thinner areas. Shield warm areas with small pieces of foil. Defrost for final ½ of time.

Juices begin to appear. Meat should look moist with glistening fat and should feel cool.

Test meat by inserting a skewer into the center. Do not insert the temperature probe until meat is completely defrosted.

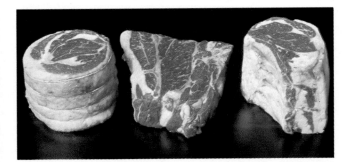

Thick roasts defrost evenly and turning over is very important. Allow some standing time to be sure interior is completely defrosted.

Flat roasts defrost quickly. Defrost for ½ of time and turn roast over.

Irregular roasts need more shielding on thinner areas. Check carefully for warm spots.

Shape of Meat as well as size influences defrosting time.

In microwaving, as in conventional cooking, less tender cuts of beef call for some liquid, tight covering, and lower power setting to make them juicy and tender. Use sirloin tip, rump, arm or blade chuck for pot roasts, and brisket or corned beef for simmered beef.

How to Microwave a Pot Roast

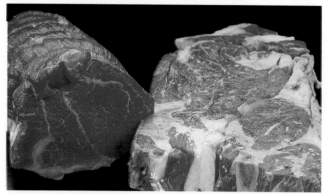

Select flat or round roast, fresh or frozen. microwave thicker roast using either time or simmer method. Thinner, flat roast microwaves best using time method.

Place 3 to 5-lb. rump or chuck roast in a roasting dish. If desired, brush all sides with a mixture of one teaspoon brown bouquet sauce and one tablespoon water. Or marinate several hours, see page 82.

How to Microwave Less Tender Roasts and Adapt Your Favorite Recipes

AUTO ROAST CODE 6 ITEM	DISH SIZE	POWER LEVEL	TIME, COOK HOURS	AUTOMATIC SIMMER AUTO ROAST CODE 6		COMMENTS
				FRESH	FROZEN	
Chuck Roast, 3 to 5 lbs.	13×9×2	Medium (5)	1½-2	4-6	6-9	Match cooking container to roast size. When not adding vegetables, you may choose to use a cooking bag. If your cooking dish does not have a vented cover, use plastic wrap, turned back at one corner to allow steam to escape.
Sirloin Tip, 3 to 3½ lbs.	3-qt. casserole	Medium (5)	1¼-1½	6-8	8-11	
Beef Brisket, 2½ to 3 lbs.	3-qt. casserole	Medium (5)	1½-1¾	6-8	8-11	
Corned Beef, 3 to 3½ lbs.	4-qt. casserole	Medium (5)	1½-1¾	6-8	8-11	

How to Automatic Simmer Less Tender Roasts (Pot Roasts):

These instructions are for models with Automatic Simmer feature, found on some models with Auto Roast. Simmering several hours produces meat which is very tender and flavorful.

Select roasts mentioned in chart above. Flat, evenly shaped roasts are best; thick sirloin tip roasts should be checked at minimum time and turned over if necessary. Always add at least ½ cup water to the roast and place tip of temperature probe in liquid in dish. Cover tightly with plastic wrap, venting around probe. See picture page 90. Set Auto Roast Code 6, and time according to chart above.

If you want vegetables with your meat, use either of two methods. One is to cook vegetables separately, either before the roast or during standing time. Add them to the meat and heat briefly. Or you may add vegetables to the meat halfway through the cooking period and mcirowave until meat and vegetables are fork tender.

Pour in ½ cup water or wine or, if roast has been marinated, use ½ cup marinade. Cover tightly with plastic wrap turning back corner to vent. **Microwave at Medium (5) 19 to 23 Minutes Per Pound.** Microwave for ½ of total cooking time.

Turn Over roast end to end after ½ cooking time.

Arrange vegetables around roast, if desired. **Cover and microwave final ½ of cooking time** or until meat is tender. Thinner roasts cook faster than thick ones.

Adapting Tips for Microwave Simmering Less Tender Meat Cuts

Place beef brisket or corned beef in large casserole. Add 1 cup water for each pound of meat. **Cover** and **Microwave at High (10) 15 to 25 Minutes.**

Turn meat over and recover. **Microwave at Medium (5) 1 to 1½ Hours,** until tender. Let stand, covered, 10 to 15 minutes.

For maximum juiciness, let beef stand in juices until partially cool.

Carve roast diagonally across the grain in thin slices for attractive, tender meat.

Recently the meat industry has updated their microwaving information to include dry roasting recommendations for round roast as well as sirloin tip and rump. That means these roasts can be microwaved just like tender beef roasts, page 92.

In the helpful hints section (right) we show how to tell by looking at your roast whether it may be classified as a tender meat roast.

Microwaving Roasts Using Temperature Probe or Automatic Simmer

To Microwave by Temperature, insert temperature probe in center of roast. Cover tightly with plastic wrap, arranging loosely around probe to vent or cover with microwave-safe dome. **Microwave at Medium (5).** Set Temp, Set 90°. When oven signals, turn roast over and continue microwaving until desired doneness.

To Microwave with Automatic Simmer, place probe, with tip submerged in liquid, next to meat in microwave ovenproof cooking dish. Cover with plastic wrap, arranging loosely around probe to vent. Set Auto Roast Code 6. Time flat roasts like chuck or arm for 4 to 6 hours. Time thicker roasts like tip or rump for 6 to 8 hours.

Flavoring Tips for Less Tender Roasts

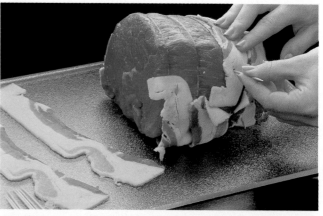

Brush high quality sirloin tip roast with bottled teriyaki sauce mixed with 1 tablespoon water, or with liquid smoke. Shake or rub seasoned pepper (lemon, garlic, herb or onion) on all surfaces. Place in cooking dish; add ½ cup red wine or water; insert temperature probe, if desired; cover and cook following directions on pages 88 and 89. On removal from the oven, the roast will appear moist but the surface will dry and darken attractively after standing. Cut diagonal slices for maximum tenderness.

Brush rolled rump roast with Worcestershire sauce and then rub with seasoned salt. Cover all except cut ends with bacon strips side by side; secure with picks. Microwave well done.

Beef Roast—Less Tender Cuts

Beef roasts that are cooked the less tender way have the advantage of flavorsome bastes or marinades. Some people prefer sprinkling a packet of dry onion soup over the roast for added flavor. Or they substitute diluted canned soup for the liquid in the recipes.

Flavoring Tip for Automatic Simmer Cooking

Cover meats to be simmered with onions, garlic, bay leaf and other seasonings. Add water, broth or wine.

Automatic Simmer is a feature included in some ovens which have Auto Roast. Cover meat with plastic wrap and add temperature probe as pictured on left. Time as on chart page 88.

New England Boiled Dinner

POWER LEVEL: High (10) and Medium (5)
MICROWAVE TIME: 3 hrs., 15 to 20 min.

3 to 3½ lb. corned beef brisket 3 cups water 1 medium onion, thinly sliced 2 cloves garlic, minced 2 bay leaves	In 3-qt. casserole place brisket with water. Slice onion over brisket and add garlic and bay leaves. Cover. **Microwave at High (10) 25 Minutes.** Turn brisket over. Recover. **Microwave at Medium (5) 60 to 70 Minutes,** turning brisket over after 30 minutes. Remove meat from broth and keep warm.
2 large potatoes, cut up 4 medium carrots, cut lengthwise 1 medium head cabbage cut in 6 wedges	Add potatoes and carrots to broth. Arrange cabbage in a pinwheel on top. Cover. **Microwave at High (10) 25 to 30 Minutes,** rearranging after 15 minutes, until vegetables are tender. Discard bay leaves to serve.

Makes 6 servings

Microwaving Less Tender Roasts Helpful Hints

"How should I test a pot roast to determine if it is done?"

Microwave for minimum time recommended on page 88. Check meat with a fork. If it is not tender and easy to pull apart, continue microwaving to maximum recommended time.

"Should less tender roasts always be covered with liquid before microwaving?"

Less tender roasts such as round, sirloin tip, or rump may be either dry roasted or simmered in liquid depending on the meat's quality. Tougher roasts should be simmered for best results. If roast has fresh color, close velvety grain with no stringy portions or large muscles, and moderate marbling, it can be dry roasted following tender roast microwaving procedures.

Since these roasts are expensive, and generally reserved for special occasions, you'll want to follow directions carefully. Select meat carefully; standards for grading beef have changed recently, which may affect grain and resulting tenderness.

Pay attention to internal temperature. Since meat continues to cook while standing, rare to medium roasts are microwaved to lower internal temperature than conventional roasts. After 10 minutes standing, both reach about the same doneness.

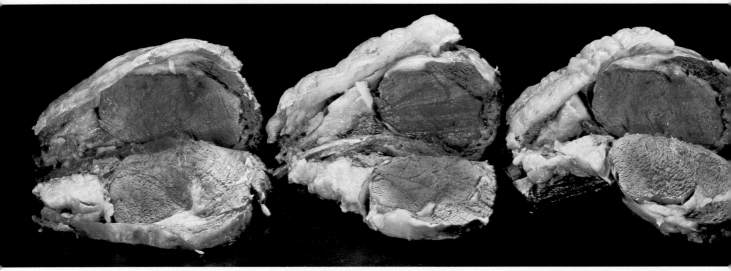

Conventionally Roasted Beef. This standing rib roast was roasted conventionally to an internal temperature of 140°. All three roasts pictured stood about 15 minutes before carving.

Microwaved Roasted Beef. This standing rib roast was microwave roasted to an internal temperature of 135°. It has the same color internally as conventionally roasted beef, although the temperature is lower. Roast was brushed with browning agent before microwaving.

Auto-Roast Roasted Beef. This standing rib roast was roasted to 140°. Unlike the microwaved roast at left which used a single power level, Auto Roast uses up to 3 power settings which automatically lower the cooking heat while food cooks, thus preventing overcooking.

Tender Roast Adapting and Cooking Chart
POWER LEVEL: **Medium (5)**

TYPE	TEMP. CONTROL SETTING	MINUTES PER POUND REFRIG.	FROZEN		COMMENTS
Standing Rib Roast, 4-6 lbs.	Rare: 120°	12-13	17-18		Place roasts on trivet, cut side up. Fo any thin ends under boneless roasts such as tenderloin, and tie with a stri Cover roast loosely with wax paper.
	Medium: 135°	14-15	19-20	Turn over all frozen roasts after first half of cooking. Insert Temp. Probe if desired at this time.	
	Well: 155°	16-17	21-22		
Rib Eye and Rolled Rib, 4-5 lbs.	Rare: 120°	12-13	19-25		
	Medium: 135°	14-15	21-26		**Allow standing time** of 10 to 15 minutes before carving.
	Well: 155°	16-17	23-28		
Sirloin Tip, 3-4 lbs.	Rare: 120°	14-15	23-24		
	Medium: 135°	16-17	24-25		Probe not recommended for roasts under 2-lbs. Time cook these roasts
	Well: 155°	18-19	25-26		
Rolled, Rump, 4-5 lbs.	Rare: 120°	12-13	24-25		
	Medium: 135°	14-15	26-27		
Tenderloin, Whole	Well: 155°	16-17	28-29		
Tenderloin, Half	Rare:	8-10	24-25*		*Cook tenderloin first 30 minutes on Medium (5), then finish at Low (3).
	Rare:	11-13	24-25*		

Small, compact and evenly shaped roasts cook best. Just as in conventional cooking a roast which is thinner on one end will be done first in that area. Long, thin roasts cook faster than short, thick ones.

If family or guests differ in preference between rare and well-done, roast the meat to the minimum doneness. Carve it, and return some slices to the microwave oven. It takes just a short time to bring a slice from rare to well-done, and all will have meat to suit their tastes.

How to Use Auto Roast

On some touch control models, this feature allows you to temperature cook fresh roasts (because of the temperature probe frozen roasts may not be used) while automatically gradually lowering the microwave power. Because of the lowered power, there is less opportunity for heat to build up around the edges of the meat and cause overcooking.

Auto Roast meat (opposite page) may be cooked to slightly higher temperature than time or temperature cooked meat because of slower, more gentle heat.

Roasts cooked with this feature take 2 to 3 more minutes cooking time per pound of meat. Coded settings corresponding to the type of meat and doneness desired are on the oven's control panel. Step by step information about Auto Roast is in the use and care book for these models.

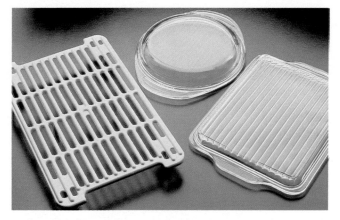

Due to the slotted design of the microwave trivet accessory shown, bottom areas of rare or medium done roasts may not be brown when meat is done. This allows greater area of rare or medium meat for serving. Flat glass or pottery trivets such as top of refrigerator dish, flat top of casserole, or china plate hold heat to bottom of roast and bottom browning will occur.

How to Microwave Tender Beef Roasts

Tie standing rib roasts across the meat to secure fat. Fold the thin end of a half tenderloin under and tie the roast to maintain an even, compact shape. Tie rib eye firmly.

Brush half tenderloin or rib eye roast with equal parts brown bouquet sauce and melted butter if desired.

Place roast on a trivet in a 12×8×2 or 13×9×2-in. cooking dish. DO NOT SALT. Cover with wax paper.

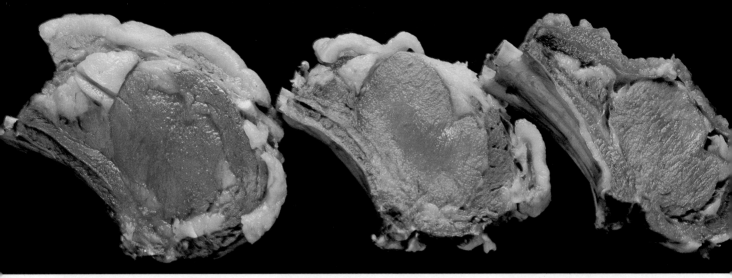

Rare. Meat microwaved to an internal temperature of 120° is red in the center, with running juices. Since microwaving is so fast, the exterior will not be browned.

Medium. Meat microwaved to an internal temperature of 135° is rosy in the center, with pink juices. Some browning occurs on the outside.

Well Done. Meat microwaved to an internal temperature of 155° is brown in the center, with clear juices.

How to Insert the Temperature Probe

Measure the distance to the center of the roast by laying the temperature probe on top of the meat. If the roast is uneven in shape or contains fat or bone, select an angle which will bring the tip of the probe to the center of the thickest meaty area without touching fat or bone.

Mark with your thumb and forefinger where the edge of the meat comes on the probe. Insert the probe horizontally up to the point marked off with your finger.

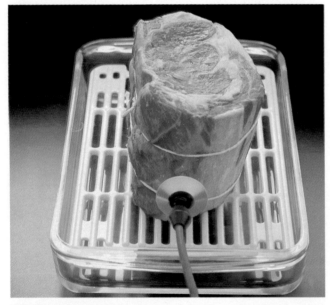

Rib Eye. Insert probe horizontally through side of roast so that tip is in the center of meat.

Rolled Rib. Insert probe horizontally into the rolled side so that tip is in the center.

NOTE: Pictures are taken without wax paper cover to best show positioning of temperature probe.

Microwaving Beef by Time

Estimate the cooking time for the type, size and desired doneness of your roast. (See chart on page 92.) After minimum time, remove roast from the oven and test temperature with a meat thermometer, following directions for probe placement given with your type of roast. Remember that microwave roasted meats are cooked to a lower temperature than conventionally roasted meats. *Do not use meat thermometer in the microwave oven unless it is specially designed or recommended for use in the microwave oven.*

Although some natural browning occurs on microwave roasts, many people prefer to deepen the color by brushing or basting a brown sauce over the outside surfaces. Recipes for 3 interesting and flavorful toppings follow below.

Other ideas include brushing the roast with liquid smoke, then seasoned pepper. Or use a teriyaki baste (bottled or recipe page 82.) Whatever browning agent is used, avoid the use of salt over meaty surfaces. Salt draws the juices out of the meat.

Shake On Browning Mix*

¼ **cup crushed**	Mix all ingredients
instant beef	together in a shaker
bouillon granules	container. Sprinkle on and
2 tablespoons flour	rub into all sides of meat
1 teaspoon paprika	using about 1 tablespoon
½ teaspoon pepper	per side.

*Courtesy, National Livestock and Meat Board.

Basting Sauces

Beefy Glaze: In a 1 cup glass measure place 6 teaspoons of beef bouillon granules or 6 beef bouillon cubes. Add ¼ cup water or sherry wine and ½ teaspoon garlic powder. Microwave at High (10) 1 to 1¼ minutes, until dissolved.

Bourbon Baste: In 1 cup measure mix ¼ cup cooking oil, ¼ cup bourbon, 2 tablespoons soy sauce, 1 teaspoon Worcestershire sauce, 1 teaspoon garlic salt and ⅛ teaspoon pepper. Good with beef steaks, roasts, veal, lamb and spareribs.

Microwaving Tender Beef Roasts Helpful Hints

"My beef roast was undercooked when the programmed temperature on the probe indicated it should be ready."

Check placement of the temperature probe. Probe should be placed horizontally in the center of roast's thickest part. See details on page 94.

"My beef roast is not as brown as I'd like. What can I do to enhance the color?"

Try shake on browning or basting recipes above, or brush with equal amounts of brown bouquet sauce and butter.

"My beef roast appeared underdone on the bottom even though I used a trivet as directed."

Many people prefer this larger area of pinkish meat. The type of trivet you use will affect doneness on the bottom of roasts. A solid glass or pyroceram trivet holds more heat next to the roast and will cook it more on the bottom than a slotted plastic trivet.

Classic Ham Loaf

Classic Ham Loaf

POWER LEVEL: High (10)　　　　　　　　TEMP: 170°
MICROWAVE TIME: 11 to 14 min.

1 lb. ground cooked **ham** **½ lb. ground fresh** **pork** **½ cup soft bread** **crumbs** **½ cup water** **2 tablespoons** **instant minced** **onion** **¼ teaspoon pepper**	Mix ground ham and pork thoroughly with crumbs, water, onion, and pepper. Mold into flat loaf in 9-in. pie plate. Insert temperature probe so tip is in center of food. Cover tightly with plastic wrap, arranging loosely around probe to vent. Attach cable end at receptacle. **Microwave at Medium. Set Temp, Set 170°.**

When oven signals, remove loaf from oven, spoon on glaze, and let stand 5 minutes before serving.

Makes 6 servings

Glaze: Stir 4 tablespoons apricot preserves until smooth; spoon and spread on hot ham loaf.

Ground Ham/Pork

Patties containing ground ham do not require use of the Brown 'N Sear Dish or a browning agent because ham has a naturally attractive pink color; however, a light brushing of brown bouquet sauce may be used.

Defrosting Ground Pork. Ground pork should be defrosted in the same way as ground beef. See page 66. Ham does not freeze well, but small quantities of leftover ground ham may be frozen for use in appetizers, casseroles or Oriental and Italian dishes which call for small amounts of ham to heighten color and flavor.

Sweet 'N' Sour Porkies

POWER LEVEL: High (10)
MICROWAVE TIME: 14 to 16 min., total

1 lb. ground cooked **ham** **½ lb. ground fresh** **pork** **½ cup soft bread** **crumbs** **½ cup water** **1 egg** **¼ cup minced celery** **2 tablespoons** **minced green** **pepper** **2 tablespoons** **instant minced** **onion** **½ teaspoon dry** **mustard** **¼ teaspoon pepper**	In large mixing bowl mix together ham, pork, crumbs, water, egg, celery, green pepper, onion, mustard and pepper. Shape mixture into 4 individual patties and place in 8-in. square dish.
8 to 12 whole cloves	Score tops of patties and place 2 or 3 whole cloves in top of each.
⅓ cup brown sugar **(packed)** **1 tablespoon** **prepared mustard** **1 tablespoon** **vinegar**	Stir together sugar, mustard and vinegar. Pour evenly over patties. Cover dish with wax paper. **Microwave at High (10) 14 to 16 Minutes.**

Makes 4 generous servings

Pork Adapting and Cooking Chart

ITEM	POWER LEVEL	TIME COOK MIN.	BROWN 'N SEAR DISH — POWER LEVEL: **High (10)**		
			PREHEAT	1st SIDE	2nd SIDE
Ground Pork/Ham loaf and patties, 1-2 lbs.	High (10)	11-16 ½ turn after 10 min.	—	—	—
Spareribs	Medium (5)	80-90	—	—	—
Pork Chops, 3-4	Medium (5)	22-28	8 min.	6 min. covered	9-11 min. covered
Pork Casserole (uncooked meat)	Medium (5)	50-60	—	—	—

Pork Spareribs

Everyone agrees that the barbecued sparerib is one of America's greatest inventions. Few agree on how it should be cooked. Whichever rib you fancy, the microwave oven cooks it fast and flavorful.

How to Defrost Spareribs

POWER LEVEL: **Defrost**

4 to 8 Minutes Per Pound

1. Place plastic or paper wrapped package in oven. **Microwave at Defrost** ½ the minimum total time.
2. Turn package over and **Defrost** second ½ of time.
3. Separate the pieces with a rubber spatula and let stand to complete defrosting, or **Microwave 1 to 2 Minutes** more.

NOTE: For a rack of ribs, let stand 15 minutes to completely defrost largest end.

Whole Rack of Spareribs should be turned over for even cooking. Rib pieces can be rearranged.

Fork Tender Spareribs

POWER LEVEL: Medium (5)
MICROWAVE TIME: 1 hr. 30 min. to 1 hr. 45 min., total

3 lb. rack of spareribs **2 cups hot tap water** **1 medium onion, very thinly sliced** **1 lemon, very thinly sliced**	In 13×9×2-in. dish place spareribs, bone side up. Add water. Cover tightly with vented plastic wrap. **Microwave at Medium (5) 80 to 90 Minutes,** rotating dish ½ turn every 20 minutes, until fork tender. Turn ribs over, distribute onion and lemon over top after 40 minutes.
1 cup barbecue sauce, bottled, or recipe page 158	Drain liquid from ribs and pour sauce over top.

Microwave at Medium (5) 10 to 15 Minutes, loosely covered with plastic wrap, until sauce has dried on top.

Makes about 4 servings

TO COOK RIBS IN PIECES: Cut into 2 or 3-rib pieces and microwave in 3-qt. covered casserole.

Teriyaki Spareribs

Ribs may be marinated in sauce several hours or overnight before cooking, if desired.

POWER LEVEL: Medium (5) and High (10)
MICROWAVE TIME: 73 to 84 min., total

3 lb. spareribs	Have butcher cut rack of spareribs in half crosswise. Cut ribs into 3-in. pieces and place in 3-qt. casserole.
¼ cup soy sauce **½ cup sliced onion** **2 tablespoons brown sugar (packed)** **1 clove garlic, minced** **1 teaspoon ground ginger** **1 teaspoon salt** **1 tablespoon sherry wine** **3 cups apricot nectar or orange juice**	In mixing bowl stir together soy sauce, onion, brown sugar, garlic, ginger, salt, sherry and nectar. Pour over ribs. Cover. **Microwave at Medium (5) 70 to 80 Minutes,** rearranging every 20 minutes. Remove ribs to platter and keep warm. Skim fat from top of liquid remaining in dish.
1½ tablespoons cornstarch **2 tablespoons water**	In small bowl, stir together cornstarch and water. Blend into liquid in dish. **Microwave at High (10) 3 to 4 Minutes,** stirring every minute until sauce is clear and thickened. Serve sauce over ribs.

Makes about 8 appetizer servings, or 4 entree servings

Pork Chops/Steaks

Microwaved pork chops or steaks need to be browned or cooked in a colorful sauce. Pictured at left from top to bottom: Conventional, Plain Microwaved, Steak Sauce and Water Topping, Brown 'N Sear Dish.

How to Defrost Chops & Steaks

POWER LEVEL: **Defrost**

4 to 8 Minutes Per Pound

1. Place plastic or paper wrapped package in oven. **Microwave at Defrost (3)** ½ the minimum time.
2. Turn package over and defrost second ½ of time.
3. Separate the pieces with a rubber spatula and let stand to complete defrosting, or **Microwave 1 to 2 Minutes** more.

Microwaving Chops or Steaks

1. Select steaks or chops about ¾-in. thick. Cut steaks into pieces about 3×4-in. Arrange in suitable dish.
2. On each chop or steak, spread 2 tablespoons of Topping. (See suggestions below.)
3. Cover tightly with plastic wrap, vent 2-in. at one side. **Microwave at Medium (5),** rotating dish ½ turn after ½ of time.
4. Add salt and pepper after microwaving, as desired.

POWER LEVEL: **Medium (5)**

NO. OF CHOPS	TIME/ MIN.	STANDING TIME/MIN.	COMMENTS
1-2	14-20	5-6	Chops should not be more than 1-in. thick.
3-4	18-25	5-10	
5-6	28-35	5-10	Rotate ½ turn after half time.

Brown 'N Sear Dish (Preheat dish for 5 min.)
POWER LEVEL: **High (10)**

NO. OF CHOPS	TIME/MINUTES 1st SIDE	2nd SIDE	COMMENTS
1-2	4	8-10	Preheat empty dish at High. Add chops; cover and cook first side. Turn chops and recover dish. Cook second side.
3-4	5-6	10-13	

Chili Pork Chops

POWER LEVEL: Medium (5)
MICROWAVE TIME: 35 to 45 min., total

4 pork chops, 1-in. thick	Score fat on chops and arrange in 3-qt. casserole so "tails" are in center. Place onion and green pepper slices on top of chops. Pour chili sauce over top. Cover. **Microwave at Medium (5) 35 to 45 Minutes,** rotating dish ½ turn after 20 minutes.
4 onion slices, ¼ to ½-in. thick	
4 green pepper rings, ¼ to ½-in. thick	
1 bottle (12-oz.) chili sauce (1½ cups)	

Makes 4 servings

Pork Chops/Steaks

Just as in conventional cooking, texture of pork chops depends upon the cooking method used. Fried chops are chewy; steamed chops are more soft. Some people prefer to brown chops in a skillet on the range top, then finish them by microwaving.

Stuffed 'N' Tender Pork Chops

Because chops are split, each layer of meat is thinner and slightly shorter cooking time may be used.

POWER LEVEL: Medium (5)
MICROWAVE TIME: 35 to 40 min., total

1. Select **4 (1-in. thick) pork chops** with pocket cut in each.
2. Fill pocket with Cornbread Stuffing or Apple Stuffing (below), dividing all of stuffing among chops. Arrange chops in 12×8×2-in. dish, with thickest meaty areas to edge and "tails" in center. Brush half of glaze (below) over top of chops. Cover with wax paper.
3. **Microwave at Medium (5) 35 to 40 Minutes,** rotating dish ½ turn after 15 minutes, until tender. Let stand 5 minutes. Brush with remaining glaze before serving.

Makes 4 servings

Cornbread Stuffing with Savory Glaze

2 cups crumbled cornbread	In mixing bowl toss together cornbread, onion, green pepper, butter, egg, pimiento, salt and pepper. Divide evenly between chops.
¼ cup chopped onion	
¼ cup chopped green pepper	
¼ cup butter, melted	
1 egg, beaten	
1 tablespoon chopped pimiento	
½ teaspoon salt	
⅛ teaspoon pepper	

Savory Glaze: Mix together ½ cup ketchup, 2 tablespoons brown sugar, 2 teaspoons prepared mustard and ¼ teaspoon chili powder.

Makes about 1½ cups

Apple Stuffing with Sweet Glaze

2 cups chopped apples	In mixing bowl combine apples, raisins, egg, butter, cinnamon, salt and pepper. Divide evenly between chops.
¼ cup raisins	
1 egg, beaten	
2 tablespoons butter, melted	
½ teaspoon cinnamon	
½ teaspoon salt	
⅛ teaspoon pepper	

Sweet Glaze: Mix together ⅓ cup currant jelly and 2 tablespoons orange juice.

Makes about 1½ cups

Cornbread Stuffed 'N' Tender Pork Chops

Pork Chops Rosado

This dish is very saucy, so plan rice or noodles to serve under chops and sauce.

POWER LEVEL: Medium (5)
MICROWAVE TIME: 40 to 50 min., total

4 center cut loin pork chops, 1-in. thick	In 12×8×2-in. dish arrange pork chops with thickest meaty areas to edge and "tails" in center. Place onion and lemon slices over top of chops.
1 large onion, cut in ¼-in. slices	
1 medium lemon or lime, cut in ⅛-in. slices	
1 cup ketchup	Combine ketchup and sour cream. Pour over top. Cover dish with plastic wrap, turning back one corner to vent.
1 cup (8-oz.) dairy sour cream	

Microwave at Medium (5) 40 to 50 Minutes, rotating dish ½ turn after 20 minutes, until pork chops are tender. Let stand, covered about 5 minutes before serving.

Makes 4 servings

100 Pork

Fresh raw pork pieces microwave well in saucy casseroles like Sweet and Sour Pork. Just like beef stew meat and other meats requiring tenderizing, they should be cooked until tender at power levels no higher than Medium (5). Casseroles with precooked pork may be reheated at High (10).

Sweet and Sour Pork

POWER LEVEL: Medium (5) and Medium High (7)
MICROWAVE TIME: 45 to 50 min., total

1½ lbs. fresh pork, cut into 1-in. cubes
1½ tablespoons instant minced onion
1 tablespoon soy sauce
1 teaspoon brown bouquet sauce
1 can (8¾-oz.) pineapple chunks

In 2-qt. casserole place pork, onion, soy sauce and bouquet sauce. Reserving juice, drain pineapple. Set aside. Add reserved juice to meat, stirring well. Cover. **Microwave at Medium (5) 30 Minutes,** stirring after 15 minutes.

1 cup water
¼ cup cider vinegar
¼ cup brown sugar (packed)
3 tablespoons cornstarch
½ teaspoon salt
1 can (5-oz.) water chestnuts, drained and sliced
1 medium green pepper, sliced in ½-in. strips

In small bowl stir together water, vinegar, brown sugar, cornstarch and salt. Add to meat along with pineapple and water chestnuts. Cover. **Microwave at Medium High (7) 15 to 20 Minutes,** stirring and adding green pepper after 8 minutes, until thickened and clear.

1 medium firm tomato, cut into chunks

Fold in tomato chunks and let stand, covered, 10 minutes before serving. Serve over rice or crisp noodles.

Makes 6 servings

Golden Pork Casserole

POWER LEVEL: High (10)
MICROWAVE TIME: 8 to 10 min., total

4 to 6 slices (½-in. thick) cooked pork roast (¾ to 1-lb.)
1 can (17-oz.) yams, drained and cut in 1-in. slices
1 cup coarsely shredded, unpeeled apple
½ cup grated sharp cheddar cheese
3 tablespoons brown sugar (packed)
1 tablespoon lemon juice
2 tablespoons butter

In 2-qt. casserole layer pork, yams, apple and cheese. Sprinkle with brown sugar and lemon juice. Dot with butter. Cover. **Microwave at High (10) 8 to 10 Minutes,** rotating dish ½ turn after 4 minutes, until hot throughout.

Makes 4 to 6 servings

Sweet and Sour Pork

Chow Mein

POWER LEVEL: High (10)
MICROWAVE TIME: 20 to 22 min., total

⅓ cup soy sauce
3 tablespoons cornstarch
2 cans (5-oz. each) water chestnuts, sliced and undrained
1 can (1-lb.) bean sprouts, undrained
1 can (7-oz.) mushroom stems and pieces, undrained
2 cups diced cooked pork or other meat
2 cups ½-in. diagonal sliced celery
1 cup thinly sliced onion.

In 3-qt. casserole stir together soy sauce and cornstarch. Stir in water chestnuts, bean sprouts and mushrooms, then meat, celery and onion. **Microwave at High (10) 20 to 22 Minutes,** stirring well after 10 minutes, until hot and thickened. Stir thoroughly and serve over cooked rice or chow mein noodles.

Makes 4 to 6 servings

Pork chops and roasts may be microwaved with the Automatic Simmer (Auto Roast Code 6) feature, which comes with some of our microwave oven models. Chops will be very tender and flavorful. Roasts will have fall-off-the bone tenderness which some people prefer for pork barbecue. Arrange chops in a flat layer with liquid and cover as on page 90; simmer 4 to 6 hours. Pork roasts may be simmered like sirloin tip, page 88.

Microwaving Pork Chops, Roasts and Ham Loaf Helpful Hints

"My microwaved pork chops were tough, but undercooked. What should I do to get good cooking results?"

The power setting used may have been too high. Pork chops microwaved at Medium (5) in a sauce, or until they lose their pinkness will be fork tender and retain their juiciness.

"If I microwave raw ground pork in a loaf shape rather than round dish, will the cooking time be affected?"

Yes; because of its depth in the loaf dish your meatloaf will require a longer cooking time, and power level should be reduced to prevent overcooking outside areas. See meatloaf, page 75.

"What's the difference in pork roast microwaved in a cooking bag from roasts microwaved without a bag?"

Roasts microwaved in a bag will be lighter in color and juicier than roasts microwaved without a bag. Use a browning sauce for added color, if desired.

How to Cook Ham Slices and Steaks

ITEM	POWER LEVEL	TIME/MIN.	COMMENTS
Ham Slice, Less than 1-in. thick	High (10)	1, per slice	Ham slices may be fried with a preheated (3½ to 4 min.) Brown 'N Sear Dish.
Ham Steak, 1 to 2-in. thick	High (10)	10-15	Add a small amount of liquid to ham steaks and cover tightly to prevent drying.

To microwave pork and ham roasts, see chart on page 108.

Slices and steaks of ready-to-eat ham are precooked, so they need only be reheated. Cooking times are short because the high sugar content attracts microwaves, but browning is not necessary, since ham has a naturally attractive color. When baking a ham slice, 1 to 2-in. thick, add some liquid to keep it juicy and cover the dish tightly with plastic wrap. Due to the salt, ham can become dry if moisture is not sealed in.

Baked Ham Slice. Use a slice of fully cooked ham, 1 to 2-in. thick. Slash the edges to prevent curling. Place ham in a baking dish large enough to hold it easily. Add a small amount of liquid. Cover the dish tightly.

Fried Ham. Thin slices and steaks of fully-cooked ham may be fried with a Brown 'N Sear Dish or griddle. Preheat the dish 3½ to 4 minutes. Cook ¼ to ½-in. thick slices 1 minute per side.

Fruited Ham Slice

POWER LEVEL: High (10)
MICROWAVE TIME: 1 to 27 min., total

1 slice fully cooked ham, 1 to 2-in. thick	Score or remove fat from ham. Depending on size of slice, place in 8-in. square dish or 12×8×2-in. dish. Drain fruit, reserving juice. Arrange fruit attractively over ham slice. Cover with wax paper. **Microwave at High (10) 10 to 15 Minutes.**
1 can (11-oz.) mandarin orange segments	
1 can (8¼-oz.) crushed pineapple	
Juice from fruits	Combine juice, sugar, cornstarch and cloves. Pour carefully over ham slice to avoid disturbing the arranged fruit. Cover. **Microwave at High (10) 8 to 12 Minutes,** until hot. Spoon juice over fruit and serve.
2 tablespoons brown sugar	
1 tablespoon cornstarch	
¼ teaspoon ground cloves	

Makes 4 to 6 servings

Bacon

Microwaving is a superior way to cook bacon. It is spatter-free. There is less curling and shrinkage than with conventional frying, and if you cook it on paper towels, there is no messy pan to wash.

When cooked until crisp, bacon will be evenly cooked and flat. Just as in conventional cooking, under-crisp bacon may be randomly cooked, with some spots fatty while others are crisp. Bacon varies in quality, depending upon the amount of sugar and salt used in curing and thickness of slices.

How to Defrost Bacon

POWER LEVEL: **Defrost (3)**

4 to 6 Minutes Per Pound

Place unopened package of bacon in oven. Microwave at Defrost for ½ of time. Turn package over. Defrost second ½ of time, just until strips can be separated with a rubber spatula.

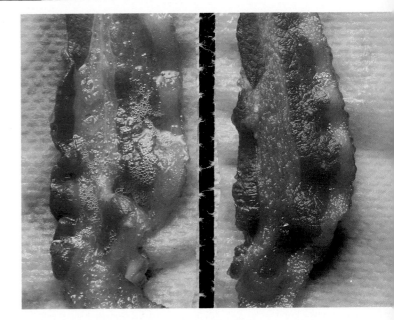

Bacon continues to brown on standing. Left, crisp-cooked bacon as it should look when removed from oven. Right, crisp-cooked bacon after standing 5 minutes.

NOTE: Brown spots on paper towel are due to sugar in the bacon. A high sugar content may also cause bacon to stick to the towel slightly.

How to Microwave Bacon

The timing below is for average cure, commercially sliced, thin bacon. Cook less time for extra-sweet bacon, more for thick slices.

POWER LEVEL: **High (10)**

¾ to 1 Minute Per Slice

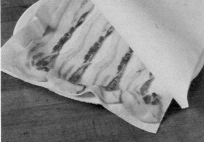

Place two layers of paper towels on paper or pottery plate without metal trim. Arrange bacon on towels and cover with another towel to prevent spatters. Microwave at High (10) ¾ to 1 minute per slice.

Layer bacon when microwaving more than 6 slices. Place 5 slices of bacon on 2 layers of paper towels in a 13×9×2-in. dish. Cover with a paper towel. Add second layer of bacon. Cover and add more layers as desired. Microwave 4 minutes for each layer of bacon. A pound of bacon takes about 15 minutes.

To Save bacon drippings for use in frying, cornbread, or microwave recipes such as wilted lettuce, cabbage or German potato salad, cook bacon on a trivet in a cooking dish. Bacon may also be cooked in a casserole or roasting dish directly in its own fat. As with conventional cooking, remove bacon to paper towel to drain and pour off drippings.

Like most ham, Canadian bacon is precooked and needs only heating to be ready to eat. Whether cooked conventionally or by microwave, Canadian bacon will be dry if it is allowed to cook until brown.

Microwaving Whole Piece of Canadian Bacon

POWER LEVEL: Medium High (7)
MICROWAVE TIME: 23 to 26 min., total

2 to 3-lb. piece Canadian bacon ¼ cup water	Remove casing from bacon and arrange in 12×8×2-in. dish. Add water.

Cover tightly with plastic wrap, turning back one corner to vent. **Microwave at Medium High (7) 23 to 25 Minutes,** turning over after 13 minutes. Let bacon stand 10 minutes before serving.

Microwaving Slices of Canadian Bacon

Place slices in single layer on dinner plate. Cover with wax paper. Timing below is for thin slices, about ¼-in. thick, such as used for Eggs Benedict, sandwiches or as a breakfast meat.

POWER LEVEL: **High (10)**

SLICES	TIME MIN.	COMMENTS
2	1-1½	No rotation necessary.
4	2-2½	Rotate ½ turn after 1 min.
6 to 8	3½-4	Rotate ½ turn after 2 min.

Whole Canadian Bacon

Sliced Canadian Bacon

Breakfast Sausage

Breakfast sausage comes in many forms. Each defrosts and cooks differently, but all will be tender, juicy and fully cooked in a very short time. Due to quick cooking, breakfast sausage doesn't brown and, since it is rarely served with a sauce, it will be more attractive if it is brushed with a browning agent before cooking. Use equal parts of brown bouquet sauce and water. If you cook sausage frequently, keep this mixture on hand in a small covered container.

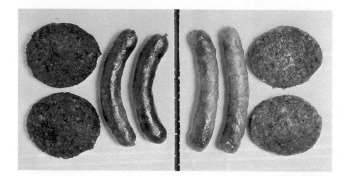

Brown 'N Sear Sausage Chart

POWER LEVEL: **High (10)**
Preheat dish 4½ to 5½ minutes.

ITEM	1st SIDE TIME MINUTES	2nd SIDE TIME MINUTES
Pork Sausage, 4 slices ½-in. thick	1 covered	1½ to 2 covered
Pork Sausage Links, 6 to 8 links, uncooked, 8-oz.	1 covered	2 to 2½ covered
Brown 'n Serve, 10 links 8-oz. pkg.	1 covered	1½ to 2 covered

Compare link and patty sausage cooked with and without a browning agent. Both are juicy and flavorful, but sausages cooked with a browning agent have more appetite appeal.

The following chart gives specific directions for different types and forms of sausage. Whatever type you are microwaving, a few basic rules are common to all. They are presented below.

Sausage Defrosting & Microwaving Chart

Defrost sausage in package, removing any metal closures. When defrosted, sausage should still be cold.

When cooking, select a utensil which is appropriate in size for the amount of sausage you wish to cook: a saucer for 1 or 2 links, a glass pie plate for an 8-oz. package, a roasting dish for a full pound of slices. Add browning agent, if desired, before cooking. Always cover the dish with wax paper to prevent spatters.

Defrosting POWER LEVEL: **Defrost**			Microwaving POWER LEVEL: **High (10)**		
ITEM	TIME MINUTES	COMMENTS	**ITEM**	TIME MINUTES	COMMENTS
Bulk (1-lb. tray)	8 to 9	Defrost like ground beef page 82	**4 patties** (½-lb.)	4 to 5	Rotate dish ½ turn after 1½ minutes
			8 Patties (1-lb.)	7½ to 8	Rotate dish ½ turn after 2 minutes.
Bulk (1-lb. roll)	4 to 6	Turn over after 1 minute	**4 Patties** (½-lb.)	4 to 5	Rotate dish ½ turn after 1½ minutes.
			8 Patties (1-lb.)	7½ to 8	Rotate dish ½ turn after 2 minutes.
Preformed Patties (12-oz. pkg.)	2 to 3	Turn over after 1 minute	**4 Patties Raw**	2½ to 3½	Rotate dish ½ turn after 1½ minutes.
			8 Patties Raw	4 to 5	Rotate dish ½ turn after 2 minutes.
Preformed Patties Brown 'n Serve (12-oz. pkg.)	2 to 3	Turn over after 1 minute	**4 Patties Brown 'n Serve**	1 to 1½	No turns.
			8 Patties Brown 'n Serve	2¼ to 2½	Rotate dish ½ turn after 1½ minutes.
Link Sausage Raw (1-lb.)	3 to 4	Turn over after 1 minute	**4 Links**	2 to 3	No turns.
			7 to 8 Links	4 to 5	Rotate dish ½ turn after 2 minutes.
Link Sausage Brown 'n Serve (8-oz.)	3 to 4	Turn over after 1 minute	**4 Links**	1	No turns.
			6 Links	1½ to 2	Rotate dish ½ turn after 1 minute.
			10 Links	2 to 2½	Rotate dish ½ turn after 1 minute.

Add sauces and condiments, such as ketchup, mustard or relish after heating. Saucy spots absorb microwave energy and may toughen the bun.

106   Franks

Frankfurters are precooked so they only need heating. They react quickly to microwave energy and many beginners overheat them because they can't believe franks will be ready in such a short time.

Defrosting. For 1-lb. of franks, place unopened package in oven. **Microwave at Defrost (3) 3 to 5 Minutes,** just until franks can be separated. For ½-lb., cut time in half.

Microwaving. Franks vary in size. Larger ones such as Polish or bratwurst, will take longer than times in chart below. For foot-long hot dogs add ¼ to ½ minute more time, and rotate them once or twice, because they tend to get overdone on the ends.

Franks Microwaving Chart

When microwaving on microwave ovenproof plate, cover with wax paper. When microwaving in bun, wrap in paper towel. Watch carefully. If ends appear dry, it means they are overdone.

If you are cooking franks in a main dish casserole, bury them under moist ingredients, such as beans or sauerkraut. If meat is on the bottom, the casserole won't need stirring.

POWER LEVEL: **High (10)**

NO. OF FRANKS	TIME MIN.	COMMENTS
2	1-2	
4	3-4	If microwaved in casserole, add ½ to ¾ cup water.
6 to 8	4-6	
10 (1-lb. pkg.)	7-9	If microwaved in buns, arrange evenly on oven floor.

How to Microwave Franks

Franks are prone to pop or explode. You can remedy this by pricking them with a fork, but diagonal slashes are especially attractive.

To Microwave a few franks on a paper or pottery plate, cover them with wax paper. Without sauce, a bun or water for shielding, ends can overcook quickly; watch carefully.

To Heat franks right in the buns, place a napkin or paper towel under the bun to absorb moisture. A bun placed directly on a plate or the oven floor gets steamy underneath.

Ham, bacon and franks are all cured meats and absorb microwave energy easily. They taste fresh and moist when properly microwaved, due to their short cooking time.

Other ways to enjoy flavorful microwaved bacon are to wrap it in a spiral fashion around hot dogs to be microwaved, or use it to encircle the edges of a hamburger pattie. In both cases, bacon should be partially cooked before wrapping, because the accompanying meat cooks so quickly.

Microwaving Bacon, Franks and Ham Helpful Hints

"The consistency of my microwaved bacon varies occasionally. What causes this?"

The thickness, sugar and fat content in bacon varies from brand to brand causing uneven cooking. Select bacon strips which are similar in thickness and in lean-to-fat content for best results.

"What causes brown spots inside microwaved frankfurters?"

Frankfurters microwaved without water, sauce, a bun, or buried in other foods can develop brown spots from excessive microwave energy. If you cook frankfurters alone, watch carefully.

"How can I prevent ham slices from curling during microwaving?"

Slashing fat around the edge of ham slices before cooking will solve this problem.

Wiener Bean Pot

POWER LEVEL: High (10)
MICROWAVE TIME: 11 to 13 min., total

2 cans (1-lb. each) pork and beans	In 2-qt. casserole stir together beans, onion, ketchup, water, brown sugar and mustard. Add wieners, pushing pieces below surface of beans to prevent overcooking. Cover. **Microwave at High (10) 11 to 13 Minutes.** Stir before serving.
⅓ cup chopped onion	
¼ cup ketchup	
¼ cup water	
2 tablespoons brown sugar (packed)	
1 tablespoon prepared mustard	
1 lb. wieners (8 to 10) cut in thirds	

Makes 6 to 8 servings

Sausage and Sauerkraut

POWER LEVEL: High (10)
MICROWAVE TIME: 10 to 12 min., total

1 lb. franks (8 to 10) scored, or 1-lb. Polish sausage (Kielbasa) cut in ½-in. pieces	In 2-qt. casserole place meat. Cover with sauerkraut mixed with onions and bouillon. Cover. **Microwave at High (10) 10 to 12 Minutes.** Stir before serving. Keep sausage covered with sauerkraut mixture.
1 can (1-lb.) sauerkraut, rinsed and drained	
2 tablespoons instant minced onion	
1 teaspoon beef bouillon granules	

Makes 4 to 6 servings

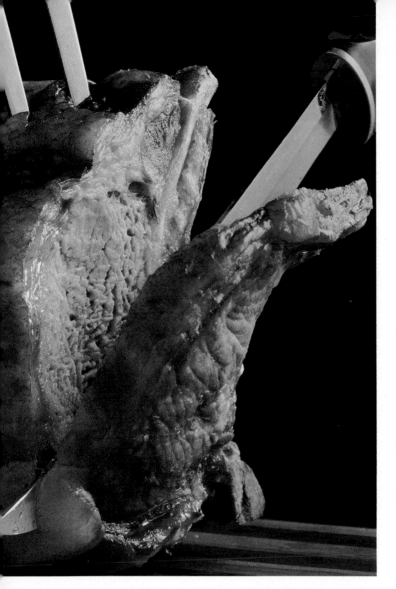

When cooking pork either conventionally or in the microwave oven, follow our directions exactly and always cook the meat to at least 170°. This assures that, in the remote possibility that trichina may be present it will be killed and the meat will be safe to eat.

Microwaving Pork Roast by Temperature

Rib end or center cut roasts. Identified by arch shaped bones on the edge of the roast and clearly defined large muscle. Insert the temperature probe slightly below center of the largest muscle, so tip is in the center of the roast.

How to Cook Pork and Ham Roasts

Be sure pork roasts are thoroughly defrosted before microwaving them.

POWER LEVEL: **Medium (5)**

ITEM	IN A COOKING BAG TIME/MIN., PER LB.	WITHOUT BAG, COVERED WITH PLASTIC WRAP OR WAX PAPER TIME/MINUTES, PER LB.	COMMENTS
Pork Loin or Rib, 4 to 5 lbs.	15-18	17-19	Roasts not cooked in a bag may be covered with plastic wrap, vented at one corner. Or, place roast in cooking dish with small amount water and wax paper cover. Microwave fat side up. Raw pork and ham should be cooked to 170°. Glazes should be spooned over roast just before serving. If using a temperature probe, insert so that tip does not touch bone.
Raw ham (half shank end) 4 to 5 lbs.	13-17	15-18	
Naturally shaped precooked ham, 5 lbs.	9-11	10-13	
Canned, precooked ham, 5 lbs.	9-11	10-13	

Pork Roasts

We recommend using a cooking bag, or small amount of water and covering with wax paper to keep roast pork tender and juicy.

Roast fat side up. When using the temperature probe, set for 170°.

Microwaved pork roasts develop browning especially when the fat coating is thin. If the roast has a heavy coating of fat, you may want to add brown bouquet sauce. Be sure to allow the entire standing time to complete cooking.

How to Defrost Pork Roast

POWER LEVEL: Defrost (3)
MICROWAVE TIME: 10 to 12 min., per pound

If roast is wrapped in paper or plastic, place the unopened package in the oven to defrost. (Foil wrapping must be removed before defrosting.) For step-by-step pictures of roast defrosting, see page 86.

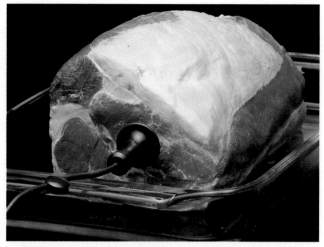

Loin end roast. Identified by circular bone at one end of the roast and rack of bones at the bottom. Insert temperature probe into end where the round bone is located, placing it ¾ to 1-in. above the bottom of the roast on the meatiest side of the round bone. Follow bone structure, angling if necessary, so that tip of probe is in the center of the roast. Do not allow tip of probe to touch bone.

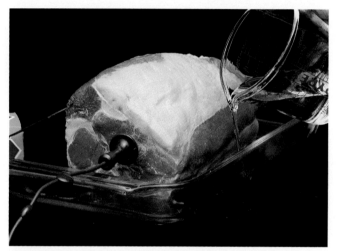

If cooking without a roasting bag, add water to roasting dish and cover with wax paper. Or, place in cooking bag without water in dish. **Microwave at Medium (5). Set Temp. Set 170°.**

Microwaving Pork Roast by Time

POWER LEVEL: Medium (5)
MICROWAVE TIME: 15 to 19 min., per pound

Do not salt roast. Place bone side up in a 13×9×2-in. dish. Add ½ cup water. Cover with wax paper, or place in a cooking bag without water.

Estimate the minimum total roasting time. **Microwave at Medium (5).** After minimum time, test internal temperature of the roast with a meat thermometer, following instructions given for probe placement. Allow 2 minutes for thermometer to register. If roast has not reached 170°, remove thermometer and return roast to the oven for a few more minutes. When cooking is completed remove and let stand 20 minutes.

Do not place conventional metal meat thermometer in microwave oven.

Cherry Almond Glaze for Pork

POWER LEVEL: High (10)
MICROWAVE TIME: 8 to 12 min., total

1 teaspoon butter **¼ cup slivered almonds**	In 8 or 9-in. pie plate place butter and almonds. **Microwave at High (10) 3 to 5 Minutes,** stirring every 2 minutes, until toasted. Set aside.
1 jar (12-oz.) cherry preserves **2 tablespoons white corn syrup** **¼ cup red wine vinegar** **¼ teaspoon salt** **¼ teaspoon cinnamon** **¼ teaspoon nutmeg** **¼ teaspoon cloves**	In 1½-qt. casserole stir together preserves, corn syrup, vinegar, salt, cinnamon, nutmeg and cloves. Cover. **Microwave at High (10) 5 to 7 Minutes,** stirring very well after 4 minutes. Mixture should be well blended. Stir in toasted almonds just before glazing.

Makes about 1¾ cups

Most hams are now precooked and need to be heated only to 115°. Take care not to overcook, which makes them dry and tough. Canned or compressed hams are very dense and especially need to be shielded around the top edge. Hams with a natural shape (shank or butt end hams) may be microwaved either by time or temperature. Again most all are precooked, but a few can be purchased raw and must be cooked before eating. Purchase hams no higher than six inches for microwaving.

How to Microwave Precooked Ham

POWER LEVEL: **Medium (5)**
12 to 14 Minutes Per Pound

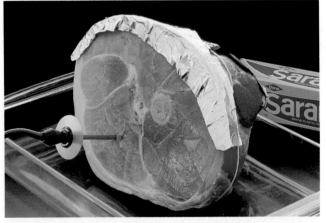

Tie string around ham to hold shape. Shield cut edge with foil (also shank bone if protruding). Place fat side up in 13×9×2-in. dish. Add ¼ cup water. Insert probe in center of lowest large muscle. Cover with plastic wrap, arranging loosely around probe to vent. **Microwave at Medium (5). Set Temp. Set 115°.** Let stand 5 to 10 minutes before carving.

How to Microwave Canned Ham

POWER LEVEL: **Medium (5)**
10 to 12 Minutes Per Pound

Shield ham (which has been tied) around top cut edges with 2-in. strip of foil. Place on trivet in 12×8×2-in. dish. Add ¼ cup water, and cover with vented plastic wrap. **Microwave at Medium (5). Set Temp. Set 115°.** Let stand 5 to 10 minutes before carving.

How to Microwave Raw (Uncooked) Ham

POWER LEVEL: **Medium (5)**
13 to 18 Minutes Per Pound

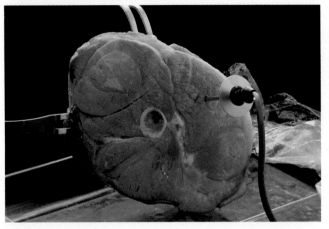

Tie ham and shield as for precooked (left). Place in 13×9×2-in. dish with ¼ cup water. Cover with plastic wrap, venting around probe. **Microwave at Medium (5). Set Temp. Set 100°.** Remove foil strips and turn over. Reshield cut edge. Continue microwaving at Medium (5) to 170°.

Kentucky Bourbon Sauce for Ham

POWER LEVEL: High (10)
MICROWAVE TIME: 4 to 5 min., total

1 jar (10-oz.) currant jelly **¼ cup butter** **½ teaspoon dry mustard** **2 teaspoons prepared mustard** **¼ cup Kentucky bourbon**	In 1-qt. casserole place jelly. **Microwave at High (10) 4 to 5 Minutes,** stirring after 2 minutes, until hot and melted. Add butter, mustards, and bourbon, stirring well.

Makes 6 to 8 servings

Currant Jelly Glaze: In small bowl stir together 1 jar (10-oz.) currant jelly, 1 tablespoon prepared mustard and 1 tablespoon brown sugar. Brush over microwaved ham. Let stand few minutes to set.

Microwaving Pork and Ham Roasts Helpful Hints

"My pork roast was undercooked in some areas. What did I do wrong?"

Correct placement of the temperature probe in pork is very important to assure roast is completely cooked before eating. With fingers, mark off correct length to insert probe (as shown right) then insert horizontally in center. Set temperature at 170°.

"When I microwave pork roast grease from the roast spatters and creates a mess inside the oven. How can this be avoided?"

Microwave your roast in a cooking bag or covered with plastic wrap. Or if you prefer a drier roast, cover it with wax paper to prevent the grease from spattering.

"Should hams and pork roasts be glazed before or after microwaving?"

It is best to glaze roasts after microwaving especially if you cover with plastic wrap. The wrap will stick to roast if it is glazed before cooking. Also, sugary glazes burn easily. Brush or spoon glaze on during standing time.

Ham-agetti Casserole

POWER LEVEL: High (10)
MICROWAVE TIME: 23 to 27 min., total

4 strips bacon . . . . With scissors, snip bacon into 1-in. pieces into 2-qt. casserole. **Microwave at High (10) 4 to 5 Minutes.** Remove approximately half the fat.

2 cups cooked ham, . . . Add ham, tomatoes, **cut into strips** spaghetti, onion, green
1 can (1-lb. 14-oz.) pepper, salt and pepper. **tomatoes** Stir well. Cover.
1 cup spaghetti, **Microwave at High broken into** **(10) 18 to 20 Minutes,**
1-in. pieces until spaghetti is tender,
½ cup chopped onion stirring after 8 minutes.
¼ cup chopped green pepper
½ teaspoon salt
⅛ teaspoon pepper

½ cup shredded . . . . Sprinkle with cheese. **cheddar cheese** **Microwave at High (10) 1 to 2 Minutes,** uncovered, until cheese is melted.

Makes 6 servings

Pineapple Ham and Yams

POWER LEVEL: High (10)
MICROWAVE TIME: 5¼ to 7½ min., total

1 tablespoon butter . . . In 1-qt. casserole place
1 can (8-oz.) yams or butter. **Microwave at**
sweet potatoes, **High (10) ¼ to ½**
drained **Minute,** to melt. Add
2 tablespoons brown drained yams and mash
sugar well. Stir in brown sugar.
4 slices (about 4-oz.) Divide mixture equally
packaged, thinly over one end of each ham
sliced cooked slice. Roll up into firm rolls.
ham *

1 can (8-oz.) sliced . . . . Drain pineapple, reserving
pineapple juice. Place pineapple
(4 slices) slices in 8-in. square dish. Cover each with ham roll, seam side down.

¼ cup coarsely . . . . Combine pecans, sugar
chopped pecans and pineapple syrup.
¼ cup light brown Spoon over ham rolls.
sugar (packed) Cover with wax paper.
¼ cup syrup reserved
from pineapple Makes 4 servings

Microwave at High (10) 5 to 7 Minutes.
*Or use thinly sliced leftover ham, about 6-in. long by 3-in. wide.

Lamb is naturally juicy and can be prepared in a variety of ways. We suggest that you try some of our pork recipes with lamb or use one of the beef marinades, page 82.

Veal is dry because it has no fat marbling. Whether cooked conventionally or microwaved, chops and cutlets should be sliced thinly or pounded to tenderize them. Chunks and pieces of veal which need long slow cooking may be substituted in stew and other main dish recipes.

Brown 'N Sear or griddle lamb chops, covered, 3 to 4 minutes on each side.

How to Microwave Lamb and Veal and Adapt Your Favorite Recipes

ITEM	POWER LEVEL	TIME/MINUTES PER POUND	BROWN 'N SEAR DISH OR BROWNING GRIDDLE PREHEAT MIN.	1st SIDE MIN.	2nd SIDE MIN.
Chops, cutlets	High (10)				
1-2		6 to 8	5 to 6	3	3 to 4
3-4		7 to 9	6 to 8	3 to 4	4 to 5
Lamb, leg or shoulder	Medium (5)	11 to 13 (Medium) 13 to 17 (Well)	— —	— —	— —
Veal rolled shoulder	Medium (5)	16 to 19 (Well)	—	—	—

How to Defrost Roasts

POWER LEVEL: **Defrost (3)**

10 to 12 Minutes Per Pound

1. If roast is wrapped in paper or plastic, place the unopened package in microwave oven. (Foil wrapping must be removed before microwaving.)
2. Defrost ½ of total time.
3. Turn roast over and finish defrosting last ½ of total time.
4. Let stand 30 minutes before microwaving or conventional cooking.

NOTE: Feel roast for warm areas after each microwaving period. Cover these areas with foil (warmth indicates they have begun to cook).

How to Defrost Chops and Cutlets

POWER LEVEL: **Defrost (3)**

4 to 8 Minutes Per Pound

1. Place plastic or paper wrapped package in oven. Microwave at Defrost.
2. Separate pieces with a table knife and let stand to complete defrosting, or microwave 1 to 2 minutes more.

How to Microwave Lamb Roasts

POWER LEVEL: **Medium (5)**

11 to 13 Minutes Per Pound for Medium
14 to 17 Minutes Per Pound for Well done

Microwaving by Temperature: If desired, brush roast with diluted brown bouquet sauce. Place roast fat side up on trivet in 13×9×2-in. dish. Insert temperature probe as directed below. Cover with wax paper. **Microwave at Medium. Set Temp, Set 130°** for medium and **180°** for well done. When oven signals, let stand 10 mintues before carving.

Microwaving by Time: Use minutes per pound, above. When oven signals, remove roast and insert conventional meat thermometer into roast in same location described for temperature probe. Check temperature after about 2 minutes; it should read 130° for medium and 180° for well done. If not, return to microwave oven a few minutes, then check again.

NOTE: Do not place conventional metal meat thermometer in microwave oven.

How to Microwave Veal Roasts

Microwaving works especially well on rolled and tied veal shoulder and other veal roasts.

POWER LEVEL: **Medium (5)**

16 to 19 Minutes Per Pound

If desired, brush roast with diluted brown bouquet sauce. Place roast fat side up in 12×8×2-in. dish. Insert temperature probe as shown below. Cover with wax paper. **Microwave at Medium (5), Set Temp, Set 155°.** When oven signals, let roast stand 10 minutes before carving.

Microwaving By Time: Use minutes per pound, above. When oven signals, remove roast and insert conventional meat thermometer into roast in same location as for temperature probe. Check temperature after about 2 minutes; it should read 155°. If not return to microwave oven a few minutes then check again.

NOTE: Do not place conventional metal meat thermometer in microwave oven.

Microwaving a Crown Lamb Roast

"Do you recommend microwaving a crown lamb roast?"

Yes; prepare and microwave crown roast with bones up as shown. Set Medium power and microwave 10 to 12 minutes per pound. Decorate top rib ends and fill center with garnish (parsley shown) after microwaving.

Chicken is naturally an excellent food for microwaving. It is tender, flavorful and juicy. It microwaves rapidly and requires little attention during cooking. Don't over cook chicken; it really will be done in the very short cooking periods given in the chart. Because they cook so quickly, chicken pieces do not get brown and crisp. Unless the chicken is cooked in a sauce, it will be more attractive if brushed with a browning agent. Plain microwaved chicken is perfect for salads and casseroles.

Compare Toppings for Microwave Chicken

Plain microwaved chicken

Well seasoned flour in Brown 'N Sear Dish

Prepared coating mix

Equal parts brown bouqet sauce and water

Adapting Tips for Chicken Pieces

Size and number of pieces in dish determine cooking time. Microwave using time and power levels on chart below.

Arrange chicken so that meatiest portions are to the outside of dish. Cover with wax paper during microwaving.

Test for doneness. Chicken should be fork tender with no pinkness next to bone. For chicken baked in sauce, remove paper after cooking and let stand 5 minutes to glaze and blend flavors.

Brown 'N Sear dish may be used to crisp skin. Heat dish for 8 minutes, then add 1 tablespoon oil and place pieces into dish, skin side down, for first ½ of cooking time. See chart below.

How to Cook Chicken and Adapt Your Favorite Recipes.

TYPE	POWER LEVEL	TIME/MINUTES FROZEN	REFRIGERATED	BROWN 'N SEAR DISH
Cut-up chicken				Coat defrosted pieces with seasoned flour and paprika. Heat dish at High (10) for 8 minutes. Add 1 tablespoon of oil to dish. Place chicken in dish, cover and Microwave 4 to 5 minutes on each side.
1-2 pieces	High	6-8*	4-6	
3-4 pieces	(10)	10-12*	7-10	
7-8 pieces		20-26*	15-18	
Quarters, halves				
4 quarters	Medium	18-20*	12-15	
2 halves	High (7)	20-22*	15-18	Not Recommended.
Whole Chicken, or Capon	Medium High (7)	42-50	25-30	Not Recommended
(3 to 4-lbs.)		(Use techniques page 122)		
Casserole, precooked chicken	Medium High (7)	16-18	8-12	—

*Times are for pieces which have been frozen in separate pieces. See page 42.

Pictured top to bottom: Sweet 'N Tangy Chicken, (page 118),
Microwaved Turkey (page 130), Cornish Hen (page 126)

Adapting Tip:
Chicken is frozen in many forms, whole or cut-up into halves, quarters or one-of-a-kind pieces, such as breasts or drum sticks. These timings are for one whole or cut-up broiler-fryer, weighing 2½ to 3½ pounds.

Several cut-up chickens or a roasting chicken will take longer. Follow directions for turkey when defrosting a large roasting chicken, or capon.

Defrost Chart
POWER LEVEL: **Defrost (3)**

ITEM	TIME/MINUTES
Broiler-fryer, cut up (2½ to 3½-lb.)	15 to 20
Broiler-fryer, whole (2½ to 3½-lb.)	19 to 24

How to Defrost a Cut-Up Chicken

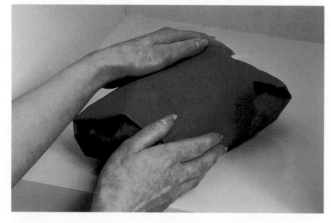

Place wrapped chicken, packaged in paper or plastic, directly on the oven shelf. If chicken is wrapped in foil, unwrap it and place it in a baking dish. Microwave at Defrost for ½ the time.

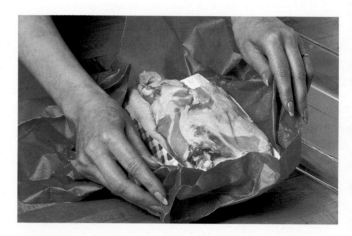

Unwrap chicken pieces and turn the block over into a baking dish. Defrost for second ½ of time, or until pieces can be separated.

How to Defrost a Whole Chicken

Whole chickens are usually frozen in a plastic bag. Remove twist tie, place package on the oven shelf and microwave at Defrost ½ the time. Unwrap chicken and turn it over into cooking dish.

Shield wing tips, tail, ends of legs and any other areas which feel warm or have begun to change color. Microwave for second ½ of time.

With frozen packages of one-of-a-kind pieces, you will need to use your judgment. Bony pieces, such as wings, will take less time than meaty pieces, such as thighs.

The defrosting steps also apply to other poultry, such as ducks or cornish game hens. Two cornish hens take about the same amount of time as one chicken.

Separate chicken pieces and let them stand until defrosted, or if faster defrosting is desired, arrange them in the cooking dish, meaty parts to the outside, and microwave 1 to 2 minutes more.

Defrosted chicken will be soft to the touch, very moist and cold, but not frosty. There may be a very small amount of running juice.

Giblets can be loosened but not removed. Chicken should be soft and cool to the touch, with a glistening surface.

Run cold water inside chicken until giblets can be freed. Interior will be cold but not icy.

The recipes on these pages are for both Time Cooking and Automatic Simmering (Auto Roast Code 6) featured on some models. Time cooking gives fast results and a fresh natural flavor. Automatic simmering is a slow cook method which gives more tenderness and developed flavor after the lengthy cooking period.

Crumb-Coated Chicken

This has the same appearance and taste as oven fried.

POWER LEVEL: High (10)
MICROWAVE TIME: 18 to 22 min., total

2 eggs . . . . In small bowl beat together
⅓ cup melted butter eggs, butter and salt.
1 teaspoon salt

1½ cups buttery In shallow dish place
flavored cracker crumbs. Coat chicken with
crumbs (about 50) crumbs, then egg mixture
1 chicken, (2½ to and crumbs again. In
3½-lb.) cut up, skin 12×8×2-in. dish arrange
removed chicken with meatiest
pieces to outside edges
of dish. Cover with wax
paper. **Microwave
at High (10) 18 to
22 Minutes.**

Makes about 4 servings

Chicken 'n Dressing

For richer flavor, use ¼ cup melted butter for part of chicken broth.

POWER LEVEL: High (10)
MICROWAVE TIME: 22 to 26 min., total

1 pkg. (8-oz.) herb . . . . In 12×8×2-in. dish toss
seasoned stuffing together stuffing mix,
mix celery, onion, pimiento,
½ cup chopped celery egg and broth.
¼ cup minced onion
2 tablespoons
chopped pimiento
1 egg
2 cups chicken broth

1 chicken (2½ to . . . . Brush chicken pieces with
3½-lb.) cut up melted butter, place on top
¼ cup butter, melted of dressing with meaty
Salt pieces to the outside
Paprika edges of dish. Sprinkle
with salt and paprika.
Cover with wax paper.

Microwave at High (10) 18 to 22 Minutes. Let
stand about 5 minutes before serving.

Makes about 4 servings

Note: For Chicken 'n Dressing oven meal, page 53, two whole chicken breasts, split, were substituted for whole chicken and 8x8x2-in. square dish was used instead of 12x8x2-in. dish.

Spanish Style Chicken

This is a version of the famous Arroz Con Pollo.

POWER LEVEL: Automatic Simmer and High (10)
MICROWAVE TIME: 4 hr. to 6 hr.

1 chicken (2½ to . . . . In 3-qt. casserole, place
3½-lb.) cut up chicken with meaty pieces
1 teaspoon salt around edges. Sprinkle
¼ teaspoon pepper with salt, pepper, chili
¼ teaspoon chili powder, garlic and saffron.
powder Add broth and sherry.
1 clove garlic, minced Insert temperature probe
⅛ teaspoon saffron so tip rests in liquid on
powder bottom of dish, halfway
2 cups chicken broth between center and side.
2 tablespoons sherry

Cover tightly with plastic wrap, arranging loosely around probe to vent. Attach cable end at receptacle.
Microwave at Automatic Simmer 4 to 6 Hours.

To Finish: To casserole, add 2 cups cooked rice, 1 pkg.
(10-oz.) defrosted frozen peas and ½ cup sliced stuffed
olives. Cover and **Microwave at High (10) 5
Minutes,** until vegetables are hot.

To Microwave by Time Cooking: Assemble
chicken, salt, pepper, chili powder, garlic, saffron, broth
and sherry in dish and cover according to recipe above.
For 1-step setting, set **Defrost at High (10) for 20
Minutes, then Time Cook at Medium High (7) for
20 to 25 Minutes,** cooking chicken until tender. Finish
as above.

Makes 4 to 6 servings

Sweet 'n Tangy Chicken

This golden glazed chicken is named for the comments it elicits. It really does taste special.

POWER LEVEL: High (10)
MICROWAVE TIME: 18 to 22 min., total

1 chicken (2½ to . . . . In 12×8×2-in. dish
3½-lb.) cut up arrange chicken with
thickest, meaty pieces to
outside edges of dish.

¼ cup mayonnaise . . . . . . In small bowl stir together
1 pkg. (½ of 2¾-oz. mayonnaise, onion soup
box) dry onion soup mix, dressing and
mix preserves. Spread over
½ cup bottled Russian chicken, coating each
dressing piece. Cover with wax
1 cup apricot- paper.
pineapple
preserves

Microwave at High (10) 18 to 22 Minutes. Allow to
stand 5 to 10 minutes before serving, so chicken
absorbs flavor of sauce. Serve with rice, if desired.

Makes about 4 servings

Crumb Coated and Spanish Style Chicken (page 118)

Chicken in Italian Sauce
Sometimes known as Chicken Marengo.

POWER LEVEL: Automatic Simmer and High (10)
MICROWAVE TIME: 4 to 6 hr.   (Auto Roast Code 6)

1 chicken (2½ to **3½-lb.) cut up** **1 pkg. (1½-oz.)** **spaghetti sauce mix** **½ cup water or dry** **white wine**	In 2-qt. casserole, place chicken with meaty pieces around edges. Stir together sauce mix and liquid; pour over top.

Insert temperature probe so tip rests in liquid on bottom of dish, halfway between center and side. Cover tightly with plastic wrap, arranging loosely around probe to vent. Attach cable end at receptable. **Microwave at Automatic Simmer 4 to 6 Hours.** Garnish as described below.

To Garnish: Stir 2 peeled fresh tomatoes, cut in quarters and ¼-lb. fresh mushrooms, cut in ½-in. slices, into chicken. **Microwave at High (10) 5 Minutes** to heat. If desired, serve with ½ cup sliced black olives and ¼ cup snipped fresh parsley. Serve over rice.

To Microwave by Time Cooking: Assemble chicken, sauce mix and water in dish and cover according to recipe above. **Microwave at High (10) 17 to 23 Minutes,** until chicken is tender. Garnish as above.

Chicken in Wine
Coq au Vin is its French name. This makes a delicious supper when served with rice and a salad.

POWER LEVEL: Automatic Simmer
MICROWAVE TIME: 4 to 6 hr.

1 medium onion **chopped (¾ cup)** **1 chicken (2½ to** **3½-lb.) cut up** **1 tablespoon paprika** **3 tablespoons minute** **tapioca** **Sauce (below)**	In 3-qt. casserole, spread onion evenly. Rub paprika on chicken then arrange chicken with meaty pieces around edges. Sprinkle with tapioca. Pour sauce (below) over all. Insert temperature probe so tip rests in sauce on bottom of dish. Cover tightly with plastic wrap, arranging loosely around the probe to vent. Attach cable end at receptacle. **Microwave at Automatic Simmer 4 to 6 Hours.**
1 lb. large fresh **mushrooms,** **quartered** **2 tablespoons fresh** **snipped parsley**	Add mushrooms and parsley to casserole. Cover and **Microwave at High (10) 5 Minutes** to heat.

Makes about 4 servings

Sauce: In small bowl stir together 1 cup white wine, ½ bay leaf, ½ teaspoon thyme, 1 teaspoon salt and ⅛ teaspoon freshly ground pepper.

To Microwave by Time Cooking: Assemble chicken, onion, paprika, tapioca, and sauce in dish and cover according to recipe above. **Microwave at Medium High (7) for 30 to 40 Minutes,** until chicken is tender. Add mushrooms and parsley and finish as in recipe above.

Oriental Chicken

POWER LEVEL: High (10)
MICROWAVE TIME: 14 to 17 min., total

2 chicken breasts **split, skinned and** **boned**	Pierce chicken breasts with cooking fork. Arrange in 3-qt. casserole.
1 tablespoon **cornstarch** **2 tablespoons brown** **sugar** **¼ teaspoon oregano** **1 clove garlic,** **crushed** **2 tablespoons** **cooking oil** **¼ cup soy sauce** **¾ cup rose wine** **⅓ cup seedless** **raisins**	In small bowl combine cornstarch, brown sugar, oregano, garlic, oil, soy sauce, wine and raisins. Pour over chicken. Cover. **Microwave at High (10) 11 to 13 Minutes.** Serve with rice if desired.

Makes 4 servings

120 Chicken

How to Stew Chicken Using Time Cook, or Automatic Simmering

Combine in 4-qt. casserole 1 cut up stewing chicken, 5 cups hot tap water, 1 onion, 1 carrot and 1 celery stem, all coarsely cut up. Add 4 peppercorns, 2 cloves and cover.

To Time Cook: Microwave at High (10) 15 Minutes. Rearrange chicken, bringing bottom pieces to the top. Cover. Microwave at Medium 2 to 2¼ Hours, rearranging chicken after 1 hour.

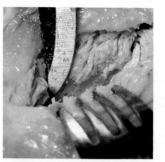

Test for doneness. Chicken should be fork tender. For maximum tenderness, let chicken cool in its broth. Meat will then be easily removed from the bones.

To Automatic Simmer (on models with this feature) stewing chicken, position temperature probe halfway between center and edge of dish and cover tightly. Set Auto Roast Code 6.

Chicken 'N Dumplings:

In 5-qt. casserole, place 4 to 6 lb. stewing chicken with 1 large onion, chopped, 4 cups water, 2 tablespoons chicken bouillon and 1 teaspoon salt. Place temperature probe in liquid halfway between center and edge of dish. Cover tightly with plastic wrap, arranging loosely around probe to vent. Attach cable end at receptacle. Microwave at Automatic Simmer (Auto Roast Code 6) for 11 to 12 hours. Or, set time cook to Microwave at Medium (5) for 2 to 2½ hours, rearranging chicken after 1 hour.

To Finish Chicken:

Let pieces stand in broth until cool. Strip off skin and remove meat from bones. Skim fat from broth. To broth, add diced meat and mixture of ¼ cup each corn starch and cold water. Microwave at High (10) 5 to 8 minutes, until hot and bubbly. Drop Dumplings (below) by tablespoonfuls around edge of dish. Microwave at Medium (5) 7 to 9 minutes, until dumplings appear set and dry.

Dumplings:

In small bowl mix together 2 cups buttermilk biscuit mix, ⅔ cup milk and 1 tablespoon parsley flakes until just moistened.

Adapting chart for stewing chicken

Microwave simmering is the best way to cook older, more tough stewing chickens because they may be tenderized over the long slower cooking period. However, you can also simmer the naturally tender young broiler-fryers with excellent results. The meat will be succulent and juicy and the extended cooking time develops a rich flavor. The meat from simmered chicken is perfect for salads, sandwiches and casseroles.

Stewing is done by Time Cooking at Medium Power for 1 to 3 hours or by automatic simmering, available on some ovens having the Auto Roast feature. Automatic simmering is controlled with the temperature probe and keeps chicken at a low steady temperature for several hours (see picture above for probe placement and covering instruction). It requires no attention and results in more tender chicken than with Time Cooking.

Time Cooked Chicken

Item	Approximate Microwave Time/Hours	
Chicken, Stewing 4 to 6 lbs.		
Fresh	2 to 2½	
Frozen	2½ to 3	Cover. Rearrange chicken after half of time.
Chicken, Broiler-Fryer (2½-3½-lbs.)		
Fresh	1 to 1½	
Frozen	2 to 2½	

Automatic Simmer Chicken

Item	Approximate Simmer Time/Hours	
Chicken, Stewing 4 to 6 lbs.		Always use at least ½ cup water. Position temperature probe halfway between center and edge of dish. Cover tightly.
Fresh	11 to 12	
Frozen	12 to 14	
Chicken, Broiler-Fryer (2½-3½-lbs.)		
Fresh	4 to 6	
Frozen	6 to 8	

Chicken

Mexican Chicken Casserole

POWER LEVEL: High (10) TEMP: 155°
MICROWAVE TIME: 15 min.

1 can (10½-oz.) . . . . **condensed cream of chicken soup** **2 tablespoons green chilies, diced** **¼ teaspoon instant minced onion** **½ cup water**	In small mixing bowl place soup, chilies, onion and water. Stir until well blended.
2 large, firm, ripe . . . . . . **tomatoes**	Slice tomatoes in ½-in. slices.
1 pkg. (6-oz.) corn . . . . . **chips** **2 cups diced, cooked chicken, or 2 cans (5-oz. each) boned chicken, diced** **1 cup (4-oz.) shredded cheddar cheese**	In 2-qt. casserole layer ½ of corn chips. Top with 1 cup chicken, then ½ of tomato slices. Pour ½ of soup mixture over chicken; sprinkle with ¾ of cheese, reserving rest for topping after cooking. Repeat layers.

Insert temperature probe so tip is in center of casserole. Attach cable end at receptacle. **Microwave at High (10). Set Temp, Set 155°.** When oven signals, sprinkle with reserved cheese and let stand 5 minutes before serving.

Makes 6 to 8 servings

Chicken a la King

The old favorite, creamed chicken, dressed up with colorful pimiento, green pepper and flavorful mushrooms. Serve over toast or in a pastry shell.

POWER LEVEL: High (10) and Medium High (7)
MICROWAVE TIME: 16 to 21 min., total

⅓ cup butter . . . . **½ cup unsifted all-purpose flour** **2 cups dairy half & half** **1 cup chicken broth**	In 2-qt. casserole place butter. **Microwave at High (10) 1 Minute,** until melted. Blend in flour. Gradually stir in half & half and broth; mix well. **Microwave at High (10) 8 to 10 Minutes,** stirring with whisk after 4 minutes, until thickened and smooth. Stir well again.
2 cups cubed, cooked chicken **1 jar (4-oz.) sliced pimiento** **1 can (4-oz.) sliced mushrooms, undrained** **½ cup diced green pepper** **1 teaspoon salt** **¼ teaspoon pepper**	Mix in chicken, pimiento, mushrooms, green pepper, salt and pepper. Cover. **Microwave at Medium High (7) 7 to 10 Minutes,** until hot. Let stand 5 to 10 minutes before serving, to blend flavors.

Makes 4 servings

Brunswick Stew

If a more highly seasoned stew is desired add about 1 teaspoon Worcestershire sauce and 3 to 5 drops hot pepper (tabasco) sauce.

POWER LEVEL: Medium High (7) and High (10)
MICROWAVE TIME: 50 to 63 min., total

1 chicken . . . . **(2½ to 3½-lb.) cut up** **2 cups water**	In 3-qt. casserole place chicken pieces and water. Cover. **Microwave at Medium High (7) 25 to 30 Minutes,** depending on weight of chicken, until tender. Remove meat from bones discarding skin. Cut meat into pieces and return to broth in casserole.
2 cups diced raw . . . . **potatoes (2 medium)** **½ cup sliced onion (1 small)** **2 teaspoons salt** **¼ teaspoon pepper**	Add potatoes, onion, salt and pepper to casserole. **Microwave at Medium High (7) 15 to 18 Minutes,** stirring after 8 minutes.
1 can (12-oz.) whole . . . . . **kernel corn, undrained** **½ cup unsifted all-purpose flour** **1 pkg. (10-oz.) frozen baby lima beans, defrosted** **1 can (16-oz.) tomatoes, drained**	Into small bowl drain liquid from corn and stir in flour, mixing well. Blend into hot mixture. Add corn, lima beans and tomatoes. **Microwave at High (10) 10 to 15 Minutes,** stirring after 5 minutes, until vegetables are hot and sauce is thickened. Let stand 5 to 10 minutes before serving, to blend flavors.

Makes about 8 servings

Chicken Almondine

POWER LEVEL: High (10)
MICROWAVE TIME: 6 to 8 min., total

½ cup celery, thinly . . . . . . **sliced** **¼ cup onion, chopped**	Combine celery and onion in 1½-qt. casserole. Cover. **Microwave 2 Minutes at High (10).**
1 can (10¾-oz.) cream . . . **of celery soup** **¼ cup milk** **½ cup sliced almonds** **1 cup cooked chicken, cubed** **¼ teaspoon Worcestershire sauce**	Add remaining ingredients. Mix well and cover. **Microwave at High (10) 4 to 5 Minutes,** stirring after 2 minutes. Serve over rice, if desired.

Makes 4 servings

When microwaving a whole chicken, be sure to select a young, plump tender bird. The skin should be smooth and have a pale, creamy color tinged with pink. If you are in doubt, choose a broiler-fryer. Avoid chickens with thick, bumpy skin and large amounts of bright yellow fat.

If you do not care to use a cooking bag, or if you prefer a drier surface, microwave chicken covered with wax paper. You may need to add 2 or more additional minutes to the total cooking time. Microwaving chicken at Medium High rather than High eliminates excessive handling and foil for shielding.

How to Microwave Whole Chicken in a Cooking Bag
POWER LEVEL: Medium High (7) 9 to 10 Minutes Per Pound

Brush chicken with a mixture of 1 tablespoon bottled brown bouquet sauce and 1 tablespoon melted butter. Cut a ½-in. strip from open end of an oven cooking bag.

Place chicken in a bag on a microwave ovenproof platter or baking dish. Add ⅓ cup water, chicken broth or wine. Tie end of bag with plastic strip. Slash bag next to closure.

Insert temperature proble, if you are using it, through the bag into meatiest part of inner thigh, from below the end of and parallel to the leg. Microwave at Medium High (7) to an internal temperature of 190°.

How to Microwave Whole Chicken Without a Cooking Bag
POWER LEVEL: Medium High (7) 9 to 10 Minutes Per Pound

Brush chicken with a mixture of 1 tablespoon bottled brown bouquet sauce and 1 tablespoon melted butter. Place breast side down on trivet in cooking dish and cover with wax paper. Microwave at Medium High (7) for ½ the minimum time.

Turn chicken breast side up. Recover with wax paper. Microwave for second ½ of time.

Test for doneness by cutting skin between inner thigh and breast. Meat should show no trace of pink, and juices should run clear.

Whole Chicken

You can dress up whole chicken in a variety of ways, simply by varying the sauce, glaze or topping.

The recipes below illustrate both time and temperature cooking. Depending on the sauce or topping you choose, select the method which gives you the best finished results. Time cooking will produce a drier surface than temperature cooking, which is microwaved in a cooking bag.

Barbecued Stuffed Chicken

We have chosen to cook this recipe by time, instead of by temperature, because of the barbecue sauce coating. The time method uses a loose covering of wax paper which allows steam to escape away from the surface of the bird. As the skin cooks, the barbecue sauce dries to form a beautiful showy glaze.

POWER LEVEL: Medium High (7)
MICROWAVE TIME: 30 to 35 min., total

4 cups day-old ½-in. bread cubes or crumbled cornbread **¼ cup minced onion** **½ cup minced celery** **1 teaspoon salt** **1 teaspoon poultry seasoning** **¼ teaspoon pepper** **⅓ cup melted butter** **⅔ cup chicken broth**	In large bowl toss together bread, onion, celery, salt, poultry seasoning, pepper, butter and chicken broth to make stuffing.
1 whole broiler-fryer, about 3-lb. **Bottled barbecue sauce**	Fill body cavity of chicken with stuffing. Tie wings flat to body with string around chicken; tie legs together. Brush all areas with barbecue sauce.

On trivet in 12×8×2-in. dish place chicken with breast side down. Cover with wax paper. **Microwave at Medium High (7) 30 to 35 Minutes,** turning chicken breast side up and brushing with barbecue sauce after 15 minutes. Chicken is done when no trace of pink shows in meat when cut is made between inner thigh and breast. Let chicken stand 10 minutes before serving.

Makes 2 to 4 servings

Simmered Chicken

One of the simplest of ways to cook chicken, and one of the best. For ovens with automatic simmer setting included with the Auto Roast feature.

POWER LEVEL: Automatic Simmer   (Auto Roast Code 6)
MICROWAVE TIME: Fresh 4 to 6 hr.—
Frozen 5 to 7 hr.

1 whole chicken (2½ to 3½-lb.) **Paprika** **1 cup chicken broth**	In 3-qt. casserole place chicken. Rub chicken with paprika. Add broth.

Insert temperature probe so tip is in liquid on bottom of dish. Cover tightly with plastic wrap, arranging loosely around probe to vent. Attach cable end at receptacle. **Microwave at Automatic Simmer 4 to 6 Hours** for fresh chicken; or **5 to 7 Hours** for frozen.

Makes 4 servings

Chicken Teriyaki

Chicken Teriyaki

POWER LEVEL: Medium High (7)   TEMP: 190°
MICROWAVE TIME: 24 to 30 min., total

¼ cup soy sauce **⅓ cup honey** **⅓ cup sherry**	In small cooking bag, mix soy sauce, honey and sherry.
1 whole broiler-fryer, about 3-lb.	Add chicken to bag and tie open end securely with plastic strip cut from open end of bag.

Turn chicken on its side and place in 12×8×2-in. dish. Marinate in refrigerator 1 to 2 hours, turning chicken over after ½ of time. To microwave, place bird breast side up in dish. Slash bag near closure. Insert temperature probe as shown at left. **Microwave at Medium High (7). Set Temp, Set 190°.** When oven signals, remove chicken. Prepare Teriyaki Sauce (below) and finish chicken as described in sauce recipe.

Makes about 4 servings

Teriyaki Sauce: In 1-pt. glass measuring cup stir together 1 tablespoon water and 2 tablespoons cornstarch. Cut off one corner of cooking bag with scissors and drain juices into cup. **Microwave at High (10) 2 to 3 Minutes,** until thick and clear, stirring after 1 minute. After 10 minutes, remove chicken from bag to serving platter. Pour sauce over chicken just before serving.

Canned convenience foods, or foods frozen in metal trays, should be removed from their containers to suitable microwave plates or casseroles. Small boil-in-bag pouches (about 5 to 10-oz.) can be placed directly in the oven. Slit or pierce the top of the pouch before microwaving and open carefully after heating to avoid burns from steam. Large boil-in-bags may be placed in a serving dish. When contents are partially defrosted, open the bag, slide food into the dish and stir before continuing to microwave.

Chicken Gravy and Main Dishes such as barbecue chicken, chicken a la king, chicken and dumplings, creamed chicken, croquettes, escalloped chicken with noodles, fried chicken, pieces or slices in gravy, stew and turkey tetrazzini may be microwaved according to chart below.

POWER LEVEL: **High (10)**

CANNED AMOUNT	TIME MIN.	COMMENTS
7½ to 10½-oz.	2-4	Cover. Stir before serving, or use temperature probe set for 150°.
14 to 24-oz.	4-6	Cover. Stir before serving, or use temperature probe set for 150°.

FROZEN AMOUNT	TIME MIN.	COMMENTS
5 to 6½-oz. pouch	3 to 4	Slit pouch before microwaving.
12-oz.	7-9	Cover.
16 to 17-oz.	11-14	Cover.
Fried Chicken 2 pieces	4	Follow procedure below. Some brands of frozen fried chicken are not fully cooked. If label does not state "fully cooked", check for doneness.
Fried Chicken 1 lb., 6 pieces	6-7	
Fried Chicken 2 lb., 10 pieces		

How to Microwave Frozen Fried Chicken

Arrange chicken pieces in a single layer on a microwave ovenproof platter or cooking dish with meatiest parts to the outside.

Cover with wax paper. Microwave at High according to times above.

Remove from oven and let stand, covered with wax paper, about 5 minutes. If package label does not state "fully cooked", check for doneness by cutting through meat to bone. Pinkness indicates more cooking is needed.

Poultry

Chicken is one of the most popular foods for microwaving. The hints below have been developed from the most commonly asked questions from new microwave oven users about cooking chicken, so check them before you microwave.

Poultry Microwaving Helpful Hints

"I love the smoky flavor of grilled chicken, but it takes so long to cook."

Cut the cooking time in half by grilling the chicken just long enough to get the smoked flavor, then finish in the microwave.

"I like to use my microwave to cook poultry, but I do not like the moist skin. What do you suggest?"

Coating the chicken with cracker crumbs helps provide somewhat crisp outsides (see page 118). Or you can crisp the skin on your poultry by using the broiler on your conventional oven after microwaving; or for less calories and cholesterol, you could remove the skin on chicken pieces before microwaving, and brush on a browning sauce.

"When I microwave poultry there is such a large amount of fat in the bottom of the dish. Should I pour this off before adding sauces?"

Sometimes microwaving renders more fat from foods than conventional cooking. Yes, you may either extract or pour off grease before adding sauces, or using drippings for gravies.

"My microwaved chicken was tough and dry. Is there a way to avoid this problem, other than adding coatings and sauces?"

When microwaved properly, chicken may have a somewhat firmer texture than conventionally cooked, but it is very moist and juicy. Tough or dry chicken is usually overcooked. For more tender texture, marinate uncooked pieces in Lemon Marinade or Teriyaki Marinade, page 82.

*Cornish Hens Stuffed with
Long Grain and Wild Rice*

How to Defrost Cornish Hens and Duckling

Delicate Cornish Hens need some extra attention during defrosting or they may start to cook. We recommend defrosting in 3 steps rather than 2.

POWER LEVEL: Defrost
10 to 14 Minutes Per Pound

1. Place unopened package in oven. (Metal closure need not be removed.) Microwave at Defrost for ⅓ the total defrosting time.

2. Turn package over. Microwave for ⅓ of time.

3. Unwrap and shield ends of legs with foil. Microwave for last ⅓ of time. If giblets do not move freely, run cold water into cavities.

Plain microwaved Cornish Hen in background contrasts with a hen brushed with teriyaki sauce before microwaving. Teriyaki sauce gives a more golden color than brown bouquet sauce.

How to Microwave Cornish Hens and Duckling, Halved

Cornish Hens are naturally tender, especially when microwaved. Because they cook so quickly, the unevenness of browning is particularly noticeable, so you will probably prefer to brush with browning sauce before microwaving.

9 to 10 Minutes Per Pound

1. Brush halves of hens with browning sauce. (Duckling should not be brushed until second ½ of cooking time.) Place hens, or duckling in cooking dish, skin side up. Cover with wax paper. Microwave at High (10) for ½ the cooking time.

2. Rotate dish ½ turn. Microwave for second ½ of time. Test for doneness by piercing inner thigh with a fork, juices should run clear.

How to Microwave Cornish Hens and Duckling, Whole

POWER LEVEL: High (10)
6 to 8 Minutes Per Pound

1. Brush hens with browning sauce. (Duckling should not be brushed until second ½ of cooking time.) Shield legs and wings with foil. Place breast side down in suitable cooking dish. Cover with wax paper. Microwave for ½ the cooking time.

2. Turn breast side up. Microwave for second ½ of time. Let stand 10 minutes to allow meat to firm. Test for doneness by piercing thigh with a fork; juices should run clear.

Rice is an excellent stuffing for Cornish Hens and Duckling. For each hen use about ½ cup cooked rice (white and/or wild), well-buttered and seasoned. Use 2 to 2¾ cups of rice for 2 to 3 pound duckling. Or , stuff poultry with Fruited Rice Stuffing below.

Fruited Rice Stuffing

This recipe may be used to stuff a whole duckling or broiler-fryer chicken (about 3 pounds).

POWER LEVEL: **High (10)**
MICROWAVE TIME: 8 to 10 minutes.

In 3-qt. casserole combine 2 cups quick-cooking (Minute) rice, 1 cup golden raisins, 1 cup finely diced celery, 1 small onion, chopped, 1¼ cups orange juice, 1 cup hot tap water, 2 tablespoons butter, 2 tablespoons grated orange peel, ½ teaspoon salt and ¼ teaspoon each pepper, thyme and marjoram. Cover. **Microwave at High (10) for 8 to 10 Minutes,** stirring after 4 minutes. Cool. Makes about 2¾ cups.

Duckling

Since duckling is so fatty, browning sauce is not brushed on before the first half of cooking because it will not adhere to the skin. Add browning agent after partial cooking or broil the bird after microwaving to crisp and brown the thick skin.

Duckling or Cornish Hens Far East Style

POWER LEVEL: High (10)
MICROWAVE TIME: 18 to 20 min., total

2 cornish hens, about 1-lb. each or 1 duckling, about 3-lbs., defrosted	Split in halves, using kitchen shears or a sharp knife. Place in 12×8×2-in. dish, skin side down.
¼ cup soy sauce **¼ cup sherry wine** **¼ cup pineapple juice** **1 clove garlic, crushed or ⅛ teaspoon garlic powder** **½ teaspoon curry powder** **¼ teaspoon dry mustard**	In small bowl mix together soy sauce, sherry, pineapple juice, garlic, curry powder and mustard. Stir to blend well and pour over meat in dish. Refrigerate 4 to 6 hours, or overnight.

To cook, turn skin side up and baste with marinade. Cover dish with wax paper. **Microwave at High (10) 8 Minutes.** Brush with marinade and rotate dish ½ turn. Recover. **Microwave at High (10) 10 to 12 Minutes** more, until meat is tender. Serve immediately.

Makes 2 to 4 servings

Duckling with Colorful Marmalade Sauce

Microwave whole duckling, opposite page. During standing time, brush generously with Colorful Marmalade Sauce, below. Let stand uncovered for about 10 minutes before serving.

POWER LEVEL: High (10)
MICROWAVE TIME: 5 to 7 min., total

1 cup sweet orange marmalade **½ cup currant jelly** **1 tablespoon chopped onion** **2 teaspoons soy sauce** **1 teaspoon ground ginger** **½ cup sliced almonds**	In 1½-qt. casserole combine marmalade, jelly, onion, soy sauce, ginger and almonds. **Microwave at High (10) 5 to 7 Minutes,** stirring every 2 minutes, until hot and well combined.

Makes about 2 cups

Duckling with Colorful Marmalade Sauce

Prick skin of breast and legs with a kitchen fork after first ½ of cooking time. Brush with diluted brown bouquet sauce, if desired. For a crisp skin, omit sauce and, after microwaving, broil under a conventional broiler until crisp and brown.

Shape as well as size influences defrosting. A broad breasted, meaty turkey takes longer to defrost than a streamlined one of the same weight. Higher areas such as the breast and legs need more shielding because they are higher in the oven.

These directions are for defrosting turkeys weighing up to 15 pounds. If you wish to start defrosting a turkey the day before you plan to roast it, defrost for ¾ time, then place in refrigerator overnight to complete defrosting.

How to Defrost Whole Turkey

POWER LEVEL: Defrost 9 to 11 Minutes Per Pound

Place unwrapped turkey, breast side down, with legs to right, in oven. It is not necessary to remove the metal closure because of the large amount of food. Microwave at Defrost for ½ the time.

Unwrap turkey and shield legs, wing tips and any warm areas with foil. Secure foil with wooden picks.

Adapting Chart for Whole Turkey and Turkey Parts

Methods: There are two methods below for whole turkey. The method using a cooking bag gives very moist turkey meat and skin; and uses the shortest time. Without the cooking bag, skin is drier and crispier, but cooking time is increased significantly. If your oven has AUTO ROAST, use cooking bag method for whole turkey and Set Auto Roast Code for poultry.

Item	MICROWAVE TIME/MINUTES To Defrost	To Microwave	Power Level	Comments
Whole Turkey 9 to 15 pounds	9 to 11 per lb.	Without a cooking bag: 20 to 22 per lb.	Medium (5)	Brush with butter and browning sauce. Cover breast area around edge of neck cavity and meaty tops of legs with foil. Place single sheet of plastic wrap over breast and wings, securing to sides of dish. Remove wrap and foil when basting after about ½ of cooking time. Let stand 20 minutes before carving. See page 130.
		With a cooking bag*: 11 to 13 per lb.	Medium (5)	See procedure on page 130-131.
Halves, Quarters and Legs, 4 to 6 lbs.	9 to 11 per lb.	11 to 13 per lb.	Medium High (7)	Must be defrosted before microwaving. Brush with butter and browning sauce and cover with wax paper. *Do Not Add Water.* Turn over after ½ of time. Let stand 20 minutes.
Whole Turkey Breast, 6 to 14 lb.	9 to 11 per lb.	9 to 11 per lb.	Medium High (7)	Microwave with temperature probe in cooking bag (see directions for whole turkey, page 130-131). Insert temperature probe from side into center of thickest meaty area. Set at 170. Breast cooks to lower finished temperature than whole turkey. Let stand 20 minutes before slicing.

*For complete meal cooking on oven shelf, select turkey no larger than 10 lbs. and use cooking bag technique only.
See pages 131 and 54.

Turn breast side up with legs to left of oven. Shield breast, neck area and tail area with foil. Defrost for second ½ of time.

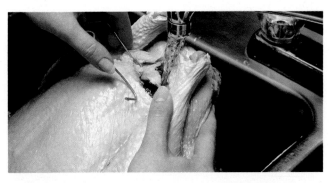

Remove metal clamp from legs. Run cold water into breast and neck cavities until giblets and neck can be removed. Turkey should feel soft and cool with a glistening surface. Interior should be cold and slightly icy.

How to Defrost Turkey Parts

POWER LEVEL: Defrost 9 to 11 Minutes Per Pound

Unwrap turkey parts if in foil. Place parts in a dish and cover with wax paper. Parts in all plastic or paper packaging can be placed in microwave without unwrapping. Microwave skin side down at Defrost for ½ time.

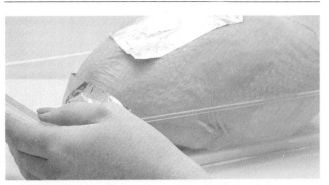

Turn parts over. Those parts microwaved in paper or plastic packaging should now be unwrapped, placed in a dish and turned over. Check for warm spots and shield, if necessary. Cover with wax paper. Microwave at Defrost for second ½ of time. Run cold water over parts until softened and pliable. When defrosted, the surface will be cool and glistening. The interior should be cold and slightly icy.

Turkeys weighing up to 15 pounds may be microwaved in two ways. For a moist turkey needing no attention during cooking, use an ovenproof cooking bag.

If you do not care to use a cooking bag, or prefer turkey with a drier surface, microwave turkey in a roasting dish partially covered with foil and plastic wrap. This method requires a longer cooking time, but skin will be crisper and meat firmer.

How to Microwave Turkey in a Cooking Bag

Brush turkey with a mixture of 1 tablespoon brown bouquet sauce and 4 tablespoons butter. Dry turkey thoroughly before brushing, or sauce will not cling to bird. Shield breastbone area and legs with strips of aluminum foil.

POWER LEVEL: Medium (5) 11 to 13 Minutes Per Pound

Place turkey in bag and arrange in a roasting dish. If desired, lightly oil inside of bag over breast to prevent sticking. Add ½ cup water, chicken broth, or wine. Close bag securely using plastic tie. Slash bag near closure.

How to Microwave Turkey Without a Cooking Bag

Brush turkey with browning sauce as directed above. Place turkey in roasting dish, breast side up tucking wings underneath.

POWER LEVEL: Medium (5) 20 to 22 Minutes Per Pound

Shield breast and legs with foil and cover breast area with plastic wrap attaching wrap to edges of dish, as shown. Place in microwave oven with legs to left of oven. Microwave at Medium (5) for ½ the cooking time.

Rotate dish ½ turn. Remove foil and plastic wrap. Baste turkey and insert temperature probe, if you are using one. Set Temp, Set 190°. Microwave second ½ of time until probe reaches 190°, or legs move freely at joints. Let stand 20 mintues before carving.

If your oven is equipped with a temperature probe, be sure to use it when microwaving turkey. The oven will signal when turkey has reached 190°. Let turkey stand 20 minutes after microwaving, before serving.

If your microwave oven has the Auto Roast feature, use it to automatically cook turkey to the proper finished temperature. Use a cooking bag and insert the probe as shown on this page. Then set Auto Roast and the code for poultry, given on your oven's control panel.

Insert temperature probe, if you are using one, through the bag into the meatiest part of the inner thigh. Position the probe below the end of, and parallel to the leg. Microwave at Medium (5), Set Temp, Set 190°. If not using the probe microwave for minimum time and check with a meat thermometer. Do not put conventional metal meat thermometer in microwave oven.

Double the capacity of your microwave oven by using the shelf. Add desserts, small casseroles or vegetables during last minutes of turkey's cooking time. Use the shelf for turkeys weighing less than 10 pounds, in a cooking bag. See page 54 for suggestions.

Savory Stuffing

Stuffed whole turkey takes about the same microwaving time as unstuffed. Use adequate broth or melted butter for turkey stuffing since microwaves are attracted to moisture. Allow about ½ cup stuffing per pound of bird. To prevent food spoilage, stuff just before cooking and remove leftover stuffing from cooked bird before storing.

POWER LEVEL: High (10)
MICROWAVE TIME: 4 to 6 min., total

8 cups bread crumbs . . . In large bowl, mix all
½ cup minced onion ingredients. Pour into an
1 cup minced celery 8-in. square baking dish.
2 teaspoons salt **Microwave at High**
2 teaspoons poultry **(10) 4 to 6 Minutes.** Use
seasoning to accompany turkey or
¼ teaspoon pepper other poultry.
⅔ cup melted butter
1 cup chicken broth, Makes about 5 cups
or strained turkey
drippings

Cranberry Sauce

The perennial favorite with roast turkey. This keeps up to a month well covered in the refrigerator.

POWER LEVEL: High (10)
MICROWAVE TIME: 18 to 20 min., total

2 cups sugar . . . . In 3-qt. casserole stir all
½ cup water ingredients together.
1 lb. cranberries, Cover. **Microwave at**
fresh, or frozen **High (10) 18 to 20**
Minutes, stirring after ½
time. Serve warm or cold.

Makes 3 to 4 cups

Hot Turkey and Cheese Sandwich

Turkey

Hot Turkey and Cheese Sandwiches

These are known in the South as "Hot Browns", created at a once-famous hotel in Louisville.

POWER LEVEL: Medium High (7)
MICROWAVE TIME: 7½ to 9 min., total

4 strips bacon . . . . On paper plate lined with double thickness paper towels, arrange bacon. Cover with single thickness paper towel. **Microwave at Medium High (7) 2½ to 3 Minutes,** until only partially cooked.

4 slices toast . . . . In 2 (7 to 9-in.) oval au gratin dishes, divide toast, arranging to cover bottoms of dishes. Place 4 to 6 large slices turkey in each dish and top each with 2 tomato slices. Divide cheese sauce over sandwiches. Sprinkle tops of sandwiches with parmesan cheese. Arrange 2 slices partially-cooked bacon over each sandwich.
8 to 12 large slices turkey breast
4 slices tomato (¼-in. thick)
1 recipe Cheese Sauce, page 158
¼ cup parmesan cheese

Place dishes side by side in microwave oven. Cover with wax paper. **Microwave at Medium High (7) 5 to 6 Minutes,** until hot.

Makes 2 sandwiches

Turkey Tetrazzini

POWER LEVEL: High (10)
MICROWAVE TIME: 24 to 27 min., total

1 pkg. (7-oz.) spaghetti . . . . Cook spaghetti (see chart, page 160), except **Microwave High (10) 9 Minutes.** Drain. Place in greased 12×8×2-in. dish.

¼ cup butter . . . . In 2-qt. casserole place butter, mushrooms, onion and lemon juice. **Microwave at High (10) 2 to 3 Minutes,** stirring after 1 minute.
1 can (4-oz.) sliced mushrooms, drained
1 small onion, chopped
1½ teaspoons lemon juice

⅓ cup flour . . . . Stir in flour, salt, paprika and nutmeg, until smooth. **Microwave at High (10) 1 Minute.** Stir well. Gradually stir in broth. **Microwave at High (10) 6 to 8 Minutes,** stirring after 3 minutes, until thickened.
1 teaspoon salt
½ teaspoon paprika
⅛ teaspoon nutmeg
2 cups turkey or chicken broth

½ cup dairy half & half . . . . Mix in half & half and turkey. Pour over spaghetti. Sprinkle with cheese and paprika. **Microwave at High (10) 7 to 9 Minutes,** until hot.
2½ cups cooked, cubed turkey
½ cup parmesan cheese
Paprika

Makes 4 to 6 servings

Saucy Turkey and Broccoli

Called Turkey Divan when made with the traditional Mornay Sauce. This makes a nice luncheon or supper dish. A salad of tomato slices is a colorful accompaniment.

POWER LEVEL: High (10)
MICROWAVE TIME: 6 to 8 min., total

1 bunch (about 1¼-lb.) broccoli, cut in spears . . . . Microwave broccoli according to directions, page 168. Drain. In 12×8×2-in. dish or microwave ovenproof platter arrange attractively.

8 large slices cooked turkey . . . . Layer turkey slices over broccoli. Cover with sauce. **Microwave at High (10) 6 to 8 Minutes,** until hot.
1 recipe Cheese Sauce, page 158

Makes 4 servings

Turkey

One of our tips below discusses browning of turkeys. In the opening pages of this section, we mention brushing with brown bouquet sauce, diluted with butter or water as perhaps the standard way to increase browning on poultry. In our most recent testing we have had excellent success with butter-soy sauce mixture, as a browning aid. Or, use a shake-on browner either purchased or homemade — see recipe page 95.

Turkey Microwaving Helpful Hints

"The pop-up thermometer that came inserted in my turkey indicated it was done; but the joints were raw when it was carved."

Pop-up thermometers are not inserted deeply enough into the turkey to give a true reading when microwaving. Use a meat thermometer or check leg joints.

"Why is such a long standing time recommended after microwaving turkeys?"

When microwaving or conventional cooking, a 20 minute standing time is necessary. During this time the turkey continues to cook at joints and meat firms for easier slicing.

"Will I get better browning if I don't microwave my turkey in a cooking bag?"

Yes; turkeys microwaved without a bag can be basted with butter and browning sauce for even color. The skin will be crisper and meat firmer.

Turkey Convenience Chart

POWER LEVEL: High (10)

ITEM	TIME/MINUTES	COMMENTS
Gravy & Sliced Turkey, Frozen (5-oz. pkg.)	3 to 4	Make 1-in. slit in top of pouch with sharp knife.
Turkey Casseroles, Frozen (12-oz. pkg.)	7 to 9	Place food in 1-qt. casserole. Cover.
Turkey Roasts, Frozen (2 to 4-lb.)	18 to 20 per lb.	Add ½ cup water. Can be microwaved from frozen without defrosting. Cover with plastic wrap. Turn over after ½ of time. Note: When a gravy pouch is included it should not be included in calculating total microwave time for turkey roast. Subtract weight of gravy from total package weight.

134 Fish and Seafood

Fish and seafood are naturally tender and require minimal cooking to preserve their delicate flavor and texture. Overcooking dries and toughens fish. We recommend that many seafoods, especially the meatier types, be cooked until the outer areas appear opaque but the centers are still slightly translucent. These areas will finish cooking as the seafood stands, while the outer areas remain tender.

How to Microwave Fish Fillets and Steaks

Arrange fillets in a cooking dish, thickest parts to outside and pour sauce over.

Brush steaks with lemon-butter. (If desired, line dish with paper towel to collect juices.)

Fish is done when meat flakes easily with a fork. Center should be slightly translucent.

Steam fillets and steaks by covering with dampened towel.

Scallop fish with cream and crumb topping. See recipe on page 138.

Brown seasoned floured fillets in preheated, oiled Brown 'N Sear dish.

Fish Cooking and Adapting Chart for Your Recipes

POWER LEVEL: **High (10)**

TYPE	TIME/MINUTES FRESH	TIME/MINUTES FROZEN	DEFROSTED FISH BROWN 'N SEAR* First Side (Time/Minutes)	DEFROSTED FISH BROWN 'N SEAR* Second side (Time/Minutes)
Fillets, or **Steaks** (½-in. thick)				
1 to 2	4 to 5	5 to 7	2-3	2½ to 3½
3 to 4	6 to 9	8 to 11	4-6	5 to 7
5 to 6	10 to 12	12 to 14	8-12	10 to 14
Whole Fish (1½ to 2½ lbs.)				
1 to 2	13 to 15	4 to 5	—	—
3 to 4	16 to 20	6 to 9	—	—

Fish Casserole, or **Stews**   Defrosted, pre-cooked fish — 10 minutes per quart
Add shellfish and other delicate fish last to prevent overcooking.
*Add 1 tsp. of oil, or butter to preheated Brown 'N Sear dish. Roll fillets in seasoned flour before microwaving.

Pictured top to bottom: *Fillets in Lemon Butter (page 138)*
Shrimp Gumbo (page 146)

136 Fish and Seafood

Fish defrosts rapidly. It is naturally delicate and tender, so care should be taken not to toughen it by over-defrosting. Remove fish from the microwave oven while it is still slightly icy.

If you or a family member like to fish, freeze your catch for fresh-tasting fish all year 'round. Seal fillets or steaks in a plastic bag with a small amount of water and freeze.

How to Defrost Fillets and Steaks

Defrosting Chart
POWER LEVEL: **Defrost**

ITEM	1st SIDE TIME MINUTES	2nd SIDE TIME MINUTES
Fillets, 1-lb.	4	4 to 6
Steaks, 6-oz. - 1	2	None
Steaks, 6-oz. - 2	2	1 to 2

Shape of package, as well as its weight influences defrosting time. Thick fillets or bulky packages take longer than flat packages of the same weight.

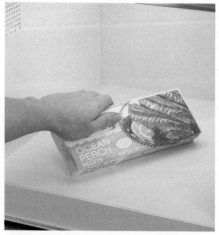

Place unopened paper or plastic package directly on oven floor. Fillets frozen at home in a bag of water should be placed in a dish to avoid leakage.

How to Defrost Whole Fish

Defrosting Chart
POWER LEVEL: **Defrost**

ITEM	1st SIDE TIME MINUTES	2nd SIDE TIME MINUTES
1 - 8 to 10-oz. Fish	2	2 to 4
2 - 8 to 10-oz. Fish	4	6 to 8
1 - 3 to 4-lb. Fish	8	12 to 14

Shape of fish, as well as weight, determines defrosting time. A short, thick fish may take longer to defrost than a long, thin one of the same weight.

Arrange fish in a cooking dish large enough to hold it easily. Microwave at Defrost for first part of time.

Clean whole fish, then dip them in water and freeze on a baking dish. The icy coating will protect fish from freezer burn. Package for freezing after icy coating forms.

When defrosting home frozen fish, use a cooking dish to collect water as it melts.

Turn package over so that the side which was closest to the back of the oven is brought to the front.

Check after minimum defrosting time. Corners should not feel warm, although outer pieces may have started to loosen.

Hold fillets under cold running water until they can be separated.

Turn fish over. Microwave for second part of minimum time.

Test fish. It should feel cold and pliable and may still be slightly icy in the cavity.

Rinse cavity with cold running water to complete defrosting.

Favorite sauces for fish fillets or steaks often include some form of lemon butter as exemplified by two of the recipes here. The third recipe has a creamy sauce, which is another popular accompaniment for fish and seafood.

Dilled Salmon Steaks

Fillets in Lemon Butter

POWER LEVEL: High (10)
MICROWAVE TIME: 9 to 12 min., total

1 lb. firm fish fillets **½ to 1 teaspoon salt** **⅛ teaspoon pepper**	In 12×8×2-in. dish, arrange fillets with thickest areas to outside edges of dish. Sprinkle with salt and pepper.
½ cup (¼-lb.) butter **½ cup chopped parsley** **1 tablespoon lemon juice** **½ cup buttery flavored cracker crumbs** **½ teaspoon paprika**	In 1-qt. casserole place butter. **Microwave at High (10) 1 to 2 Minutes,** until melted. Blend in parsley and lemon juice and pour over fish. Top with crumbs, then sprinkle on paprika. **Microwave at High (10) 8 to 10 Minutes.**

Makes 4 servings

Dilled Salmon Steaks

POWER LEVEL: High (10)
MICROWAVE TIME: 6 to 7 min., total

4 (½-in. thick) salmon steaks (1-lb.) **2 tablespoons melted butter** **2 teaspoons lemon juice** **½ teaspoon dill weed**	In paper towel lined 12×8×2-in. dish place steaks. Brush with melted butter mixed with lemon juice. Sprinkle with dill. Cover dish with wax paper.

Microwave at High (10) 6 to 7 Minutes. When done, fish will flake easily with fork. Turn fish over onto serving plate. (Paper towel absorbs juices for best appearance of fish.) Garnish top of steaks with sprinkling of paprika or parsley and additional melted butter, if desired.

Makes 4 servings

Scalloped Fish or Scallops

POWER LEVEL: High (10)
MICROWAVE TIME: 7 to 9 min., total

1 lb. white fish fillets or scallops	On microwave ovenproof platter or 9-in. pie plate place fish fillets or scallops with thickest areas to outside edges of dish. Cover with dampened paper towel which has most of water squeezed out. **Microwave at High (10) 4 Minutes.**
½ cup (¼-lb.) butter **1 cup soft bread crumbs** **1 cup saltine cracker crumbs**	Remove platter from oven and let stand covered with paper towel while preparing buttered crumbs. In 1-qt. glass measure place butter. **Microwave at High (10) 1 Minute,** or until melted. Add bread and cracker crumbs. Mix with fork.
1 teaspoon salt **⅛ teaspoon freshly ground pepper** **⅓ cup milk or cream**	Remove paper towel from fish and sprinkle evenly with salt and pepper, then buttered crumbs. Pour milk evenly over top. **Microwave at High (10) 2 to 4 Minutes** more.

Makes 4 servings

The speed and moisture retention of microwaving are decided advantages when cooking fish. Plan a standing time of about 5 minutes after cooking, and keep the fish well covered while standing. Select a delicate sauce so as not to mask the fresh natural flavor.

Fish Microwaving Helpful Hints

"When I microwave fish it turns dark and dry. What am I doing wrong?"

Overcooking is the problem. When microwaving overlap thin ends of fillets and place thick areas toward side of dish. Microwave only for minimum suggested time, then check for doneness. When properly cooked, after standing, fish should flake easily and thick areas should look opaque.

"What should I do to give my microwaved fish a browned appearance similar to the way it looks when broiled."

Microwave floured fillets or steaks in Brown 'N Sear dish. Or, mix coating sauce like brown bouquet, teriyaki or soy sauce with butter and brush over fish before microwaving.

"My microwaved fish develops white coagulated juices that form in the dish bottom. What should I do to avoid this problem?"

Try lining the dish with a paper towel which will collect the coagulated juices, or...

Elevate fish fillets and steaks on a trivet.

Tuna Noodle Casserole

POWER LEVEL: High (10)
MICROWAVE TIME: 31 to 36 min., total

1 pkg. (8-oz.) fine **egg noodles**	Microwave noodles (see chart, page 160), except cook 10 minutes.
3 tablespoons butter **1 clove garlic,** **minced** **½ cup finely chopped** **green onions** **½ teaspoon salt** **⅛ teaspoon pepper**	In 3-qt. casserole place butter, garlic, onion, salt and pepper. **Microwave at High (10) 2 to 3 Minutes,** stirring after 1 minute, until onion is softened.
¼ cup unsifted **all-purpose flour** **1½ cups milk**	Stir in flour until smooth. Gradually stir in milk. **Microwave at High (10) 4 to 6 Minutes,** stirring every 2 minutes, until smooth and thickened.
2 cans (7-oz. each) **tuna, drained**	Gently stir tuna and noodles into sauce. Cover. **Microwave at High (10) 15 to 17 Minutes,** stirring after 8 minutes, until hot.
⅓ cup cracker **crumbs** **2 tablespoons** **minced parsley** **2 tablespoons** **melted butter**	In small bowl, mix together crumbs, parsley and butter. Sprinkle over casserole before serving.

Makes 6 to 8 servings

Scalloped Tuna and Chips

POWER LEVEL: High (10)
MICROWAVE TIME: 15 to 17 min., total

1 can (10½-oz.) **condensed cream of** **celery soup** **1 can (7 to 8-oz.)** **mushrooms, stems** **and pieces** **1 teaspoon instant** **minced onion** **1 tablespoon** **chopped parsley** **1 cup milk** **1 tablespoon lemon** **juice**	Mix soup, undrained mushrooms, onion, parsley, milk and lemon juice.
3 cups crushed **potato chips** **2 cans (7-oz. each)** **tuna, drained and** **flaked**	In 2-qt. greased casserole layer 1 cup crushed chips, ½ of tuna, ½ of soup mixture. Repeat layers and top with potato chips. **Microwave at High (10) 15 to 17 Minutes,** until bubbly.

Makes 6 servings

Tuna dishes essentially require only reheating by microwave energy because the ingredients are precooked. The three recipes on this page are popular favorites to save you time with family meals.

Tuna Wedges

Tuna Wedges

A tuna loaf, microwaved in a round shape. Garnish with tomato slices and sprinkle with grated cheese if desired.

POWER LEVEL: High (10)
MICROWAVE TIME: 10 to 12 min., total

2 eggs **1½ cups cooked rice** **6 green onions,** **finely chopped** **2 cans (7-oz.) solid** **pack tuna**	In large mixing bowl beat eggs with fork. Add rice, onions and undrained tuna. Mix well.
½ cup (¼-lb.) butter **¼ teaspoon thyme** **1 cup fine dry bread** **crumbs**	In small glass bowl place butter. **Microwave at High (10) 1 Minute,** until melted. Add to tuna along with thyme and crumbs. Mix well.

Spread mixture evenly in lightly greased 9-in. pie plate. Cover with wax paper. **Microwave at High (10) 9 to 11 Minutes,** rotating dish ½ turn after 5 minutes. Serve in wedges.

Makes about 6 servings

Whole fish makes a dramatic presentation and microwaving is a superior way of preparing it. With a tight cover fish steam in their own natural moisture and are delicate and juicy.

Although the head is not eaten, it should be shielded with foil to maintain its appearance for serving. The eye, which turns white during cooking, can be covered with an olive slice.

How to Insert the Temperature Probe

Insert Probe just above gill into meatiest area, parallel to backbone. Probe should be on side of fish closest to dish.

How to Microwave a Whole Fish by Temperature Cooking

(Striped Bass, Snapper, etc. 2½ to 4 pounds)

Brush entire fish with a mixture of 1 tablespoon browning sauce and 1 tablespoon water, then with melted butter; or brush with lemon-butter sauce. Add stuffing, if desired. Insert temperature probe.

Shield head and thin tail area with foil. Make sure foil on head is no closer than ¾-in. from probe disc.

Cover dish tightly with plastic wrap, arranging loosely around probe to vent. Attach cable end at receptable. **Microwave at High (10). Set Temperature 170°.**

How to Microwave a Whole Fish by Time

POWER LEVEL: **High (10)**
4 to 7 Minutes Per Pound

Brush fish with sauce as directed in the recipe.

Shield head and thin tail area with foil.

Cover tightly with plastic wrap, turning back one corner to vent.

Stuffed Red Snapper

POWER LEVEL: High (10)
MICROWAVE TIME: 13 to 15 min., total

1 red snapper (1½ to 2½-lbs.) cleaned and gutted	Place fish on microwave safe platter or in 12×8×2-in. dish.
Vegetable Stuffing	Stuff cavity with Vegetable Stuffing.
2 tablespoons bottled brown bouquet sauce	Brush all areas with mixture of brown bouquet sauce and butter.
¼ cup butter, melted	

Cover head and thin tail end with strips of aluminum foil. Cover platter or dish with plastic wrap, turning back one corner to vent. **Microwave at High (10) 13 to 15 Minutes,** until fish flakes easily with fork. While letting stand 5 minutes, brush again with butter, if desired.

Makes 2 servings

Vegetable Stuffing

½ cup (¼-lb.) butter, melted	In 2-qt. casserole place butter, onion, carrots, mushrooms, parsley, bread crumbs, egg, lemon juice, salt and pepper. Toss to mix well. Pack lightly into fish.
½ cup finely chopped onion	
½ cup finely grated carrots	
½ cup chopped raw mushrooms	
¼ cup finely minced parsley	
½ cup fine dry bread crumbs	
1 egg, beaten	
1 tablespoon lemon juice	
1 teaspoon salt	
⅛ teaspoon pepper	

Makes about 2 cups

142 Shellfish

Shellfish is expensive in some areas of the country, and care should be taken to preserve its freshness when freezing.

Small pieces of shellfish are especially vulnerable to freezer burns and should be very well wrapped.

POWER LEVEL: **Defrost**

How to Defrost Small Loose Pieces of Shellfish

TYPE	TIME MINUTES
Crab Fingers (1-lb.)	6 to 7
Scallops (1-lb.)	6 to 7
Shrimp (1-lb.)	6 to 7

Small pieces of loose-packed shellfish, such as shrimp, scallops or crab fingers, are easiest to defrost, since they c▪ spread out in a single layer and absorb microwave energy evenly. Check at minimum time.

How to Defrost Shellfish Frozen in Blocks

TYPE	TIME MINUTES
Crab Meat (6-oz. pkg.)	4 to 5
Crab Meat (2 6-oz. pkgs.)	6 to 7
Crab Meat (1-lb. can)	14 to 16
Oysters (12-oz. can)	8 to 10
Oysters (3 12-oz. cans)	18 to 20
Scallops (1-lb. pkg.)	7 to 9

Blocks of shellfish, such as crab meat and scallops can b▪ defrosted in their paper packages. Oysters and crab meat ▪ in cans must be removed to a covered dish. Break up these dense blocks as soon as possible.

How to Defrost Large Shellfish

TYPE	TIME MINUTES
Crab Legs (8 to 10-oz.) 1 to 2	5 to 7
Crab Legs (8 to 10-oz.) 3 to 4	10 to 12
Lobster Tails (6 to 9-oz.) 1 to 2	5 to 7
Lobster Tails (6 to 9-oz.) 3 to 4	10 to 12
Lobster Tails (12 to 16-oz.) 1 to 2	8 to 10
Whole Lobster, or Crab (1½-lb.)	16 to 18 (approx. 12 min. per pound)

Large pieces such as whole lobster, lobster tails, whole cr▪ large crab legs should be removed from the oven while still slightly icy and allowed to stand a few minutes.

Shellfish

No special attention is needed while defrosting shellfish. However, to avoid overdefrosting, it is best to check at minimum time. Loose small pieces of seafood can be microwaved from frozen to done when arranged in a ring shape, drizzled with melted butter and tightly covered with plastic wrap, see picture below. Extend microwave time 2 to 3 minutes.

Adapting Tips for Defrosting and Cooking Shrimp

Defrost shellfish in baking dish in single layer.

Test after minimum time. Shellfish · should be cool, soft, translucent.

Continue cooking immediately for serving, if desired.

Adapting Tips for Defrosting and Cooking Oysters

Place block in a covered casserole. Defrost for half the time.

Turn block over second half of time, breaking off pieces as they loosen.

Pieces should be loose and still feel icy. Let stand to complete defrosting.

Adapting Tips for Defrosting and Cooking Lobster

Arrange in a baking dish with darker side up.

Defrosted lobster should be flexible, transparent, cool.

Slit shells to expose meat for cooking.

144 Shellfish

Steaming is the classic method for cooking shellfish. In the microwave oven most shellfish steam without water in a cooking dish covered with plastic wrap, or wax paper. A dampened paper towel provides sufficient steam for scallops. Clams, lobster tails and crab legs steam in their own natural moisture, in their shells. Whole lobster needs some water because of its size. We recommend cooking unpeeled shrimp in water with a bay leaf and vinegar to reduce cooking odors.

How to Microwave Shrimp, Clams and Scallops

Arrange cleaned, peeled and deveined shrimp in a ring. Cover tightly with plastic wrap, turning back 2-in. to vent. Microwave at High (10) for 5 minutes.

Cook 1 to 2 pounds unpeeled, raw shrimp in a 2-qt. glass casserole dish with 2½ cups water, 1 bay leaf, 1 tablespoon vinegar. Microwave at High (10) for 6 to 10 minutes.

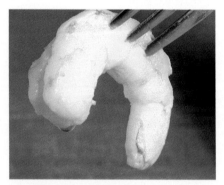

Check appearance of shrimp for doneness. It will turn from translucent to opaque.

Place 6 clams (3 to 5-oz.) in ring with hinged side out. Microwave at High (10) for 3 to 5 minutes.

Remove clams from oven as soon as the shells open partially. Tightly closed shells contain bad clams and should be discarded.

Steam scallops. Cover with a damp paper towel. Arrange 1 pound scallops in single layer and Microwave at High (10) for 5 to 7 minutes.

Shellfish Adapting Chart

POWER LEVEL: **High (10)**

TYPE	TIME (MIN.)	TYPE	TIME (MIN.)
Clams (3 to 5-oz.) 6	3-5	Lobster Tails (8 to 10-oz.) 4	10-12
Crab Legs (8 to 10-oz.) 2	5-6	Whole Lobster (1½ to 2-lb.) 1	10-12
(8 to 10-oz.) 4	9-11	Scallops (1-lb.)	5-7
Lobster Tail (12 to 16-oz.) 1	6-7	Shrimp, peeled (1-lb.)	5
Lobster Tails (8 to 10-oz.) 2	6-7	Shrimp, unpeeled (1 to 2-lb.)	6-10

Let stand for 5 minutes. Cooking will be completed during standing time.

How to Microwave Lobster Tails and Crab Legs

Brush lobster meat with mixture of 1 tablespoon melted butter and 1 tablespoon lemon juice.

Arrange crab legs in baking dish with dark colored side up. Do not add water.

Cover lobster tails, or crab legs with wax paper and Microwave at High (10), see chart page 144. When done, meat is white, not translucent.

How to Microwave Whole Lobster

Plunge the tip of a heavy knife into live lobster between the head and first segment to sever the spinal cord, which kills lobster. Lobster may show signs of movement for a few minutes.

Peg the tail to prevent curling by inserting a wooden skewer lengthwise through the meat. At this time, or after lobster is cooked, cut through the undershell of the body and remove the intestinal vein and small sack below the head.

Arrange lobster in a baking dish with back side up and add ½ cup hot water. Cover tightly with plastic wrap, turning back a corner to vent. **Microwave at High (10) 9 to 11 Minutes.**

Crab Legs and Lobster Tail

Shrimp Gumbo

For spicy flavor, tie 1 to 2 teaspoons crab boil in a cheesecloth bag and add along with shrimp. For bright color accent, save out about ¼ of green pepper to stir into finished gumbo.

POWER LEVEL: High (10) and Medium High (7)
MICROWAVE TIME: 29 to 30 min., total

1 medium onion, sliced (about ½ cup) **¼ cup butter (use bacon fat, if desired)**	In 3-qt. casserole place onion and butter. **Microwave at High (10) 3 Minutes,** stirring after 2 minutes, until onion is limp.
2 tablespoons cornstarch **1 cup water** **2 cans (16-oz. each) stewed tomatoes** **1 cup diced green pepper (2 medium)** **2 cloves garlic, crushed** **2 teaspoons salt** **1 teaspoon ground nutmeg** **¼ teaspoon pepper** **1 pound raw shrimp, shelled, deveined** **2 pkgs. (10-oz. each) frozen okra, defrosted, cut into 1-in. pieces**	In small bowl stir together cornstarch and water. Add to onion along with tomatoes, green pepper, garlic, salt, nutmeg, pepper, shrimp and okra. Stir well. Cover **Microwave at Medium High (7) 29 to 31 Minutes,** stiring and recovering after ½ of time.

Makes 6 to 8 servings

Scalloped Oysters

POWER LEVEL: High (10)
MICROWAVE TIME: 12 to 14 min., total

3 cans (12-oz. each) frozen oysters, thawed (about 4 cups)	Drain oysters, reserving ¼ cup liquid.
¾ cup butter, melted **2 cups fine soda cracker crumbs (about 40 small squares)** **1 teaspoon salt** **⅛ teaspoon pepper** **⅛ teaspoon nutmeg**	In small mixing bowl mix together butter and crumbs. In 10×6×2-in. dish layer ⅓ of crumb mixture, ½ of drained oysters, ½ of seasonings, then ⅓ of remaining crumbs, rest of oysters, seasonings and crumbs.
¼ cup milk	Mix milk with oyster liquid and pour evenly over top.

With knife, poke 3 to 4 holes through layers so liquid goes to bottom. **Microwave at High (10) 7 Minutes.** Sprinkle with ¼ cup parsley. Rotate dish ½ turn. **Microwave 6 to 8 Minutes,** until oysters are firm when pierced with fork.

Makes about 6 servings

Creamed Scallops

The classic dish often known as Coquille St. Jacques. Large scallop shells are natural microwave utensils.

POWER LEVEL: High (10), Med. (5) and Med. High (7)
MICROWAVE TIME: 17 to 20 min., total

3 tablespoons butter **1 jar (4-oz.) sliced mushrooms** **2 green onions, sliced** **¼ cup chopped celery**	In 2-qt. casserole place butter, mushrooms, onions and celery. **Microwave at High (10) 2 to 3 Minutes,** stirring after 1 minute.
2 tablespoons flour **½ teaspoon salt** **¼ teaspoon thyme** **1 tablespoon pimiento, chopped** **⅓ cup white wine** **1 lb. raw scallops**	Stir in flour, salt, thyme and pimiento well, then wine and scallops, stirring again. **Microwave at High (10) 5 to 6 Minutes,** stirring after 3 minutes, until thickened.
¼ cup dairy half & half **1 egg yolk, beaten**	Stir in half & half and egg yolk. **Microwave at Medium (5) 3 to 4 Minutes,** stirring after 2 minutes.

Divide mixture among 4 scallop shells. Top with Crumb Mixture (below). Cover with wax paper. **Microwave at medium high (7) 7 to 9 Minutes,** rearranging after 4 minutes, until hot.

Makes 4 servings

Crumb Mixture: In small bowl, place 2 tablespoons butter. **Microwave at High (10) ¼ to ½ Minute,** until melted. Stir in ¼ cup fine dry bread crumbs and 2 tablespoons Parmesan cheese.

Sweet and Sour Shrimp

Garnish with chopped bacon and green onion slices.

POWER LEVEL: High (10)
MICROWAVE TIME: 6 to 8 min., total

1 recipe Sweet and Sour Sauce, page 156 **1 lb. cleaned and cooked shrimp** **1 can (8-oz.) pineapple slices, drained**	Stir together Sweet and Sour Sauce, shrimp and drained pineapple slices. **Microwave at High (10) 6 to 8 Minutes,** stirring gently after 3 minutes.

Makes 4 to 5 servings

The Sweet and Sour Shrimp recipe, opposite page, shows how the seafood can be enhanced by combining with a sauce from our Sauce chapter pages 156-159.

Shrimp, lobster and crabmeat go well with cheese sauce, barbecue sauce and classic Italian sauce. For oysters, clams and scallops, use a mild butter sauce, flavored with garlic and parsley.

Shellfish Microwaving Helpful Hints

"If my microwaved clams don't open, should they be eaten?"

Throw them away. Clams that don't open during cooking probably aren't safe to eat.

"How can crableg meat be removed easily from the shell?"

Use a nutcracker to loosen shell, or slit with a sharp knife. The crabmeat will slide right out.

"After I microwave and shell shrimp, is there any additional preparation needed?"

Many people prefer to devein (remove) the dark mud vein with a sharp knife before serving.

Fish and Shellfish Convenience Chart
POWER LEVEL: **High (10)**

ITEM	TIME MIN.	COMMENTS	ITEM	TIME MIN.	COMMENTS
Deviled Crabs (6-oz. pkg.)	3-4	Will not be crisp.	Fish Sticks (9-oz. pkg.)	4-5	Distribute evenly in dish. Will not be crisp.
Fish 'N' Chips	7-9	Distribute evenly in large dish. Will not be crisp.	Shrimp Newburg (6½-oz. pkg.)	4-5	Puncture top with fork to vent.
Fish Fillets with Crumb Coating (8-oz. pkg.)	4-5	Distribute evenly in dish. Will not be crisp.	Tuna Noodle Casserole (11½-oz. pkg.)	6-8	Place in 1-qt. casserole with cover. Stir before serving.

Eggs microwave rapidly, and since they are a delicate food, toughen when overcooked. The yolks, which have a higher fat content, cook faster than the whites.

When yolks and whites are mixed together, eggs may be cooked at higher power settings. Omelets, which need time to set, are cooked at Medium, while scrambled eggs, which are stirred, are microwaved at High. Scrambled eggs are one of many foods which microwave better than they cook conventionally.

Eggs Benedict

POWER LEVEL: High (10) and Medium (5)
MICROWAVE TIME: 13 to 14 min., total

4 poached eggs (pg. 150)	Poach eggs and allow to stand as directed.
2 egg yolks **1 tablespoon lemon juice** **½ teaspoon dry mustard** **⅛ teaspoon salt** **½ cup (¼-lb.) butter**	While eggs are standing, make Hollandaise sauce. In container of electric blender measure egg yolks, lemon juice, mustard and salt. In 1-qt. glass measure place butter. **Microwave at High (10) 1 Minute** until hot and bubbly. Turn electric blender to highest speed and gradually add butter, blending until creamy and thickened.
8 thin slices (¼-in. thick) Canadian bacon	Just before serving, microwave Canadian bacon which has been arranged in single layer on microwave ovenproof plate. **Microwave at High (10) 4 Minutes.**
4 English muffins, split and toasted	Assemble Eggs Benedict by arranging 2 slices of Canadian bacon, then a poached egg over each of 4 English muffin halves. Top eggs with Hollandaise Sauce. Butter remaining muffin halves and serve as accompaniment. Decorate with parsley if desired.

Makes 4 servings

Fluffy Cheese Omelet

POWER LEVEL: High (10) and Medium (5)
MICROWAVE TIME: 7½ to 10 min., total

3 eggs, separated **⅓ cup mayonnaise** **2 tablespoons water**	In largest mixer bowl beat egg whites at highest speed of mixer, until soft peaks form. Then in smaller bowl, using same beaters, beat yolks, mayonnaise and water. Gently pour yolk mixture over beaten whites. Fold together carefully.
2 tablespoons butter	In 9-in. pie plate place butter. **Microwave at High (10) 1 Minute,** swirl to coat dish. Carefully pour egg mixture into pie plate. **Microwave at Medium (5) 6 to 8 Minutes.**
½ cup finely shredded cheddar cheese	Sprinkle cheese over omelet.

Microwave at Medium (5) ½ to 1 Minute, until cheese is slightly melted. Quickly run spatula or turner around sides and bottom of dish. Fold half of omelet over the other half. Gently slide onto serving plate. Sprinkle with chives, if desired.

Makes 1 to 2 servings

Jelly Omelet variation: Microwave ¼ to ⅓ cup jelly at **High (10) 1 Minute,** until jelly is soft and can be stirred smooth. Set aside. Follow Fluffy Omelet recipe above **omitting** cheese and mayonnaise. Spoon jelly over half of omelet when set but still glossy on top. Fold plain half of omelet over jelly half. If desired, sprinkle cinnamon-sugar over omelet before serving.

Makes 1 to 2 servings

Egg and Cheese Adapting Chart (Use Microwave safe containers)

ITEM	POWER LEVEL	TIME MIN.	COMMENTS
Scrambled Eggs, 2	High (10)	1½ to 2	Stir 2 to 3 times.
Scrambled Egg Substitutes (9-oz.)	High (10)	3½ to 4½	Stir 2 to 3 times till smooth.
Poached Eggs, 2	Medium (5)	7 to 8	Eggs poach ¾-1 min. per egg.
Omelet, 3 eggs	Medium (5)	4 to 6	Recipe idea above.
Quiche (9-in.)	Medium (5)	16 to 18	Recipe idea, page 152.
Souffle (2-qt.)	Low (3)	22 to 25	Recipe idea, page 153.
Cheese Fondue (1¼-lb. cheese)	High (10) & Medium (5)	7 to 8	Heat wine at (10), melt cheese and finish at (5).

Pictured top to bottom: Eggs Benedict
Fluffy Cheese Omelet

150 Eggs

Eggs are versatile; they can be prepared in a variety of ways, each with its own character. Microwaving techniques and times can vary greatly depending on the recipe. Here we present the basic ways of cooking eggs.

All but hard boiled eggs microwave well. Do not try to hard boil eggs in the microwave oven. They expand during cooking and burst the shell.

How to Microwave Scrambled Eggs

Place 1 teaspoon butter per egg in a glass measure or casserole. Microwave at High (10) until melted.

Add eggs and 1 tablespoon milk per egg, beat until well blended.
Microwave at High (10) ¾ minute per egg for ½ of total time.

Stir set portions from the outside to the center. Repeat 1 or 2 times during remaining cooking period.

How to Microwave Basic Eggs

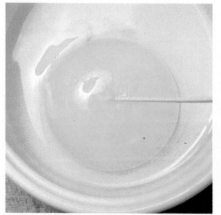

Puncture membrane of yolk to prevent bursting when microwaving shirred or poached eggs.

Microwave shirred eggs in buttered custard cups. Puncture membrane and cover with plastic wrap. Microwave 1 minute per egg at Medium Power (5).

Poach eggs by microwaving 2 cups hot tap water 5 to 6 minutes at High (10), until boiling. Break eggs onto plate; puncture membrane. Swirl boiling water with spoon. Slip in eggs gently. Cover. Microwave at Medium (5) 1 minute per egg; ¾ minute per egg for more than 1 egg. Let stand in water a few minutes.

Some of our microwave oven models are equipped with a shelf which increases the cooking space.

If your oven has this feature, try the breakfast idea below. As a variation, substitute 2 bowls of instant hot cereal, mixed with required water, for the bacon.

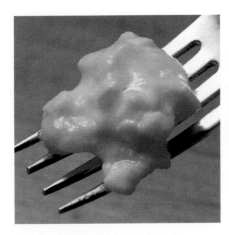

When done, eggs should be just past the runny stage.

After standing 1 or 2 minutes, eggs will be set.

To make Scrambled Eggs and Bacon Breakfast, arrange 4 strips of bacon between paper towels on a plate. Place on oven shelf. Add measuring cup containing 4 eggs scrambled with 2 tablespoons melted butter and ¼ cup milk. Microwave at High (10) 4 minutes. Stir eggs and add frozen coffee cake to oven floor. Microwave 3-4 minutes more. Microwave bacon only 1 to 2 minutes more.

Fry eggs in the Brown 'n Sear dish. Preheat dish at High (10) 1 minute per egg. Add ½ tablespoon butter per egg. Break eggs into dish, cover and microwave ¾ minute per egg, or to desired doneness.

Fluffy omelets are microwaved in a pie plate and folded over a filling. See recipes on page 148.

Never attempt to hard-cook eggs or reheat eggs in shells.

Quiche is so versatile that wedges make a hearty supper, while small pieces provide a distinctive appetizer.

Microwaved Quiche Lorraine differs from conventionally baked because the milk or cream is heated before the custard is prepared. The warm filling microwaves more evenly, allowing the center to set without overcooking the edges.

How to Microwave Quiche Lorraine

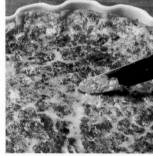

Brush pastry with a mixture of 1 egg yolk and 1 teaspoon Worcestershire sauce. Microwave at High.

Fill pastry with crumbled cooked bacon, grated cheese and green onions. Pour in hot custard mixture. Microwave at Medium High (7).

Metal knife inserted in the center will come out coated with partially cooked custard when quiche is done. Center will set during the 5 minutes of standing time.

Classic Quiche Lorraine

POWER LEVEL: Medium High (7)
MICROWAVE TIME: 14 to 18 min., total

6 strips crisp cooked bacon, crumbled **½ cup grated Swiss cheese** **3 green onions, chopped** **1 Quiche Pastry, pg. 197**	Reserve 2 tablespoons each of bacon and cheese and 1 tablespoon onion. Sprinkle remaining bacon, cheese and onion over bottom of microwaved pastry crust.
1½ tablespoons flour **¼ teaspoon salt** **¼ teaspoon nutmeg** **Dash cayenne** **1 cup milk** **1 cup whipping cream**	In 1-qt. measure mix flour, salt, nutmeg and cayenne. Gradually stir in milk and cream. **Microwave at Medium High (7) 7 to 8 Minutes.** Stir every 2 minutes.
4 eggs	In 1-qt. casserole beat eggs. Stir in hot liquid.

Microwave at Medium High (7) 2 to 3 Minutes, stirring every ½ minute, until thick. Pour into pastry. Top with bacon, cheese, onion and, if desired, paprika. **Microwave at Medium High (7) 6 to 8 Minutes,** until almost set. Let stand 5 minutes.

Makes 1 (9-in) quiche, about 6 servings

Golden Onion Quiche

Golden Onion Quiche

POWER LEVEL: High (10) and Medium (5)
MICROWAVE TIME: 16 to 18 min., total

1 commercially frozen pie crust **Worcestershire sauce (about 2 teaspoons)**	Remove pastry from foil pan to glass 8-in. pie plate. **Microwave at High (10) 1 Minute,** until softened. With fingers, press firmly in pie plate. Brush inside with Worcestershire sauce. Prick pastry. **Microwave at High (10) 4 Minutes.**
1 cup (4-oz.) shredded Mozzarella or pizza cheese	Sprinkle cheese over bottom of pie shell.
3 eggs **½ cup whipping cream** **3 drops hot pepper sauce (tabasco)**	With fork, beat together eggs, cream and hot pepper sauce. Pour over cheese in pie shell.
1 can (3-oz.) French fried onions	With sharp knife, cut through onions in can to chop medium fine. Pour over top and lightly press down.
1 tablespoon dried or frozen chives, or chopped green onion	Sprinkle chives, or onion over top.

Microwave at Medium (5) 11 to 13 Minutes. Let stand about 5 minutes to firm slightly before serving.

Makes 1 (8-in.) pie, about 6 servings

Souffles must be specially formulated for microwaving, so you **cannot** adapt conventional recipes. Because it cooks so quickly, a microwaved souffle needs to be stabilized. For this reason we use evaporated milk in making the cream sauce base.

A microwaved souffle rises very high because it does not form a crust. A 2½-qt. souffle dish is the minimum size for a 6-egg souffle.

When done, the souffle will be dry on top with a creamy meringue in the center.

Tips for Microwaving a Souffle

Beat egg whites until stiff and beginning to dry. Set aside, and with the same beaters, beat egg yolks until thick and lemon colored. Mix yolks with prepared cheese sauce.

Fold egg-cheese mixture into whites, using a rubber spatula to cut down to bottom of dish, move across the bottom, and lift the egg whites up over top of sauce.

Pour into souffle dish. Rotate dish every 5 minutes. Microwave at Low (3) 10 minutes, then Microwave at Medium (5) 12 to 14 minutes, until top appears dry.

Cheese Souffle

Cheese Souffle

POWER LEVEL: High (10), Low (3) and Medium (5)
MICROWAVE TIME: 30 to 35 min., total

¼ cup flour ¾ teaspoon salt ½ teaspoon dry mustard ⅛ teaspoon paprika 1 can (13-oz.) evaporated milk	In 1½-qt. casserole blend together flour, salt, mustard and paprika. Stir in evaporated milk. **Microwave at High (10) 4 to 6 Minutes,** stirring every 2 minutes, until thickened.
2 cups (8-oz.) sharp cheddar cheese	Stir cheese into hot sauce. **Microwave at High (10) 1 to 2 Minutes,** until smooth.
6 eggs, separated 1½ teaspoons cream of tartar 1 teaspoon sugar	In large mixer bowl beat egg whites with cream of tartar and sugar until stiff but not dry. Set aside and, using same beaters, beat yolks in medium mixer bowl until thick and lemon colored.

Slowly pour cheese mixture over beaten yolks, beating until well combined. Gently pour over beaten egg whites, fold together gently just until blended. Pour into ungreased 2½-qt. souffle dish. **Microwave at Low (3) 22 to 25 Minutes** rotating dish ¼ turn every 5 minutes, until puffed top edges are beginning to appear dry and souffle has "set" appearance. Serve immediately.

Makes 6 to 8 servings

Natural cheese reacts to microwaving much as it does to conventional cooking, but faster. Because of its high fat content it melts quickly and tends to become stringy when overcooked. Where cheese must be cooked for more than a few moments, layer it between other ingredients and use Medium Power (5), or use process cheese, which is less apt to become stringy.

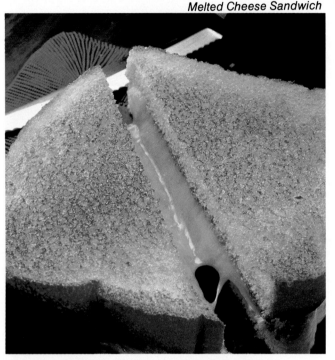

Melted Cheese Sandwich

Lo-Cal Melted Cheese Sandwich

This is lower in calories than grilled sandwiches.

POWER LEVEL: Medium High (7)
MICROWAVE TIME: 20 seconds, total

2 slices bread	In conventional toaster, toast bread.
2 slices processed cheese	Assemble sandwich; wrap in paper towel, **Microwave at Medium High (7) for 20 seconds.** Makes 1 sandwich.

Cheese Fondue with Natural Cheese

It is important to whisk or stir the fondue every minute.

POWER LEVEL: High (10) and Medium (5)
MICROWAVE TIME: 7 to 8 min., total

1 cup dry white wine **2 tablespoons kirsch (optional)**	In 2-qt. microwave fondue pot place wine and kirsch. **Microwave at High (10) 4 Minutes.**
5 cups (20-oz.) **shredded gruyere cheese or Swiss cheese** **3 tablespoons flour** **⅛ teaspoon pepper** **Dash nutmeg**	Toss cheeses with flour, pepper and nutmeg, until coated. Stir into hot wine. Cover. **Microwave at Medium (5) 3 to 4 Minutes,** stir briskly every minute, until melted. Serve with cubes of crusty bread.

Makes about 4 servings

Cheese Enchiladas

POWER LEVEL: High (10)
MICROWAVE TIME: 12½ to 15¾ min., total

1 lb. ricotta cheese **1 egg** **1 cup chopped green onions** **2 tablespoons chopped green chilies** **1 teaspoon cumin** **1 cup (4-oz.) shredded Jack cheese**	In mixing bowl stir together ricotta, egg, onions, chilies, cumin and Jack cheese.
8 fresh corn or flour tortillas, (about 6-in. diameter) or, 10 to 12 canned tortillas (5-in. diameter)	Wrap tortillas in towel. **Microwave at High (10) ½ to ¾ Minute,** until pliable. Divide filling among tortillas. Roll up each one tightly.
1 can (10-oz.) enchilada sauce	In lightly greased 12×8×2-in. dish place rolls, seam side down. Pour sauce over rolls. **Microwave at High (10) 11 to 13 Minutes.**
2 cups (8-oz.) shredded cheddar cheese	Cover with cheddar cheese. **Microwave at High (10) 1 to 2 Minutes,** until cheese is almost melted.
Sour cream and chopped green onions	Garnish with sour cream and green onions.

Makes 4 generous servings

Cheese Rarebit

Rarebit is a rich cheese sauce served over toast.

POWER LEVEL: High (10) and Medium (5)
MICROWAVE TIME: 7 to 10 min., total

8 oz. pasturized processed cheese, diced **1 tablespoon butter**	In 1-qt. casserole place cheese and butter. **Microwave at High (10) 2 to 3 Minutes,** stirring every minute, until smooth.
¼ teaspoon salt **¼ teaspoon dry mustard** **½ teaspoon Worcestershire sauce** **Dash cayenne pepper** **¼ cup dairy half & half** **1 egg yolk, beaten**	Add salt, mustard, Worcestershire sauce and cayenne pepper. Quickly stir in half & half and egg yolk. **Microwave at Medium (5) 5 to 7 Minutes,** stirring every minute, until hot.

Makes 3 to 4 servings

Eggs and Cheese

Because eggs are a protein food, they can toughen when overcooked just as in conventional cooking. One of the tips below discusses how to avoid overcooking.

Since the standing time for most eggs is just 1 to 2 minutes, the wait is not inconvenient.

Egg Microwaving Helpful Hints

"What causes my eggs to be dry and tough after standing time?"

They were probably microwaved too long. Eggs should be checked after minimum time and removed from the oven when they begin to set.

"How can I keep my souffle from falling even before I remove it from the oven?"

Egg whites for microwaved souffles must be beaten until thick and stiff to obtain the best results. Also, use evaporated milk to stabilize.

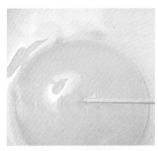

"How can I keep poached and shirred eggs from exploding during microwaving?"

Always remember to puncture the egg yolk of whole eggs before microwaving.

"Is there a fast easy way to microwave several eggs at a time?"

Yes, you can microwave several eggs quickly by using a buttered non-perforated microwave safe muffin pan, or glass custard cups.

Eggs & Cheese Convenience Chart

ITEM	POWER LEVEL	TIME MINUTES	COMMENTS
Egg Substitute (egg beaters) (8-oz. carton)	Defrost	4 to 4½	Time 3 minutes, turn over after 1½ minutes. Open carton and stir every ½ minute.
Cheese Souffle (12-oz. pkg.)	Defrost & Medium High	10 to 14 9 to 11	To Defrost: Place in 8-in. pie plate. Stir. To Cook: Divide between 4 buttered custard cups; 6-oz. Rearrange after 4 minutes. When done center is set.

Gravies and sauces microwave easily because there is no scorching or lumping or constant stirring. They save time in cooking and clean-up too.

Make them right in the cup you use for measuring or in the microwave oven proof sauce boat you use for serving.

Poultry Giblet Gravy

POWER LEVEL: Medium (5) and High (10)
MICROWAVE TIME: 21 to 29 min., total

Giblets from a 3-lb. chicken 1 cup water	In 1-qt. casserole place giblets. Prick with fork. Add water. Cover. **Microwave at Medium (5) 16 to 20 Minutes,** stirring after 10 minutes until tender. Chop medium fine.
¼ cup poultry drippings ¼ cup flour ½ teaspoon salt ¼ teaspoon celery salt Dash pepper	In separate 1-qt. casserole place drippings. **Microwave at High (10) 1 to 2 Minutes,** until hot. Stir in flour, salt, celery salt and pepper until smooth.
Broth from giblets plus water to make 1¼ cups	Stir in broth. **Microwave at High (10) 2 to 4 Minutes,** stirring every minute. Add giblets. **Microwave at High (10) 2 to 3 Minutes** more, stirring every minute, until thickened.

Makes about 2½ cups

Creamy Horseradish Sauce

POWER LEVEL: High (10)
MICROWAVE TIME: 4 to 5 min., total

| 1 egg
1½ cups milk
2 tablespoons cornstarch
2 tablespoons powdered horseradish
¼ cup vinegar
1 tablespoon sugar | In 1½-qt. casserole, beat egg with milk. Stir in cornstarch, horseradish, vinegar, and sugar. **Microwave at High (10) for 4 to 5 Minutes.** |
| 2 tablespoons butter | Stir in butter. Serve with roast beef sandwiches. |

Makes about 1¾ cups

Sweet and Sour Sauce

This piquant sauce is so versatile that it goes with just about every type of meat, poultry and seafood.

POWER LEVEL: High (10)
MICROWAVE TIME: 5 to 7 min., total

| ½ cup sugar
2 tablespoons cornstarch
¼ cup cold water | In 1½-qt. casserole stir together sugar, cornstarch and water, until well blended. |
| 1 can (8-oz.) crushed pineapple
½ cup chopped green pepper
¼ cup (4-oz. can) chopped pimiento
½ clove garlic, mashed
½ cup cider vinegar
2 tablespoons soy sauce
10 drops liquid pepper seasoning (tabasco) | Stir in pineapple, pepper, pimiento, garlic, vinegar, soy sauce and pepper seasoning. **Microwave at High (10) 5 to 7 Minutes,** stirring every 2 minutes, until clear and thickened. Let sauce stand 5 to 10 minutes, to develop flavor, before serving. |

Makes about 1¾ cups

Milk Gravy

Be sure to use a 1-qt. utensil to prevent boilover. These proportions are for gravy which runs easily from spoon. For thicker gravy use ⅓ cup flour.

POWER LEVEL: High (10)
MICROWAVE TIME: 7 to 10 min., total

| ¼ cup chicken or beef drippings
¼ cup flour
¼ teaspoon salt
1¼ cups milk | In 1-qt. glass measure, measure drippings. **Microwave at High (10) 1 to 2 Minutes,** until hot. Add flour and salt. Stir well. Stir in milk slowly. **Microwave at High (10) 6 to 8 Minutes,** stirring every minute. |

Makes about 1½ cups

How to Adapt Homemade and Convenience Gravies and Sauces

POWER LEVEL: **High (10)**

ITEM	TIME MIN.	COMMENTS
Butter or oil, based sauces or gravies — 1 cup	4 to 5	To increase recipe add 1 to 2 more minutes microwave time per cup of sauce.
Thin liquid sauces — 1 cup Au Jus, Clam, etc.	2 to 3	
Melted Butter sauces — ½ cup Clarified Butter	½ to 1	For clarified butter, let melted butter stand until separated. Clear top layer is clarified butter. Pour off.

Pictured top to bottom: Poultry Giblet Gravy (page 156)
Sweet and Sour Sauce (page 156)
Cheese Sauce (White Sauce Variation) (page 158)
Classic Italian Sauce (page 158)

Basic White Sauce

POWER LEVEL: High (10)
MICROWAVE TIME: 5½ to 6½ min., total

2 tablespoons butter **2 tablespoons flour** **½ teaspoon salt**	In 1-qt. glass measure place butter, flour and salt. **Microwave at High (10) 2 Minutes** stirring after 1 minute.
1 cup milk	Gradually stir in milk. **Microwave at High (10) 3½ to 4½ Minutes,** stirring every minute until thick and bubbly ... For thicker sauce, use 3 tablespoons flour instead of 2 tablespoons.

Makes 1 cup

Cheese Sauce Variation: Add 2 cups (8-oz.) shredded sharp cheese and a dash of cayenne pepper to White Sauce. Stir to melt cheese after microwaving as above.

Barbecue Sauce

The traditional sauce to use when cooking ribs and chicken. Or, slice leftover beef or pork into barbecue sauce and serve warm as an entree or sandwich filling.

POWER LEVEL: High (10)
MICROWAVE TIME: 5 to 6 min., total

1 cup chili sauce **½ cup water** **¼ cup lemon juice** **1 tablespoon cooking oil** **2 tablespoons brown sugar (packed)** **½ teaspoon salt** **¼ teaspoon paprika** **¼ teaspoon liquid pepper seasoning** **1 tablespoon Worcestershire sauce**	In 1-qt. casserole thoroughly combine chili sauce, water, lemon juice, cooking oil, brown sugar, salt, paprika, pepper seasoning and Worcestershire sauce. Cover. **Microwave at High (10) 5 to 7 Minutes,** stirring after 3 minutes, until hot. Use as desired.

Makes 2 cups

Clam Sauce

This clear sauce is popular on pasta.

POWER LEVEL: High (10)
MICROWAVE TIME: 7 to 8 min., total

2 tablespoons olive oil **3 cloves garlic, minced** **¼ teaspoon salt**	In 1-qt. casserole place oil, garlic and salt. **Microwave at High (10) 3 Minutes,** until softened.
2 cans (6.5-oz. each) minced clams **¼ cup water** **1 tablespoon cornstarch** **¼ cup minced parsley**	Drain clams, reserving juice. Set aside. Stir together water and cornstarch. Add to garlic along with clam juice and parsley. **Microwave at High (10) 3 Minutes,** stirring after 2 minutes, until thickened. Stir in clams. **Microwave at High (10) 1 to 2 Minutes,** until hot.

Makes about 2 cups

Classic Italian Sauce

POWER LEVEL: High (10)
MICROWAVE TIME: 15 to 18 min., total

1 large onion, chopped **3 tablespoons olive or cooking oil** **3 cloves garlic, minced**	In 3-qt. casserole place onion, oil and garlic. **Microwave at High (10) 3 to 4 Minutes,** stirring after 2 minutes, until onion is limp.
2 cans (15-oz. each) tomato sauce **2 cans (6-oz. each) tomato paste** **⅔ cup burgundy, beef broth or tomato juice** **2 tablespoons brown sugar** **2 teaspoons Worcestershire sauce** **1 teaspoon oregano** **1 teaspoon basil** **1 teaspoon salt** **½ teaspoon pepper**	Add tomato sauce, tomato paste, wine, broth or juice, brown suagr, Worcestershire sauce, oregano, basil, salt and pepper. Mix together well. Cover. **Microwave at High (10) 12 to 14 Minutes,** stirring after 6 minutes, until very hot.

Makes about 2 quarts

Other Sauce Ideas

Lemon Butter Sauce is good with carrots and other vegetables as well as fish. Place ½ cup butter in glass measure. Microwave High (10) for ½ to 1 minute to melt. Stir in 1 tablespoon lemon juice, 1 tablespoon snipped parsley and dash of pepper. Keep warm.

Almond Butter Sauce accents fish and vegetables. Place ¼ cup almonds in 9-in. pie plate with 1 teaspoon butter. Microwave at High (10) for 5 to 6 minutes, stirring every 2 minutes. Add ½ cup butter. Microwave at High (10) for 1 minute to melt.

Sweet Mustard Sauce complements ham, or pork and is a zippy dip for fried appetizers like egg rolls. Empty 1 jar (10-oz.) cherry or currant jelly in small mixing bowl. Microwave at High (10) for 2 to 3 minutes. Add ⅓ cup mustard, and ¼ cup bourbon or liqueur. Stir.

Brown Roux may be microwaved for Creole gumbo or French stews. Stir together ½ cup all-purpose flour and ½ cup oil in 2-qt. casserole. Microwave at High (10) for 7 to 9 minutes; stir after 4 minutes. Caramel colored roux will be gritty with fat slightly separated.

Gravy and Sauce Microwaving Helpful Hints

"I tried white sauce in my microwave, but it seems thinner than usual. Why is this?"

Microwaved sauces and gravies evaporate less than on range top, they may be thinner than when conventionally cooked. To increase thickening, add an extra teaspoon to 1 tablespoon flour or cornstarch for each cup of liquid.

"What container is recommended for microwaving sauces or gravies?"

Less than 2 cups of sauce with a butter base can be microwaved in a glass measure for convenience and easy clean-up. Larger amounts should be microwaved in a large microwave safe bowl or casserole. Because you frequently stir sauces to prevent lumping, handles on sauce containers (as shown) are convenient.

"How can I keep my gravy from being lumpy and thick on the outside?"

Stir frequently with a wire whisk so that a smooth consistency throughout is obtained.

160 Pasta, Rice & Cereal

Most pasta, rice and cereal dishes require two cooking steps — first cooking the grain, then combining with other ingredients. They take the same amount of time to soften, whether you cook them by microwave or conventionally.

Advocates of microwaved pasta insist that they have a better flavor and firm, "al dente" texture.

Tightly covered with plastic wrap, pasta and rice reheat to a "fresh cooked" flavor and texture.

How to Adapt Pasta & Rice

Combine pasta or rice with hottest tap water and salt in the recommended cooking dish. Add oil if needed.

Cover tightly with casserole cover or plastic wrap, turned back at one corner to vent. Microwave at High (10).

Stir or rearrange after ½ time. Recover and continue microwaving. Drain immediately.

Pasta & Rice Microwaving Chart

POWER LEVEL: **High (10)**

FOOD TYPE	AMOUNT	UTENSIL	WATER SALT & OIL	TIME MIN.	GENERAL DIRECTIONS
Macaroni	6 to 8-oz. pkg.	2-qt. casserole	3 cups water 2 teaspoons salt	15 to 18	Stir after 10 minutes.
Rotini	16-oz. pkg.	3-qt. casserole	6 cups water 1 teaspoon salt	13 to 16	Stir after 10 minutes. Check rotini after 10 minutes as it cooks faster than other pasta.
Spaghetti or Linguine	16-oz. pkg.	13×9×2-in. dish	6 to 7 cups water 1 tablespoon salt 1 tablespoon oil	16 to 19	Rearrange after 10 minutes.
Egg Noodles, Narrow	3 cups or 6-oz.	8-in. square dish	3 cups water 1 teaspoon salt	13 to 16	Time is the same for spinach or regular.
Egg Noodles, Wide	8-oz.	3-qt. casserole	8 cups water 1 teaspoon salt 1 teaspoon oil	23 to 25	Stir after 10 minutes.
Lasagna	8 to 16-oz. pkg.	13×9×2-in. dish	Cover with water placing ½ teaspoon salt in bottom of dish 1 tablespoon oil	11 to 16	Rearrange after 7 minutes.
Manicotti	10 to 12 pieces, about 5-oz. pkg.	12×8×2-in. dish	Brush with oil first then cover with water	22 to 25	Using fork turn over every 5 minutes to prevent sticking.
Long Grain Rice	1 cup	3-qt. casserole	2¼ cups water 1 teaspoon salt	18 to 21	Stir after 10 minutes.
Minute Rice	1½ cups	2-qt. casserole	1½ cups water ½ teaspoon salt	4 to 6	Stir after 2 minutes.
Rice-Vermicelli Mixes	8-oz. pkg.	2-qt. casserole	Follow package directions	18 to 22	Stir every 6 minutes. Let stand 5 minutes before serving.
Brown Rice	1 cup	3-qt. casserole	3 cups water 1 teaspoon salt 1 tablespoon oil	30 to 35	Stir after 20 minutes.

NOTE: Many of our recipes in the main dish sections call for quick cooking rice, because regular rice will not be cooked in the short times needed for the other ingredients. Make this same substitution in adapting your own recipes.

Pictured top to bottom: *Jiffy Spanish Rice (page 162)*
Easy Method Lasagna (page 163)
Old Fashioned Oatmeal (page 164)

Cheese Stuffed Manicotti

POWER LEVEL: High (10)
MICROWAVE TIME: 35 to 38 min., total

10 manicotti	Cook manicotti (see chart, page 160), except **Microwave 20 Minutes.**
1 pkg. (6-oz.) sliced . . . . **Mozzarella cheese** **2 cups (1-pt.) ricotta cheese** **½ cup romano cheese** **1 can (7¾-oz.) spinach, drained** **½ teaspoon garlic powder** **½ teaspoon salt** **¼ teaspoon pepper**	Dice cheese into ½-in. cubes before separating slices. Reserve about ⅓ cup for topping. Combine rest of Mozzarella with ricotta, romano, spinach, garlic, salt and pepper. Stuff cooked manicotti with cheese filling. Rearrange in 12×8×2-in. dish.
1 can (15-oz.) tomato sauce **Marjoram**	Pour tomato sauce over top. Sprinkle with cheese and marjoram. Cover with wax paper.

Microwave at High (10) 15 to 18 Minutes.

Makes 4 servings

Noodles Romanoff

A traditional combination of noodles, cheese and sour cream.

POWER LEVEL: High (10)
MICROWAVE TIME: 19 to 21 min., total

1 pkg. (7 to 8-oz.) . . . . . . **narrow noodles**	Cook noodles (see chart, page 160), except **Microwave 9 Minutes.** Place in 3-qt. casserole.
1 cup cottage cheese **1 cup (8-oz.) dairy sour cream** **½ cup chopped stuffed olives** **1 teaspoon instant minced onion** **½ teaspoon salt** **½ teaspoon Worcestershire sauce** **Dash liquid pepper seasoning (tabasco)**	Add cheese, sour cream, olives, onion, salt, Worcestershire sauce and liquid pepper. Mix well. Cover. **Microwave at High (10) 8 Minutes,** until hot.
1 cup (4-oz.) . . . . **shredded sharp cheese**	Sprinkle cheese on top. **Microwave at High (10) 2 to 4 Minutes** more, uncovered.

Makes 6 servings

Jiffy Spanish Rice

POWER LEVEL: High (10)
MICROWAVE TIME: 13 to 17 min., total

1 lb. ground chuck beef **1 cup precooked rice** **1 can (1-lb. 12-oz.) tomatoes, undrained, cut up** **1 tablespoon instant minced onion** **1 or 2 tablespoons chili powder** **2 teaspoons salt** **⅛ teaspoon pepper**	In 3-qt. casserole crumble beef. **Microwave at High (10) 5 to 6 Minutes,** stirring after 3 minutes. Drain. Add rice, tomatoes, onion, chili powder, salt and pepper. Cover. **Microwave at High (10) 8 to 11 Minutes.** Stir well. Let stand, covered, about 5 to 10 minutes before serving.

Makes 4 to 6 servings

Creamy Macaroni and Cheese

POWER LEVEL: High (10) and Medium High (7)
MICROWAVE TIME: 23 to 27 min., total

1 pkg. (7-oz.) elbow macaroni	Cook macaroni (see chart page 160), except **Microwave 10 Minutes.** Drain well and return to same casserole.
¼ cup butter	In 1-qt. measure place butter. **Microwave at High (10) ½ to 1 Minute,** to melt.
6 tablespoons flour . . . . **1 teaspoon salt** **2 cups milk**	Blend in flour and salt. Stir in milk until smooth. **Microwave at High (10) 5½ to 6 Minutes,** stirring with table fork every minute, until thickened.
2 cups (8-oz.) grated sharp cheddar cheese	Stir in cheese until completely melted.

Stir sauce into drained macaroni, mixing well. **Microwave at Medium High (7) 7 to 10 Minutes,** stirring after 4 minutes. If desired, sprinkle top with paprika or buttered crumbs before serving.

Makes 6 to 8 servings

Quick and Easy Macaroni and Cheese variation:
Omit sauce ingredients from above recipe. To cooked macaroni add 1 lb. pkg. process cheese spread, cut in cubes, and 1 can (5⅓ oz.) condensed milk. **Microwave at High (10) 6 to 8 Minutes.** Stir and serve.

Makes 6 to 8 servings

Green Rice Casserole

Green Rice Casserole

POWER LEVEL: High (10)
MICROWAVE TIME: 20 to 24 min., total

1 pkg. chopped . . . .
  spinach, frozen
  (10-oz.)
3 eggs
1 can evaporated
  milk (13-oz.)
⅔ cup Minute rice
Pasteurized pro-
  cess cheese spread
  (8-oz. pkg.) cut in
  cubes
½ teaspoon salt
¼ teaspoon pepper
	Microwave spinach in a
	1-qt. casserole at **High
	(10) 5 to 6 Minutes.**
	Drain well and set aside.
	Mix eggs, milk, rice,
	cheese, salt and pepper in
	2-qt. casserole.
	**Microwave at High
	(10) 5 to 6 Minutes,**
	stirring after 2 minutes
	until cheese melts.

¼ cup chopped onion . .	Add onion and spinach to rice mixture and pour into a 10×6×2-in. baking dish. **Microwave at High (10) 10 to 12 Minutes** until center is set.

Makes 6 to 8 servings

Easy Method Lasagna

This spicy version does not require pre-cooking noodles. Noodles will have a firm al dente texture.

POWER LEVEL: High (10) and Medium (5)
MICROWAVE TIME: 43 to 44 min., total

½ lb. ground chuck. . . ½ lb. ground pork	Place meat in colander, set over a casserole bowl. **Microwave at High (10) 5 to 6 Minutes.** Break up drained, cooked meat with fork; discard fat.

1 can (6-oz.) tomato. . . .
  juice
1 can (8-oz.) tomato
  sauce
2 cans (6-oz. each)
  tomato paste
1 medium onion,
  chopped
1 tablespoon oregano
2 teaspoons basil
1 teaspoon salt
½ teaspoon pepper
2 garlic cloves,
  minced
2 teaspoons brown
  sugar
1 tablespoon
  Worcestershire
  sauce
	In large bowl mix together
	tomato juice, tomato sauce,
	tomato paste, onion,
	oregano, basil, salt,
	pepper, garlic, brown sugar
	and Worcestershire sauce.
	Stir in drained meat.
	Spread ⅓ cup meat sauce
	over bottom of 12×8×2-in.
	dish.

½ pkg. (½ lb.) . . . .
  lasagna noodles
2 cups (1-pt.) ricotta
  cheese
2 pkg. (6-oz.) sliced
  Mozzarella cheese
	Place ½ the uncooked
	noodles over sauce and top
	with ½ the ricotta cheese;
	then half of Mozzarella
	cheese. Repeat layers and
	cover with remaining
	sauce.

1 cup grated Parmesan cheese . . .	Sprinkle with Parmesan cheese. **Microwave at Medium (5) for 35 Minutes** uncovered. Place remaining Mozzarella cheese on top and continue **Microwaving at Medium (5) for 3 Minutes,** or until cheese is melted. Let lasagna stand 5 minutes before slicing.

Quick and Easy Lasagna Variation:
Microwave and drain ground chuck and pork as directed
above. Mix meat with 2 (15½-oz.) jars of commercial
spaghetti sauce. Layer meat sauce with noodles and
cheese (use amounts and types called for in above
recipe) and Microwave as directed above.

Makes 6 to 8 servings

Cereals microwave in a simple, 1-step process. You don't have to boil the water first, or stir frequently during cooking. Microwaved cereals are easy to clean up since the cereal does not stick to the cooking dish. Family members can microwave single servings of instant cereal in paper bowls. There'll be no dirty dishes in the sink after breakfast.

How to Adapt Cereals

Mix cereal and **hottest** tap water in a bowl large enough to prevent boil-over. Microwave at High (10), uncovered.

Stir half way through the cooking time. For softer cereal, let stand a few minutes after microwaving.

Cereal Adapting Chart

POWER LEVEL: **High (10)**

TYPE CEREAL	NO. OF SERVINGS	INGREDIENTS				TIME MIN.
		WATER	SALT	CEREAL	CONTAINER	
Oatmeal, Quick*	1	¾ cup	¼ teaspoon	⅓ cup	16-oz. cereal bowl	1 to 2
	2	1½ cups	½ teaspoon	⅔ cup	1½-qt. casserole	2 to 3
	4	3 cups	¾ teaspoon	1⅓ cups	2-qt. casserole	5 to 6
	6	4 cups	1 teaspoon	2 cups	3-qt. casserole	7 to 8
Oatmeal, Old-fashioned	1	¾ cup	¼ teaspoon	⅓ cup	1-qt. casserole	3 to 5
	2	1½ cups	½ teaspoon	⅔ cup	2-qt. casserole	6 to 7
	4	3 cups	¾ teaspoon	1⅓ cups	3-qt. casserole	8 to 9
	6	4 cups	1 teaspoon	2 cups	3-qt. casserole	10 to 11
Cornmeal	1	⅔ cup	¼ teaspoon	3 tbsp.	16-oz. cereal bowl	1½ to 2
	2	1⅓ cups	½ teaspoon	⅓ cup	1½-qt. casserole	2½ to 3
	4	2⅔ cups	¾ teaspoon	⅔ cup	2-qt. casserole	3½ to 4
	6	4 cups	1 teaspoon	1 cup	2-qt. casserole	4½ to 5
Grits, Quick*	1	¾ cup	Dash	3 tbsp.	16-oz. cereal bowl	3 to 4
	2	1⅓ cups	¼ teaspoon	⅓ cup	1½-qt. casserole	6 to 7
	4	2⅔ cups	¾ teaspoon	⅔ cup	2-qt. casserole	8 to 9
	6	4 cups	1 teaspoon	1 cup	2-qt. casserole	10 to 11
Cream of Wheat	1	1 cup	⅛ teaspoon	2½ tbsp.	1-qt. caserole	3 to 4
	2	1¾ cups	¼ teaspoon	⅓ cup	2-qt. casserole	5 to 6
	4	3½ cups	½ teaspoon	⅔ cup	3-qt. casserole	7 to 8
	6	5 cups	1 teaspoon	1 cup	3-qt. casserole	9 to 10
Cream of Rice	1	¾ cup	Dash	3 tbsp.	16-oz. cereal bowl	1½ to 2
	2	1⅓ cups	¼ teaspoon	⅓ cup	1½-qt. casserole	2 to 3
	4	2⅔ cups	½ teaspoon	⅔ cup	2-qt. casserole	3½ to 4½
	6	4 cups	1 teaspoon	1 cup	2-qt. casserole	6 to 7

*Single servings of instant oatmeal or grits (about 1-oz. pkg.):   Follow package directions for amount of water.
Microwave at High (10) ½ to 1 Minute.

When microwaving pasta, remember that you can make rich-tasting pasta sauces in the microwave oven, too. Italian and clam sauces, page 158 are traditional.

Microwave the sauce first then cover and let stand while microwaving the pasta.

Pasta, Rice and Cereal Helpful Hints

"How can I keep my pasta from sticking together?"

Add 1 teaspoon of oil at the beginning of cooking time.

"How do I adapt pasta to keep it from boiling over during microwaving?"

Try using a larger dish and just enough water to cover the pasta. Remember, the water doesn't evaporate in microwaving as readily as it does when boiling foods on the surface unit.

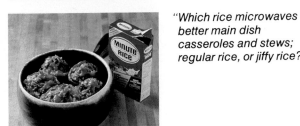

"Which rice microwaves better main dish casseroles and stews; regular rice, or jiffy rice?"

Jiffy rice is recommended for most casseroles since just as in conventional cooking it cooks faster than regular rice. Microwave regular rice (see chart page 160) before adding to most casseroles, except those which cook 1¼ hours or longer.

Pasta and Rice Convenience Foods

ITEM	POWER LEVEL	TIME, MIN.	COMMENTS
Canned Macaroni & Cheese, Ravioli, Spaghetti, Spanish Rice (12 to 15-oz.)	High (10)	3-5*	Microwave. Stir before serving.
Canned Lasagna (40-oz.)	High (10)	4-7*	Microwave. Stir before serving.
Frozen Rice in (10-oz.) pouch	High (10)	6-8	Puncture pouch. Stir to fluff before serving.
Frozen Macaroni & Cheese, Macaroni & Beef (8-oz. pkg.)	Med-High (7)	6-8	Stir before serving.
Frozen Macaroni & Cheese, Stuffed Shells, Spaghetti & Meatballs (11 to 14-oz.)	Med-High (7)	12-14	Stir before serving.
Frozen Macaroni & Cheese (2-lb. box)	Med-High (7)	18-24	Stir before serving.
Frozen Lasagna, (21 oz. box),	High (10)	15-20	Two boxes may be microwaved together in 10×6-in. dish for 25 to 30 minutes.

*Or use microwave food temperature control, set to 150°.

166 Vegetables

Microwave ovens have earned a reputation for cooking crisp, yet tender vegetables and for maintaining vegetables' bright colors and nutritive value.

Nutrition research indicates that many microwaved vegetables and fruits lose less water-soluble vitamin C than when cooked conventionally. This is due to shorter cooking time and to the fact that less cooking water is needed when microwaving fruits and vegetables.

How to Microwave Potatoes

Pierce vegetables cooked in skins, such as potatoes or squash, with a fork.

Arrange potatoes about 1-in. apart in a star shape as shown above.

Salt vegetables after cooking, or put salt in the casserole with the water before adding vegetables. Salting the tops of vegetables before microwaving causes darkened, dried-out spots.

Touch potatoes at end of cooking time. They may feel somewhat firm, but will complete cooking in about 5 minutes standing time.

How to Adapt Other Vegetables

Rearrange stacked vegetables like corn on the cob after ½ the cooking time. Move ears in the center which receive less microwave energy, to the outside.

Cover vegetables in a dish with a casserole lid or with vented plastic wrap. The peel or husks of some vegetables provide a natural covering, while others may simply be wrapped in plastic without using a dish.

Adding water creates steam around fresh vegetables microwaved in a covered casserole. Steam surrounding individual pieces contributes both speed and even heating. If you wish to salt vegetables before microwaving them, put salt in dish before the vegetables and water.

Pictured top to bottom: *Twice Baked Potatoes (page 181)*
Corn on Cob (page 170)
Yellow Squash and Zucchini Combination (page 171)

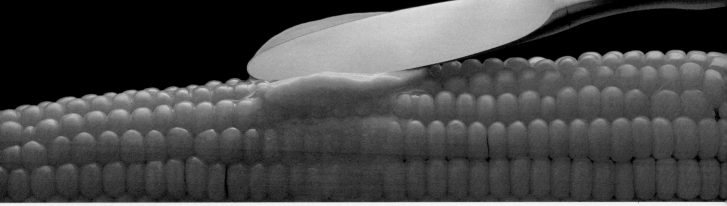

Vegetable Microwaving Chart

VEGETABLE	AMOUNT	PROCEDURE	POWER LEVEL	TIME MINUTES	COMMENTS
Artichokes Fresh	4 medium	Prepare by discarding tough outer leaves. Snip tips with scissors and cut off stems. In 3-qt. casserole place 1 cup water and ½ teaspoon salt. Add artichokes. Cover. Rotate dish ½ turn after 7 minutes. Test for doneness: At minimum time, try to pull a leaf from whole artichoke. If it comes away freely, artichoke is done.	High (10)	14 to 15	Drain artichokes upside down before serving. Curry mayonnaise is easy accompaniment; mix 1 cup mayonnaise with 1 to 2 teaspoons curry powder. Artichokes are eaten by pulling off leaves and, with teeth, scraping tender green inner leaf; cut heart into chunks and eat.
Asparagus Fresh Cuts	1 lb. (3 cups, cut into 1 to 2-in. pieces)	In 2-qt. casserole place ¼ cup water and ½ teaspoon salt; add asparagus. Cover. Stir asparagus every 3 minutes.	High (10)	9 to 11	If pieces are longer than 4-in. lengths microwave at Medium following technique below.
Asparagus Fresh Spears	1-lb.	In 10×6×2-in. dish place ¼ cup water and ¼ teaspoon salt. Add asparagus, arranging thicker pieces to outside of dish with tender tops to center. Cover dish with plastic wrap turning back corner to vent. Rotate dish ½ turn after 5 minutes.	Medium High (7)	15 to 17	Larger, more mature stem ends should be peeled.
Asparagus Frozen Spears	10-oz. pkg.	In 1-qt. casserole place ½ teaspoon salt and asparagus spears. Cover. Rearrange after 4 minutes.	High (10)	8 to 10	No water is needed with this frozen vegetable.
Beans Dry	1 lb.	In 3-qt. casserole place beans, 4 cups water, ham hock, 1 cup coarsely chopped celery, 1 small sliced onion, 2 teaspoons salt, and ¼ teaspoon pepper. Cover.	High (10) Medium (5)	1 hour and 30 min.	Microwave at High (10) for 30 minutes until boiling, then at Medium (5) until tender. Stir every 30 minutes. May add more water during cooking.
Beans Fresh Green & Wax	1 lb. cut in half	In 1½-qt. casserole place ½ cup water and ½ teaspoon salt. Add beans. Cover. Stir beans after 7 minutes.	High (10)	15 to 17	Tenderness in beans varies. Test beans after 15 minutes to determine if more cooking is needed.
Beans Frozen French Cut Green & Wax	10-oz. pkg. (about 2 cups)	In 1-qt. casserole place 2 tablespoons water and ½ teaspoon salt. Add beans. Stir beans after 5 minutes.	High (10)	10 to 12	For 2 packages or about 4 cups frozen beans microwave 15 to 18 minutes.
Beans Frozen Lima	10-oz. pkg (about 2 cups)	In 1-qt. casserole place ¼ cup water and ½ teaspoon salt. Add limas. Stir beans after 4 minutes.	High (10)	7 to 8	For 2 packages or about 4 cups frozen limas microwave 10 to 12 minutes.
Beets Fresh Whole	1 bunch (5 medium)	In 2-qt. casserole place ½ cup water and ½ teaspoon salt; add beets. Cover. Stir beets after 11 minutes.	High (10)	22 to 25	After cooking, skins peel easily. Slice or dice and season.
Broccoli Fresh Spears	1 bunch (1¼ to 1½ lb.)	In 13×9×2-in. dish place ¼ cup water and ½ teaspoon salt. Arrange broccoli spears with stalks to outside of dish and flowerets in center. Cover with plastic wrap, turning back one corner to vent. Rotate dish ½ turn after 6 minutes.	Medium High (7)	15 to 17	Larger, more mature stalks should be peeled. As an alternate arrangement place in circular dish, flowers to center, stalks to edges.
Broccoli Fresh Cut	1 bunch (1¼ to 1½ lb.) cut into 1-in. piece	In 2-qt. casserole place ½ cup water, ½ teaspoon salt and broccoli. Cover. Stir after 6 minutes.	High (10)	12 to 14	Broccoli cooks most evenly cut in 1-in. pieces.

Broccoli Frozen Chopped	10-oz. pkg. (about 2 cups)	In 1-qt. casserole place 2 tablespoons water, ½ teaspoon salt and broccoli. Cover. Stir after 7 minutes.	High (10)	8 to 10	For 2 packages or about 4 cups frozen broccoli microwave 12 to 15 minutes.
Broccoli Frozen Spears	10-oz. pkg.	In 1-qt. casserole place 3 tablespoons water and ½ teaspoon salt. Add broccoli. Cover. Rearrange broccoli after 4 minutes.	High (10)	8 to 10	Broccoli should be rearranged carefully to avoid breaking tender flower tips.
Brussels Sprouts Fresh	1 lb.	In 1½-qt. casserole, place ¼ cup water and ½ teaspoon salt. Add brussels sprouts. Cover. Stir brussels sprouts after 4 minutes.	High (10)	7 to 9	Trim dry or old outer leaves and cut extra-large sprouts in half before cooking.
Brussels Sprouts Frozen	10-oz. pkg. (1½ to 2 cups)	In 1-qt. casserole place 2 tablespoons water and ½ teaspoon salt. Add brussels sprouts. Cover. Stir brussels sprouts after 4 minutes.	High (10)	8 to 10	For 2 packages or about 3 to 4 cups frozen brussels sprouts microwave 12 to 15 minutes.
Cabbage Fresh Chopped	1 medium head (about 2 lbs.)	In 1½ or 2-qt. casserole place ¼ cup water and ½ teaspoon salt. Add cabbage. Stir cabbage after 5 minutes.	High (10)	9 to 11	Use large enough casserole so cabbage fits loosely.
Cabbage Fresh Wedges	1 medium head (about 2 lbs.)	In 2 or 3-qt. casserole place ¼ cup water and ½ teaspoon salt. Add cabbage. Cover. Rearrange cabbage after 7 minutes.	High (10)	13 to 15	Use large enough casserole so cabbage fits loosely.
Carrots Fresh Whole	1 to 2 lb. (see time column)	In 1½-qt. casserole place ½ cup water and ¼ teaspoon salt; add carrots. Cover. Rearrange carrots after half of time.	High (10)	1 lb. - 12 to 14 2 lb. - 18 to 20	Size of carrots affects cooking time; larger carrots take longer time.
Carrots Fresh Sliced	1 lb. (6 to 8 carrots)	In 1½-qt. casserole place ¼ cup water and ½ teaspoon salt; add slices. Cover. Stir carrots after 7 minutes.	High (10)	12 to 14	Cut slices about ½-in. thick. Old carrots take longer to cook. Diagonally sliced carrots reduce cooking time by about 2 minutes.
Carrots Frozen Sliced	10-oz. pkg. (about 2 cups)	In 1-qt. casserole place 2 tablespoons water and ½ teaspoon salt. Add carrots. Stir carrots after 4 minutes.	High (10)	8 to 10	
Cauliflower Fresh Whole	1 medium head (about 1½ lb.)	In 1½-qt. casserole place ½ cup water and ¼ teaspoon salt. Place cauliflower stem side down. Cover. Turn cauliflower over after 7 minutes.	Medium High (7)	13 to 17	Let stand about 5 minutes before serving. If desired, surround on platter with French style green beans.
Cauliflower Fresh Flowerets	1 medium head (about 1½ lb.) cut into flowerets	In 1½-qt. casserole place ½ cup water and ¼ teaspoon salt; add flowerets. Cover. Stir cauliflower after 6 minutes.	High (10)	12 to 14	
Cauliflower Frozen Flowerets	10-oz. pkg. (about 1½ cups)	In 1-qt. casserole place 2 tablespoons water and ½ teaspoon salt. Add flowerets. Stir cauliflower after 4 minutes.	High (10)	8 to 9	For 2 packages or about 3 cups flowerets microwave 12 to 14 minutes.
Celery Fresh	4 cups ½-in. slices	In 2-qt. casserole place ¼ cup water and ¼ teaspoon salt; add celery. Cover. Stir celery after 6 minutes.	High (10)	11 to 13	Celery is crisp-tender when cooked.

Vegetable	Amount	Procedure	Power Level	Time in Minutes	Comments
Corn Frozen Kernel	10-oz. pkg. (about 2 cups)	In 1-qt. casserole place 2 tablespoons water and ½ teaspoon salt; add corn. Stir corn after 3 minutes.	High (10)	5 to 7	For 2 packages or about 4 cups microwave 9 to 11 minutes.
Corn on the Cob Fresh	1 to 5 ears (see time column)	In 2 or 3-qt. casserole place corn. If corn is in husk, use no water; if corn has been husked add ¼ cup water. Cover. If ears are stacked in casserole rearrange after half of time.	High (10)	3 to 4 per ear	For convenience and freshest flavor, microwave corn in husk.
Corn on the Cob Frozen	1 to 6 ears (see time column)	In 2 or 3-qt. casserole place corn. (No additional water needed.) Cover tightly with lid or plastic wrap. Turn over after half of time. Let stand 5 minutes after microwaving.	High (10)	1 ear 5 to 6 min., over 1 ear 3 to 4 min. per ear	Corn should lay flat in dish. Use oblong glass casserole if necessary.
Eggplant Fresh	1 medium (about 1 lb.) 4 cups cubed	In 2-qt. casserole place 2 tablespoons water and ¼ teaspoon salt; add peeled, diced eggplant. Cover. Stir eggplant after 3 minutes.	High (10)	5 to 6	If peeled, cubed vegetable is prepared ahead of cooking, cover with salted water to retain color and flavor. Let stand 5 minutes.
Mushrooms Fresh Sliced	½ to 1 lb. (see time column)	In 1½-qt. casserole place 2 tablespoons butter or water for each ½ lb. mushrooms. Add mushrooms. Cover. Stir mushrooms after half of time.	High (10)	½-lb. - 3 to 5 1 lb. - 5 to 8	Don't overcook. As soon as color begins to darken remove from oven and let stand a few minutes before serving. If mushrooms are thinly sliced they will take minimum time.
Onions Fresh	4 to 8 medium quartered	In 1 or 2-qt. casserole place ½ cup water and ½ teaspoon salt; add onions. Cover. Stir onions after half of time.	High (10)	4 - 10 to 12 8 - 14 to 16	Timing gives tender but not mushy onions.
Okra Frozen Whole	10-oz. pkg.	In 1-qt. casserole place 2 tablespoons water and ½ teaspoon salt; add okra. Cover. Rearrange every 3 minutes.	High (10)	7 to 9	
Parsnips Fresh	1 lb. (2 to 3 cups cubed)	In 1½-qt. casserole place ¼ cup water and ¼ teaspoon salt; add peeled, cubed parsnips. Cover. Stir parsnips after 4 minutes.	High (10)	8 to 10	Age of parsnips affects microwaving time.
Peas Fresh Shelled	2 lb.	In 1-qt. casserole place ¼ cup water and ½ teaspoon salt; add peas. Cover. Stir peas after 6 minutes. After microwaving, add 1 tablespoon butter and let stand 5 minutes.	High (10)*	12 to 14	*Fresh young peas microwave best at High. Mature peas (yellow color, some sprouts) should be microwaved at Low Power for longer time.
Peas Frozen Shelled	10-oz. pkg. (about 2 cups)	In 1-qt. casserole place 2 tablespoons water and ½ teaspoon salt; add peas. Cover. Stir peas after 3 minutes.	High (10)	5 to 6	For 2 packages or about 4 cups microwave 8 to 10 minutes.
Potatoes Fresh Whole Sweet or White	6 to 8-oz. each (see time column)	Pierce with cooking fork. Place on paper towel on shelf of microwave oven, 1-in. apart.	High (10)	1 - 4 to 6 2 - 6 to 8 3 - 8 to 12 4 - 12 to 16 5 - 16 to 20	Potatoes may still feel firm when done; let stand to soften. Dry or old potatoes do not microwave well whole. Peel and dice them before microwaving.

See page 166 for step-by-step picture directions.

NOTE: When microwaving more than 2 potatoes, moisture can collect in oven. This does not harm food or oven and will evaporate (or may be wiped with cloth) when door is opened. Cook potatoes just until done. Excessive cooking dehydrates them.

NOTE: Not all potatoes are suitable for baking. Dry or old potatoes do not bake well, either conventionally or by microwaving, and are best peeled, cubed and cooked with water.

Potatoes Fresh Cubed White	4 potatoes (6 to 8-oz. each)	Peel potatoes and cut into small pieces (1-in cubes). Place in 2-qt. casserole with ½ cup water. Cover. Stir potatoes after 6 minutes.	High (10)	12 to 14	Drain potatoes and mash with electric mixer, adding 1 teaspoon salt, ¾ cup milk and 2 tablespoons butter.
Spinach Fresh	10 to 16-oz. washed	In 2-qt. casserole place ¼ teaspoon salt; add washed spinach (no extra water needed). Cover. Stir spinach after 4 minutes.	High (10)	7 to 9	Water which clings to leaves is enough moisture to create steam for cooking.
Spinach Frozen Chopped & Leaf	10-oz. pkg.	In 1-qt. casserole place 3 tablespoons water and ½ teaspoon salt. Add spinach. Break up and stir well after 5 minutes.	High (10)	7 to 8	
Squash* Fresh Summer & Yellow	1 lb. sliced or cubed	In 1½-1t. casserole place ¼ cup water and ½ teaspoon salt; add squash. Cover. Stir squash after 5 minutes.	High (10)	10 to 12	If desired, add 2 tablespoons butter to water before microwaving.
Squash Fresh Winter (Acorn or Butternut)	1 to 2 squash (about 1 lb. each)	Cut in half and remove fibrous membranes. In 8-in. square dish or 12×8×2-in. oblong dish, place squash cut side down. Cover with wax paper. Turn cut side up and brush with butter (sprinkle with brown sugar if desired) after 8 minutes.	High (10)	9 to 14	Wax paper cover is best to hold right amount of steam. Let stand 5 minutes.
Squash Frozen Summer	10-oz. pkg. (about 1½ cups)	In 1-qt. casserole place ½ teaspoon salt and squash (no extra water needed). Cover. Stir squash after 3 minutes.)	High (10)	5 to 7	Ice crystals in frozen squash provide enough moisture for microwaving. For 2 packages or about 3 cups microwave 8 to 11 minutes.
Succotash Frozen	10-oz. pkg. (about 2 cups)	In 1-qt. casserole place 2 tablespoons water and ½ teaspoon salt; add succotash. Cover. Stir succotash after 4 minutes.	High (10)	8 to 9	For 2 packages or 4 cups frozen succotash microwave 12 to 14 minutes.
Turnips Fresh	1 lb. cubed (2 to 3 medium)	In 1½-qt. casserole place 3 tablespoons water and ¼ teaspoon salt; add peeled cubed turnips. Cover. Stir turnips after 5 minutes.	High (10)	10 to 12	If desired, turnips can be mashed with added butter after microwaving.
Vegetables, Mixed Frozen	10-oz. pkg. (about 2 cups)	In 1-qt. casserole place 3 tablespoons water and ½ teaspoon salt; add vegetables. Cover. Stir vegetables after 5 minutes.	High (10)	9 to 10	Lima beans are last vegetable to cook; check them for tenderness. Stir and let stand 5 minutes before serving. For 2 packages or 4 cups frozen mixed vegetables microwave 14 to 16 minutes.
Zucchini* Fresh	1 lb. sliced or cubed	In 1½-qt. casserole place ¼ cup water and ½ teaspoon salt; add zucchini. Cover. Stir zucchini after 5 minutes.	High (10)	10 to 12	If desired, add 2 tablespoons butter to water before microwaving.

***Yellow Squash and Zucchini Combination:** In 2-qt. casserole arrange chunks from 1 lb. (4 medium) zucchini and 1 lb. (4 medium) yellow squash. Alternate colors for attractive appearance. Arrange drained strips from 1 jar (2 oz.) pimiento on top. Add 2 tablespoons water; dot with 2 tablespoons butter. Insert temperature probe on center bottom of casserole. Cover with plastic wrap, arranging loosely around probe to vent. Attach cable end at receptacle. **Microwave at High (10). Set Temp. Set 200°.** When oven signals, let squash stand about 10 minutes. Toss to mix, if desired.

Note: To time cook this casserole, **Microwave at High (10) for 12 to 15 Minutes.**

More and more packages of convenience vegetables contain microwave directions for heating or cooking them. Check this information, as well as the chart below, when reconstituting these products.

How to Adapt Convenience Vegetables

Starting Temperatures vary for different convenience vegetables and determine cooking time. A canned vegetable, for example, requires less heating time than its frozen counterpart.

A Trivet uncovered, is useful for microwaving frozen vegetables like breaded zucchini which need a crisp, dry exterior. Cook them conventionally if a very crisp texture is desired.

Vegetable Convenience Foods

VEGETABLE	PROCEDURE	POWER LEVEL	TIME MIN.
Breaded Vegetables 7 oz. pkg., Frozen	Place on trivet, or plate suitable for microwaving. Cook uncovered. Breading will not be crisp. Cook conventionally for crispness.	High (10)	3 to 4
Canned Vegetables	Place lightly drained vegetables in microwave proof serving dish. Cover with plastic wrap. Check at minimum time. Stir and serve. Or use temperature probe set to 150°.	High (10)	8 to 16-oz. - 1½ to 3 28 to 32-oz. - 5 to 7
Casserole, Vegetable 8 to 12-oz. pkg., Frozen	Place in 1-qt. casserole. Cover.	High (10)	5 to 8
Potatoes Baked, Stuffed, Frozen	Examine potatoes to see that mashed filling is encased in potato skin, NOT FOIL. Place potatoe(s) on plate suitable for microwave oven. Cover with wax paper.	High (10)	1-3 to 4 2-5 to 6 3-7 to 8 4-8 to 9
Potatoes Instant Mashed	Use utensil size and amounts of water, milk, butter and salt on package. Cover. After heating, briskly stir in potatoes, adding extra 1 to 2 tablespoons dry mix.	High (10)	5 (Or heat liquid with temperature probe set to 200°.)
Souffle 11-oz. pkg., Frozen	To Defrost: Place food in 8-in pie plate. Stir. To Cook: Divide equally between 3 or 4 buttered custard cups (6 or 7-oz.). Rearrange after 4 minutes. Souffles are done when center is set. Invert on serving plate.	Low (3) Medium High (7)	9 to 11 9 to 11

Vegetables come in such a variety of shapes and sizes that there are many tips and techniques for microwaving them.

Regardless of their size, try to time vegetable cooking just before eating to preserve texture, flavor and bright natural color.

Vegetable Microwaving Helpful Hints

"When I microwave broccoli, the flower overcooks before the stems are tender."

Large and uneven pieces should be arranged with thinner or more tender portions toward the center of the dish.

"When I cook vegetable mixtures, they seem to be unevenly done."

Vegetable mixtures may be unevenly done either because vegetable pieces are different sizes or different densities. Since large or dry vegetables take longer to cook than small or watery vegetables, start the longest cooking pieces first and add shorter cooking vegetables later. If vegetables are of equal moisture content, cut pieces into equal sizes.

"How can I get my microwaved vegetables to taste more southern-style; like in slow cooking?"

Minimum cooking time suggested in this book is for a crisp crunchy texture. If you prefer softer vegetables, cook to the maximum time indicated, or longer. Or, if your oven has the Automatic Simmer feature (on some models with Auto Roast), use this feature to simmer vegetables several hours.

"May I use my microwave oven shelf to cook enough potatoes for several people at once?"

Yes, by arranging up to 4 potatoes on the shelf and up to 4 on the oven floor.

"Can I microwave corn on the cob in the husk?"

Yes, by all means leave the husk on. Your corn will be more flavorful and nutritious than when boiled in large amounts of water.

Today's prevailing tastes are for crisp and crunchy food textures, which explains the wide popularity of stir frying.

Many of the techniques for wok cooking apply to microwaving, especially the sequence of adding harder vegetables before the softer ones. We have added precooked meat to the recipe below, but you can substitute pieces of shellfish or poultry if desired.

How to Stir Fry Vegetables

Select crisp, firm vegetables like onions, carrots, cauliflower buds, celery, broccoli or green peppers. Thinly sliced diagonal pieces or strips are attractive. Combine vegetables that cook at the same rate.

Substitute 1 tablespoon oil (any cooking oil, including olive or peanut oil) and 1 tablespoon butter for water recommended in cooking directions. Microwave according to directions for stir fry recipe.

Add softer vegetables like mushrooms or tomatoes and precooked meat, poultry or seafood when you stir or turn vegetable after cooking for half the time.

Stir Fry Vegetables

POWER LEVEL: High (10)
MICROWAVE TIME: 11 to 15 min., total

1 tablespoon oil **1 tablespoon butter** **3 medium onions,** **quartered** **lengthwise**	In 3-qt. glass casserole place oil, butter and onions. **Microwave uncovered at High (10) for 3 Minutes** until hot.
1 medium green **pepper, cut in ¼-in.** **wide strips** **3 cups thinly-sliced** **cabbage** **1 cup carrots** **(3 medium) sliced** **diagonally** **¼ cup (1 bunch) sliced** **green onions** **1 cup broccoli** **flowerets** **1 cup cauliflower** **flowerets** **3 stalks celery,** **diagonally sliced** **1 pkg. (10 oz.) frozen** **pea pods**	Stir in and mix well green pepper, cabbage, carrots, green onions, broccoli, cauliflower, celery, and pea pods. **Microwave at High (10) covered for 4 Minutes.**
½ cup thinly-sliced **cooked meat** **½ cup sliced** **mushrooms**	Add meat and mushrooms and continue to **Microwave uncovered for 4 to 6 Minutes** more.

Makes 6 to 8 servings

Stir Fry Vegetables

Variation: Peeled and deveined raw shrimp, or chopped cooked chicken can be substituted for meat.

The high price of meat and interest in nutrition have led many Americans to increase the amount and variety of vegetables they eat. There is no reason that vegetables have to be boring.

Throughout this chapter we have suggested ways to vary the flavor of vegetables. Here are a few topping ideas you can adapt for your favorite vegetables.

Tips on How to Vary Vegetables

Pour sauce over cooked vegetables and toss gently to coat. For Zesty Sauce shown here, Microwave at High (10) in 1-qt. casserole 1 tablespoon butter and ¼ cup grated onion for 3 minutes. Add 1 cup mayonnaise, ¼ cup horseradish, ½ teaspoon salt, ¼ teaspoon pepper and mix well. Pour over vegetables.

Top vegetables with bacon bits, crumbled hard-boiled egg, toasted nuts, or a Butter Crumb Topping of ¼ cup melted butter, 1 cup fine bread crumbs and ¼ teaspoon dill weed or other dried herb microwaved in a 1-qt. glass casserole at High (10) for 2 to 3 minutes.

Glaze yams or other vegetables. In 1½-qt. casserole stir together ¼ cup brown sugar, 2 tablespoons butter, 1 tablespoon water and ¼ teaspoon salt. Microwave at High (10) for 2 to 3 minutes. Stir well; add 1 pound hot, cooked vegetables. Stir gently to coat.

Marinate lightly-microwaved vegetables in bottled Italian salad dressing in refrigerator for several hours. Use as a salad garnish.

Fill vegetable shells like tomato halves with braised celery and peas. In 2-qt. casserole microwave at High 6 minutes, 2 cups celery slices, ⅓ cup chopped onion, 2 tablespoons water and ½ teaspoon salt. Add 1 pkg. (10-oz.) frozen peas, cover and microwave at High 6 to 8 minutes more. Makes 3½ cups.

Fresh Tomato Garnish is a good topping for vegetables and hamburgers. In 1½-qt. casserole microwave at High (10) 1 tablespoon prepared mustard, 1 tablespoon brown sugar (packed), 2 teaspoons white vinegar and ½ teaspoon seasoned salt. Add 2 cups tomatoes, ½ cup celery, ½ cup green pepper and ¼ cup green onion — all finely chopped. Microwave at High for 2 more minutes, uncovered. Stir well and refrigerate at least 1 hour before serving.

More Ways to Vary Vegetables

Vegetable Lasagna

Cook lasagna noodles (see page 160) before beginning to assemble this nutritious entree.

POWER LEVEL: Low (3) and Medium High (7)
MICROWAVE TIME: 31 to 35 min.

1 pkg. (10-oz.) frozen chopped spinach	In 12×8×2-in. glass dish place unwrapped frozen blocks of spinach. **Microwave at Low (3) for 12 to 14 Minutes,** breaking apart after 10 minutes until thawed. Drain.
2 cans (8-oz. each) tomato sauce **1 can (6-oz.) tomato paste** **1 can (4-oz) sliced mushrooms** **¼ cup onion, finely chopped** **2 teaspoons leaf oregano** **1 teaspoon basil** **1 teaspon salt** **¼ teaspoon garlic powder** **½ pkg. (16-oz.) lasagna noodles, cooked** **2 cups (1-pt.) small curd cottage cheese** **1 pkg. (6-oz.) grated mozzarella cheese**	In small bowl mix together tomato sauce, tomato paste, mushrooms, onion, oregano, basil, salt and garlic powder. Spread ½ cup sauce over bottom of 12×8×2-in. dish. Over sauce layer half lasagna noodles laid lengthwise, with spinach, half of cottage cheese, half of mozzarella cheese, half of tomato sauce in dish. Repeat layers, with noodles laid horizontally. **Microwave at Medium-High (7) for 19 to 21 minutes.**

Makes 6 to 8 servings

Creamed Vegetables

Prepare and cook vegetables according to directions. Pour sauce over cooked vegetables.

POWER LEVEL: High (10)
MICROWAVE TIME: 5 to 6½ min., total

2 tablespoons butter **2 tablespoons flour** **½ teaspoon salt**	In 1½-qt. glass casserole place butter, flour and salt. **Microwave at High (10) for 1 to 1½ Minutes,** whisking well.
1¼ cups milk or Half & Half	Gradually stir in milk. **Microwave at High (10) for 4 to 5 Minutes,** stirring every minute until thick and bubbly. Covers 1 to 2 pounds vegetables.

Makes 1¼ cups sauce

Vegetable Ring

POWER LEVEL: Medium High (7)
MICROWAVE TIME: 10 to 12 min., total

Good with a variety of vegetables — fresh, frozen or even left-over, cooked vegetables. Season with ¼ to ½ teaspoon complementary spice or herb suggested with individual vegetable charts. Cracker crumbs can be saltine or the buttery round or oval type; flavor will vary depending on which you use. To serve, unmold and fill the center with another favorite vegetable if desired.

¼ cup melted butter
1 cup milk
3 eggs, well beaten
1 tablespoon grated onion
½ teaspoon salt
¼ teaspoon pepper
¾ cup cracker crumbs
1 to 1¼ cup raw or cooked vegetables (grated or mashed)

In mixing bowl combine butter, milk, eggs, onion, salt and pepper. Beat well with fork. Stir in cracker crumbs and vegetables. Pour into well greased 5-cup glass or microwave safe plastic ring mold. **Microwave at Medium-High (7) for 10 to 12 Minutes.**

Makes about 4 servings.

Vegetable Medley

POWER LEVEL: High (10)
MICROWAVE TIME: 17 to 19 min., total

1 head cauliflower
1 bunch broccoli (1¼ to 1½-lb.) cut into spears
3 to 4 carrots, diagonally sliced ¼ inch

On 15-in. round glass or ceramic dish place head of cauliflower in center. Arrange broccoli and carrots around outside.

½ cup butter, melted
½ teaspoon garlic salt
¼ teaspoon pepper

Pour butter over vegetables. Sprinkle with garlic salt and pepper. Cover with plastic wrap turning back one edge to vent. **Microwave at High (10) for 17 to 19 Minutes.** Let stand, covered, 5 minutes. Vegetables should be crisp but tender.

Makes 6 to 8 servings

Harvard Beets

POWER LEVEL: High (10)
MICROWAVE TIME: 18 to 24 min., total

1 medium bunch . . . . **beets (about 1-lb.)** **1 cup warm tap water**	Wash and remove tops from beets. Place beets and water in 1½-qt. casserole. Cover. **Microwave at High (10) 10 to 12 Minutes,** until fork tender. Remove beets from oven and place in cool water. Peel and slice or cube as desired.
1 tablespoon . . . . **cornstarch** **1 tablespoon sugar** **¾ teaspoon salt** **Dash pepper** **⅔ cup water** **¼ cup vinegar**	In same 1½-qt. casserole stir together cornstarch, sugar, salt, pepper, water and vinegar. **Microwave at High (10) 3 to 4 Minutes,** until thickened. Add beets and **Microwave at High (10) 5 to 8 Minutes,** until hot, or, if desired, serve cold.

Makes 4 servings

Pinto Beans

POWER LEVEL: High (10)
MICROWAVE TIME: 2 hours, 10 to 20 min., total

1 pkg. (1-lb.) beans, ... **rinsed** **4 cups water** **1 ham hock** **1 small onion, sliced**	In 3-qt. casserole place beans, water, ham hock and onion. Cover. **Microwave at High (10) 30 Minutes,** stirring after ½ time. **Microwave at Medium (5) 1 Hour 40 Minutes to 1 Hour 50 Minutes,** until tender.

For "Let's Eat" Bean Soup: Remove ham hock. Cut meat into small pieces and return to casserole. Add water to thin soup as desired. Microwave to heat.

Makes 6 to 8 servings

Split Peas

POWER LEVEL: High (10)
MICROWAVE TIME: 1 hour, 13 to 15 min., total

1 cup split peas . . . . **4 cups water** **1 ham hock** **1 rib celery, cut in half** **1 small onion, sliced** **1 tablespoon lemon juice**	In 3-qt. casserole place peas, water, ham hock, celery, onion and lemon juice. Cover. **Microwave at High (10) 15 Minutes.** Stir well. **Microwave at Medium (5) 58 to 60 Minutes,** until tender.

For Split Pea Soup: Dice meat from ham hock. Slice celery. Return to dish. Stir in 1 cup water. Cover. **Microwave at Medium (5) 5 to 10 Minutes,** until hot.

Makes 6 to 8 servings

Popular Green Bean Casserole

POWER LEVEL: Low (3) and High (10)   TEMP: 170°
APPROX. MICROWAVE TIME: 12 to 15 min.

3 pkgs. (10-oz. each) . . . . **frozen French-style green beans**	Defrost beans by placing packages in single layer in microwave oven. **Microwave at Low (3) 10 to 12 Minutes,** turning over and rearranging packages every 2 to 3 minutes.
1 can (10-oz.) cream . . . . **of mushroom soup** **½ cup milk** **1 jar (2-oz.) pimiento, sliced and drained**	Separate beans into 1½-qt. casserole. Mix with canned soup, milk and pimiento to blend well.

Insert temperature probe so tip rests on center bottom of dish. Cover with plastic wrap, arranging loosely around probe to vent. Attach cable end at receptacle. **Microwave at High (10). Set Temp, Set 170°.** When oven signals let stand, covered, about 10 minutes.

Arrange Topping of **1 can (3-oz.) French fried onions** in a ring around edge of dish. Toss to mix, if desired.

Makes about 8 servings

Creamy Cauliflower

POWER LEVEL: High (10)
MICROWAVE TIME: 16 to 19 min., total

½ teaspoon salt . . . . **2 tablespoons water** **2 pkgs. (10-oz. each) frozen cauliflower**	In 2-qt. casserole place salt and water. Add cauliflower. **Microwave at High (10) 5 to 7 Minutes,** until just done. Place in strainer or colander to drain.
1 tablespoon butter, . . . **softened** **1 tablespoon flour** **½ cup milk** **1 cup small curd cottage cheese** **½ cup shredded cheddar cheese** **1 tablespoon chopped pimiento** **½ teaspoon salt** **⅛ teaspoon pepper**	In same 2-qt. casserole, stir to mix butter and flour. Stir in milk, cheeses, pimiento and seasonings. **Microwave at High (10) 6 Minutes,** until cheese melts and mixture thickens.
½ cup crushed corn . . . . . **flakes** **½ teaspoon paprika** **½ teaspoon dill weed**	Mix cauliflower gently into sauce and sprinkle top with corn flakes mixed with paprika and dill weed. **Microwave at High (10) 5 to 6 Minutes,** until hot.

Makes 6 servings

Hot Bean Salad

Hot Bean Salad

This sweet-sour bean salad tastes even better when made in advance. Reheat before serving.

POWER LEVEL: High (10)
MICROWAVE TIME: 12 to 14 min., total

4 strips bacon	Using scissors, snip bacon strips into small pieces into 2-qt. casserole. **Microwave at High (10) 3 to 4 Minutes,** stirring after 2 minutes. With slotted spoon, remove cooked bacon pieces to paper towels to drain.
½ cup sugar . . . . **1 tablespoon cornstarch** **1 teaspoon salt** **¼ teaspoon pepper** **⅔ cup vinegar**	To bacon drippings in casserole, add sugar and cornstarch, blending well. Stir in salt, pepper and vinegar. **Microwave at High (10) 3 to 4 Minutes,** until thick.
1 can (1-lb.) cut green . . . **beans, drained** **1 can (1-lb.) cut wax beans, drained** **1 can (15-oz.) red kidney beans, drained** **1 onion, sliced**	Add drained beans and onion slices to sauce in casserole, stirring well. Cover. **Microwave at High (10) 6 Minutes.** Let compote stand 10 minutes before serving to blend flavors. Sprinkle cooked bacon pieces over top and serve.

Makes 8 to 10 first course servings
or 4 to 5 servings as vegetable

Cheezy Broccoli

POWER LEVEL: High (10)
MICROWAVE TIME: See Recipe

2 pkgs. (10-oz. each) . . . . **frozen chopped broccoli**	Place unopened packages of broccoli on end in microwave oven. **Microwave at High (10) 4 to 5 Minutes,** turning over after 2 minutes. Set aside.
2 cups packaged . . . . . . **precooked (minute) rice** **2 cans (10¾-oz. each) cream of chicken soup** **1 cup milk** **1 jar (16-oz.) pasteurized processed cheese food** **1 tablespoon salt** **½ teaspoon pepper**	In 3-qt. casserole combine rice, soup, milk, cheese, salt, pepper. **Microwave at High (10) 2 to 4 Minutes,** until cheese melts and can be blended easily.
½ cup chopped onion . . . **1 cup chopped celery** **1 can (6-oz.) water chestnuts, drained and sliced**	To cheese mixture, add onion, celery, water chestnuts and broccoli. Stir thoroughly. Divide evenly between 2 lightly greased 10×6×2-in. dishes. microwave one dish at a time. **Microwave at High (10) 12 to 14 Minutes.** Let stand 5 minutes before serving.

Corn Pudding

POWER LEVEL: Medium High (7)
MICROWAVE TIME: 18 to 21 min., total

1 egg	Place egg in 1½-qt. casserole and beat well with fork. Stir in milk, sugar, corn, crackers and butter. **Microwave at Medium High (7) 7 Minutes** and stir well.
½ cup milk	
1 tablespoon sugar	
1 can (16-oz.) creamstyle corn	
¾ cup crushed crackers	
2 tablespoons butter, cut in pieces	
Paprika	Sprinkle with paprika. **Microwave at Medium High (7) 11 to 14 Minutes.** When done, center will be just barely set.

Makes 4 servings

Wilted Spinach Salad

Hot German Potato Salad

POWER LEVEL: High (10)
MICROWAVE TIME: 19 to 22 min., total

4 medium potatoes	Wash and pierce potatoes through with fork. Place on paper towel in microwave oven. **Microwave at High (10) 10 to 12 Minutes,** until tender. Remove from oven, cool slightly, peel potatoes and cut in ⅛-in. slices.
6 strips bacon	In 2-qt. casserole cut bacon in small pieces. Cover with paper towel. **Microwave at High (10) about 6 Minutes,** until crisp. With slotted spoon remove bacon to paper towels to drain. Set aside.
2 tablespoons flour	Stir flour, sugar and seasonings into bacon fat until smooth. **Microwave at High (10) 1 to 2 Minutes,** until bubbly.
¼ cup sugar	
1½ teaspoons salt	
½ teaspoon celery seed	
⅛ teaspoon pepper	
1 cup water	Add water and vinegar to flour mixture. **Microwave at High (10) 4 Minutes,** until mixture boils and thickens. Remove from oven and stir smooth. Add potatoes and bacon; stir gently so potatoes hold their shape. Cover casserole and let stand until ready to serve.
½ cup vinegar	

Makes 4 to 6 servings

Wilted Spinach Salad

POWER LEVEL: High (10)
MICROWAVE TIME: 5 to 6 min., total

3 strips bacon	With scissors, snip bacon into 1-in. pieces into 3-qt. casserole. **Microwave at High (10) 3 Minutes,** until crisp. With slotted spoon, remove bacon to paper towels to drain.
¼ cup vinegar	To drippings in casserole add vinegar, sugar, salt, pepper and tarragon. **Microwave at High (10) 2 to 3 Minutes** to boil. Stir in celery and onion.
2 teaspoons sugar	
¼ teaspoon salt	
⅛ teaspoon pepper	
⅛ teaspoon crushed dried tarragon	
¼ cup chopped celery	
1 tablespoon sliced green onion	
1 pkg. of fresh spinach leaves, torn (about 8 cups total)	Gradually add spinach to hot dressing, tossing to coat each piece, just until slightly wilted. Add orange segments and crisp bacon pieces and toss again lightly. Serve immediately.
2 medium oranges, sectioned, each section seeded and cut in half*	

Makes 8 to 10 servings

*Or substitute 1 can (11-oz.) Mandarin oranges, drained.

Scalloped Potatoes

If desired, sprinkle top with paprika and/or ½ cup shredded sharp cheese after cooking. Cheese melts as casserole stands.

POWER LEVEL: High (10)
MICROWAVE TIME: 25½ to 29½ min., total

3 tablespoons butter...	Place butter in 1-qt. measuring cup. **Microwave at High (10) ½ Minute,** or until melted. Blend in flour and seasonings. Gradually stir in milk. **Microwave at High (10) 8 to 10 Minutes,** stirring after 4 minutes.
2 tablespoons flour	
1 teaspoon salt	
¼ teaspoon pepper	
2 cups milk	
3½ to 4 cups thinly sliced white potatoes (about 3 medium)	Layer half of potatoes, onion and sauce in greased 2-qt. casserole. Repeat layers. Cover.
2 tablespoons minced onion	

Microwave at High (10) 17 to 19 Minutes. Remove from oven and let stand 5 minutes before serving.

Makes 4 to 6 servings

Twice Baked Potatoes

POWER LEVEL: High (10)
MICROWAVE TIME: See Recipe

Potatoes	Microwave desired number of potatoes according to chart, page 170. Slice the top from each potato. With teaspoon, remove center of potatoes to mixing bowl, leaving shells intact.
For each potato	Add to mixing bowl butter, sour cream, salt and pepper. Mix with electric mixer until smooth. Divide potato mixture evenly among shells, mounding, if necessary. Sprinkle with chives if desired. Place potatoes on plate suitable for microwave oven. Potatoes may be refrigerated at this point if desired.
2 tablespoons butter	
2 tablespoons sour cream	
¼ teaspoon salt	
Dash pepper	

If potatoes are microwaved immediately, **Microwave at High (10) 1 Minute** per potato. If more than 2 potatoes are microwaved at one time, arrange in a circle.

If potatoes are microwaved from refrigerator temperature, increase time for each potato by ½ minute.

Eggplant Italiano

This hearty vegetable casserole goes well with plain meats such as roasts, lamb, ham or chicken.

POWER LEVEL: High (10)
MICROWAVE TIME: 15 to 18 min., total

1 medium eggplant	Pare eggplant; slice ⅛-in. thick.
2 cans (8-oz. each) tomato sauce	Spread 2 tablespoons tomato sauce in bottom of 2-qt. casserole. Layer half of eggplant, 1 can tomato sauce, half of oregano and half of sharp cheese. Repeat layers. Cover. **Microwave at High (10) 14 to 16 Minutes.**
1 to 2 teaspoons oregano	
½ cup shredded sharp cheese, optional	
1 pkg. (6-oz)	Add mozzarella cheese. **Microwave at High (10) 1 to 2 Minutes,** until cheese has melted.
mozzarella cheese, sliced	

Makes 4 to 6 servings

Zippy Zucchini

Covering the custard mixture during the first 4 to 5 minutes of microwaving helps it to cook evenly and shortens the total time.

POWER LEVEL: High (10) and Medium High (7)
MICROWAVE TIME: 15 to 17 min., total

4 cups zucchini, cut into chunks (2 medium)	Place zucchini and onion in 10×6×2-in. dish. Cover with plastic wrap, turning one edge back slightly to vent. **Microwave at High (10) 7 Minutes.** Drain.
½ medium onion, thinly sliced	
4 eggs, beaten	In large bowl mix together eggs, cheese, pimiento, salt and pepper. Add zucchini and onions, stirring well. Grease dish in which vegetables were cooked. Pour mixture into dish and cover with paper towel. **Microwave at Medium High (7) 8 to 10 Minutes,** removing paper towel after 4 minutes, until center is set.
1½ cups (6-oz.) shredded cheddar cheese	
1 jar (2-oz.) pimiento, drained	
½ teaspoon salt	
⅛ teaspoon pepper	

Makes 4 servings

182 Quick Breads

Quick breads really are quick with microwaving. Whether you start from scratch or use a mix, you'll have fresh, hot muffins, breads or coffee cakes in minutes. Microwaved quick breads have an even texture and greater volume than conventionally baked, but they do not brown. Use batters with color, such as corn, bran or spice bread, or a topping. For "up-side-down" breads, butter the baking dish and coat the bottom and sides with topping. Savory or sweet toppings add eye appeal as well.

Sweet and Savory Toppings Add Eye Appeal

Conventional   Microwaved   Nut-Crunch Topping   Microwaved Toasted Coconut   Cinnamon & Sugar   Chopped Nuts

How to Microwave Muffins

Cupcaker, especially designed for microwaving, assures good shape and even cooking for muffins and cupcakes; or, make your own muffin cups.

Cut The Tops from paper hot drink cups, leaving 1-in. sides. Line each with a fluted paper baking cup. Arrange in a ring on a flat plate.

Fill Cups half full. Microwaved muffins rise higher than conventionally baked.

Test after minimum time. A wooden pick inserted in center comes out clean. Muffins will appear barely set; there may be moist spots on the surface.

How to Adapt Breads for Microwave Cooking

ITEM	TIME/MIN.	POWER LEVEL	COMMENTS
Muffins 1 2-4 5-6 Note: Do not use foil muffin liners.	½ to 1 1 to 2½ 2½ to 4	Medium High (7)	For best shape use microwave cupcaker or make reusable "homemade muffin cups" by cutting down paper hot drink cups. Check for doneness at minimum time. Rich thick batters may take longest time.
Quick Breads, scratch and from a mix	9 to 12	Medium High (7)	Prepare according to recipe, or package directions. Toothpick inserted in center should come out clean. Top surface will look glossy and will set during standing time of about 15 minutes.
Coffee Cakes, scratch and from a mix	8 to 10	High (10)	
Cornbread	9 to 11	Medium High (7)	
Coffee Cakes, from refrigerated biscuits	8 to 10	High (10) and Medium (5)	Microwave topping ½ to ¾ minute at High (10). Add biscuits and microwave 6 to 8 minutes at Medium (5) until biscuits spring back when lightly touched.
Yeast Breads	10 to 12 min.	Medium (5)	Use a larger loaf dish than usual because microwaved yeast breads rise higher than when conventionally baked.

Pictured top to bottom: *Cherry Caramel Ring (page 187)*
Cornbread Ring (page 184)
Bran-nut Muffins (page 184)
Savory Cheese Bread (page 189)

Thick, fluffy muffin batters, like the ones below microwave best. Because they are somewhat rich and sweet, they absorb microwave energy evenly. Muffin mixes, which are usually less rich, should be checked and rotated ½ turn if necessary after half of time.

Both muffin recipes below can be varied by changing the fruits and nuts. For cornmeal muffins, use the muffin techniques with batter from Cornbread Ring.

Fluffy Muffins

POWER LEVEL: Medium High (7)
MICROWAVE TIME: Use chart on page 184

2 cups unsifted all-purpose flour **½ cup sugar** **3 teaspoons baking powder** **½ teaspoon salt**	In mixing bowl stir flour with sugar, baking powder and salt. Make a well in center of dry mixture.
2 eggs, beaten **½ cup cooking oil** **½ cup milk**	Combine eggs, oil and milk. Add all at once to dry ingredients and stir just to moisten. Fill paper lined microwave containers ½ full; see comments. Cook according to chart page 182. Muffins are done when toothpick stuck in center comes out clean.

Blueberry Muffins Variation: Fold ½ cup rinsed, well drained blueberries into batter. Top with cinnamon sugar.

Makes 12 large muffins

Bran Nut Muffins

POWER LEVEL: Medium High (7)
MICROWAVE TIME: Use chart on page 182

1½ cups unsifted all-purpose flour **1 cup sugar** **5 teaspoons baking powder** **1½ teaspoons salt** **2 cups whole bran cereal** **1 cup chopped nuts (or raisins)**	In large mixing bowl stir together flour, sugar, baking powder, salt, bran and nuts or raisins.
2 eggs **1½ cups milk** **½ cup cooking oil**	Combine eggs, milk and oil. Stir into dry mixture just until all flour is dampened. Fill paper lined muffin cups ½ full.
¼ cup crushed bran cereal or chopped nuts	Sprinkle muffins with cereal or nuts. **Microwave at Medium High (7),** using chart page 182.

Makes about 24 muffins

Bran Nut Bread Variation

Prepare batter for Bran Nut Muffins. Pour into well greased 10-in microwave fluted ring mold. **Microwave at Medium High (7) 14 to 16 Minutes.** Let stand 5 minutes, then turn out onto cooling rack. Serve warm or cool.

Makes 1 (10-in.) fluted ring

Fluffy Blueberry Muffins

Cornbread Ring

POWER LEVEL: Medium High (7)
MICROWAVE TIME: 9 to 11 min., total

1 cup yellow corn meal **1 cup unsifted all-purpose flour** **2 tablespoons sugar** **4 teaspoons baking powder** **½ teaspoon salt**	In large mixing bowl, stir together cornmeal, flour, sugar, baking powder and salt.
1 egg **1 cup milk** **½ cup cooking oil**	Add egg, milk and cooking oil. Beat until smooth, about 1 minute.
1 can finely crushed French fried onions (3-oz. can) **2 tablespoons Parmesan cheese**	Place onions and cheese in well-greased 8-in ring mold. Tilt to coat all sides reserving excess crumbs. Pour batter into ring mold and sprinkle with reserved crumbs.

Microwave at Medium-High (7) for 9 to 11 Minutes until toothpick inserted in center comes out clean. Turn out on cooling rack or serving plate. Serve warm.

Makes 1 (8-in.) ring

Many muffin batters refrigerate well for several days, and can be used to microwave a few fresh hot muffins at a moment's notice.

Quick Bread Cooking Helpful Hints

"My friend makes a delicious coffee cake from refrigerated biscuits in the microwave; but mine was dry and chewy. Why is this?"

Your coffee cake was either cooked too long or at too high a power level. Use Medium (5) power level and check after minimum time. Dough should spring back when lightly touched. It will look moist. See page 186.

"I have tried to adapt my favorite coffee cake batter to microwaving, but have trouble telling when it is done."

A toothpick inserted in the center should come out clean when coffee cake is done.

"May I use my microwave shelf for microwaving twice as many breads or muffins?"

Yes, but time will also double. After half of time, reverse the locations of the breads by placing shelf food on oven floor and floor food on shelf.

"How can I garnish muffins so they will look more like conventionally baked?"

Try our suggested sweet and savory topping ideas on page 182. Select toppings that will best suit the muffin recipe you are using.

"Does reheating day old bakery products really freshen them?"

Yes, the flavor of bakery products is just as good as when freshly baked after the first reheating. However, reheating causes moisture loss. Numerous reheatings will cause bakery products to dry out and toughen.

Coffee cakes may be microwaved in a round dish, rather than a ring. The richer, sweeter batter cooks evenly, so there will be no depression in the center. Like other quick breads, coffee cakes do not brown, and need a colorful topping or simple icing to give them a finished appearance.

Everyday Coffee Cake

Biscuit mix recipe.

POWER LEVEL: High (10)
MICROWAVE TIME: 5 to 7 min., total

1½ cups buttermilk biscuit mix **¼ cup sugar**	In mixing bowl stir together biscuit mix and sugar.
½ cup milk **1 egg** **2 tablespoons cooking oil**	Add milk, egg and oil. Beat by hand, mixing well. Pour into greased 8-in. round dish.
⅓ cup buttermilk biscuit mix **⅓ cup brown sugar (packed)** **2 tablespoons butter** **1 teaspoon cinnamon** **¼ cup chopped nuts**	Blend biscuit mix, brown sugar, butter and cinnamon until crumbly. Sprinkle over batter and sprinkle with nuts. **Microwave at High (10) 5 to 7 Minutes.** Cool 15 minutes; drizzle with Fine Glaze. Serve warm.

Fine Glaze: Stir together ¾ cup confectioners sugar and 1 tablespoon milk. From tip of spoon, drizzle glaze over cake in spoke fashion.

Makes 1 (8-in. round) cake

Cherry Caramel Ring

POWER LEVEL: High (10) and Medium (5)
MICROWAVE TIME: 8½ to 10¾ min., total

¼ cup butter	Place butter in 8-in. round dish. **Microwave at High (10) ½ to ¾ Minute,** until melted.
½ cup brown sugar (packed) **2 tablespoons light corn syrup** **½ cup pecan halves** **¼ cup maraschino cherries, quartered**	Sprinkle sugar over butter and add corn syrup. Stir well with fork. Place drinking glass open-side-up in center of dish. Sprinkle with pecans and cherries.
1 roll (10-oz.) refrigerated buttermilk biscuits	Arrange biscuits over mixture in dish in petal shape, squeezing to fit, if necessary. **Microwave at Medium (5) 6 to 8 Minutes.** Remove glass and invert onto serving plate. Let dish stand over rolls a few minutes so remaining syrup in dish may drizzle over rolls. Serve warm.

Makes 1 (8-in.) ring

How to Microwave a Caramel Biscuit Ring

Prepare topping in bottom of improvised tube pan made by placing a drinking glass about 4-in. high or inverted 6-oz. custard cup, in an 8-in. dish. Or, use plastic ring mold designed for microwaving.

Arrange biscuits over topping and around glass center.

Inverted onto a serving plate, the ring has a rich caramel-colored syrup over the top and sides, although the bottoms of the biscuits are not brown.

One of the best uses for the microwave oven is defrosting frozen convenience breads and warming bakery products. The Defrost setting provides rapid defrosting and warming, yet keeps breads tender.

Coffeecakes packaged in foil should be removed from the container. If the cardboard cover is not foil-lined it may be used as a plate under cake. Other breads may be placed on pottery or paper plates before heating.

Metal Twist Ties must be removed before package of rolls or bread is placed in oven. Under some conditions, metal twist ties can cause package to catch fire.

Convenience Breads Defrosting and Warming Chart
POWER LEVEL: **Defrost (3)**

ITEM	TIME MINUTES	COMMENTS	ITEM	TIME MINUTES	COMMENTS
DEFROSTING — POWER LEVEL 3			Doughnuts (1 to 3)	1 to 2½	
Bread, Buns or Muffins (1-lb. pkg.)	3 or 4	Turn over after 2 minutes.	Doughnuts (4 to 6)	2½ to 3½	
Heat & Serve Rolls (7-oz. pkg.)	2 to 3		Doughnuts (1 box of 12 glazed)	3½ to 4½	
Coffee Cake (11 to 13-oz. pkg.)	5½ to 6	No turn needed.	French Toast (2 slices)	5½ to 6½	No turn needed.
Coffee Cake (6½-oz. pkg.)	2 to 3		French Toast (4 slices)	9 to 10	
Coffee Ring (10-oz. pkg.)	3½ to 4		**WARMING (room temperature) POWER LEVEL: 5**		
			Dinner Rolls(1 to 3)	¼ to 1½	
			Dinner Rolls(4 to 6)	1½ to 2½	
Sweet Rolls, Crumb Cakes, Pull-aparts (8¾ to 12-oz. pkg.)	2½ to 3½		Doughnuts	1 to 2	Rotate more than 6.

Cherry Caramel Ring

Yeast Breads

The microwave oven can be used to defrost frozen yeast bread and, if you wish, to cook the dough. However, its appearance will not be the same as if it were conventionally baked.

Microwaved yeast bread toppings add eye appeal.

Toppings on microwaved breads made from frozen dough are shown at the left in comparison with conventional and microwaved breads without toppings. From the top: Conventional, Microwaved, Taco Seasoning Mix with Cornmeal, Toasted Sesame Seeds, Cinnamon Sugar, Crushed Canned Onion Rings.

Toast Sesame Seeds in a small bowl or 10-oz. custard cup, using 1 teaspoon of butter and 1 jar (2¾-oz.) seeds. **Microwave at High 4 to 5 Minutes.**

How to Defrost Frozen Bread Dough

 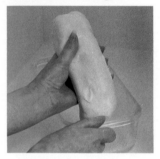

Brush 1 tablespoon melted butter over frozen bread dough. Place dough in 9×5×3-in. loaf dish. (For conventional baking use 8×4×3-in. dish).

Defrost at power level (1) for a total time of 30 minutes, turning loaf over and rotating dish ¼ turn after ½ time.

To Proof: Microwave at Warm (2) for 30 Minutes. Rotate ¼ turn after ½ time. Proofed bread should be about 1-in. below top of dish.

After defrosting and proofing frozen bread dough **Microwave at Medium (5) 10 to 12 Minutes,** rotating loaf ¼ turn after 5 minutes.

Breads cooked in the microwave oven do not brown or develop a crust as they do conventionally because there is no hot air in the oven to dry out the surfaces. Microwaved bread raises higher during cooking than conventionally baked bread, because it does not have a firm crust to prevent it from rising too much. For this reason bread must be microwaved in a larger loaf dish. When properly microwaved, breads look set and dry on top and, when touched, the surface springs back.

Colorfully Topped Cheese Bread, below, created for microwaving contains butter and cheese for richness.

Low shape provides maximum exposure to microwave energy for even cooking.

How to Proof Bread Dough

For regular Basic Bread Dough from scratch:
Step 1. Microwave 3-cups of water in 1-qt. measure at High (10) for 2 to 3 minutes until steaming hot.

Step 2. Place bowl of dough in oven next to water. Cover bowl lightly with towel. **Microwave at Warm (1) for 20 to 24 minutes.**

Step 3. Test for rising by making an indention with fingers; dough should **not** spring back and surface should be dry.

Step 4. Microwave as directed in recipe. Bread will not brown. Check for doneness by touching top lightly until it springs back.

Frozen Bread Dough: See directions on page 188.

Savory Cheese Bread

POWER LEVEL: Medium (5)
MICROWAVE TIME: 10 to 12 min. per loaf

2¾ cups unsifted all-purpose flour 2 tablespoons sugar ½ teaspoon salt ½ cup (¼-lb.) butter	In large mixing bowl place flour, sugar, salt and butter. Cut through mixture with pastry blender until mixture resembles coarse meal.
1 pkg. (¼-oz.) active dry yeast ¼ cup warm water 1 cup milk 1 egg, beaten	Dissolve yeast in warm water. Add to crumbly mixture along with milk and egg. Beat with spoon until well blended.
1 pkg. (½ of 2¾-oz. box) dry onion soup mix 1 cup (4-oz. pkg.) shredded cheddar cheese	Mix together 2 tablespoons onion soup mix and ¼ cup shredded cheese. Set aside. Add remaining soup mix and cheese to batter. Stir well.

Divide batter evenly between 2 well greased 8×4×3-in. dishes. Sprinkle loaves with reserved cheese mixture. Cover lightly and let rise in warm place 1½ to 2 hours, just until dough is slightly puffy.

Microwave one loaf at a time. **Microwave at Medium (5) 10 to 12 Minutes.** Carefully remove breads to cooling rack.

Serve warm or cool.

Makes 2 (8×4×3-in.) loaves

190 Fruit Desserts

Many times fruits are served as an accompaniment to a main dish. But since they are naturally sweet, we have included them with other desserts. Fruit is tasty when microwaved because its flavor stays so fresh. Because fruits are naturally juicy, they microwave efficiently preserving water-soluble nutrients such as vitamin C. We have included separate chapters for custards, pies, cakes, cookies and dessert sauces. You will find some basic adapting tips, recipes and helpful hints in each dessert chapter.

How to Adapt Fruit Desserts for Microwave Cooking

Defrosted fruit will be cold, firm and slightly icy. Pouch will be flexible and juices liquid.

Fruit over Pound Cake (defrosted 2 min.) makes a quick easy dessert. Top with whipped topping defrosted (2 min.), if desired.

Stewed Fruit: Mix 4 cups fruit, ¾ cup sugar and ¼ cup light corn syrup in 3-qt. casserole. Cover. Microwave at High (10) 9 minutes.

For Applesauce, place 6 pared, cored and quartered apples in a 2-qt. casserole with ¼ cup water. Cover. Microwave at High Power (10) for 8 min., until tender. Into blender container, place apple mixture, ⅓ cup sugar, ⅛ teaspoon salt and ⅛ teaspoon cinnamon. Blend until smooth. Makes 3 to 4 cups.

Apples or Pears should be cored and slit to prevent bursting. **Fill** each fruit with 2 tablespoons brown sugar, ⅛ teaspoon cinnamon and 1 teaspoon butter. **Pour** 2 tablespoons water for each fruit in bottom of casserole. Microwave according to chart below.

Easy Fruit Pudding: Spread 1 can (20 to 22-oz.) fruit pie filling in 8-in. square dish. Microwave at High (10) 4 minutes, until heated through. Sprinkle 1 box 1-layer white, yellow, or spice cake mix evenly over fruit. Dot with ¼ cup butter. Mix 2 tablespoons sugar with 1 teaspoon cinnamon and ¼ cup finely chopped nuts. Sprinkle mixture over top of butter. Microwave at High (10) 11 to 13 minutes. Makes 6 servings.

Fruit Defrosting Chart

Properly defrosted fruit should be cold, firm and slightly icy for best flavor and texture. Remove any metal or foil from package and, if necessary, place fruit in a casserole. Be sure to check at minimum time and break up with a fork. Flex package to speed defrosting of fruit frozen in plastic pouches.

Type	Power Level	Time Min.
Fruit (10 to 16-oz. pkg.)	Defrost	5-10
Fruit, plastic pouch (1 to 2 10-oz. pkgs.)	Defrost	5-10
Escalloped Apples (12-oz. pkg.)	High	6-8, covered

Adapting Chart for Baked Fresh Fruit

Number of Fruit	Casserole Size	Microwave Power Level	Time, Min.
1	1-qt.	High (10)	2-4
2	1½-qt.	High (10)	4-5½
3	2-qt.	High (10)	6-8
4	2-qt.	High (10)	9-10

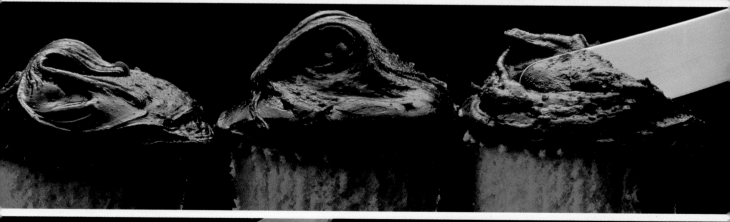

Many fruit recipes are versatile enough to accommodate other fruits for a flavor change. The streuseled apple recipe below microwaves well when pears or peaches are substituted for apples.

The butterscotch bananas may be turned into a tasty pineapple sauce by replacing banana pieces with drained canned pineapple slices or chunks. Instead of orange and maraschino cherries in the filled pineapple, try snipped dried apricots and bing cherries for a tart-sweet effect.

Fruit Filled Pineapple

Streuseled Apples

Known conventionally as Apple Crisp. Vary this recipe by substituting other fresh or canned fruits for apples.

POWER LEVEL: High (10)
MICROWAVE TIME: 9 to 12 min., total

6 cups sliced, peeled apples	In 8-in. square dish place apples and sugar.
¾ cup brown sugar (packed)	
½ cup unsifted all-purpose flour	With pastry blender mix flour, sugar, oats, butter and cinnamon until crumbly. Sprinkle over top of apples.
⅓ cup brown sugar (packed)	
⅓ cup quick-cooking oats	
¼ cup butter	
½ teaspoon cinnamon	

Microwave at High (10) 9 to 12 Minutes. Let stand few minutes before serving.

Makes 6 to 8 servings

Note: In oven meal shown on page 54, use 2-qt. casserole instead of 8-in. square dish.

Fruit-Filled Pineapple

The Temperature Probe, Set to 120°, will signal when the pineapple is warm enough to develop flavor and be flamed.

POWER LEVEL: High (10)   TEMP: 120°
APPROX. MICROWAVE TIME: 10 to 12 min.

1 medium fresh pineapple	Cut pineapple, including leafy crown, in half lengthwise. Cut out fruit, leaving outside shell intact. Remove woody core; cut remaining fruit in chunks.
1 cup (3 to 4-oz.) shredded coconut	Toss pineapple chunks with coconut, almonds, oranges, cherries and marmalade. Place pineapple shells in 13×9×2-in. dish or on serving plate suitable for microwave oven. Fill shells with fruit mixture. Insert temperature probe so tip is in center of one of pineapple halves. Cover with wax paper. Attach cable end at receptacle. **Microwave at High (10), 10 to 12 Minutes.**
½ cup toasted sliced almonds	
1 can (11-oz.) mandarin orange sections, drained	
½ cup maraschino cherries without stems, drained	
½ cup sweet orange marmalade	
¼ cup light rum	Measure rum into glass measure. **Microwave at High (10) 15 Seconds.** Remove 1 metal tablespoonful. Pour rest of rum over pineapple. Ignite rum in spoon and pour over pineapple to flame.

Makes 6 servings

Custards and puddings are a microwave specialty. Conventionally baked custard must be set in a pan of water, which provides moisture to prevent drying and browning. On the range top you must stir custard and pudding constantly to keep it free from lumps. Delicate custard microwaves smooth and creamy with a minimum of stirring.

Basic Custard and Chocolate Pudding

Basic Casserole Custard

POWER LEVEL: High (10) and Low (3)
MICROWAVE TIME: 13 to 16 min., total

3 eggs **¼ cup sugar** **1 teaspoon vanilla** **⅛ teaspoon salt**	In 1-qt. casserole beat eggs, sugar, vanilla and salt with wire whisk, until very well blended and sugar is dissolved.
1½ cups milk	Scald milk in glass measure. **Microwave at High (10) 3 to 4 Minutes.** Gradually add to egg mixture, stirring well.

Cover dish and **Microwave at Low (3) 10 to 12 Minutes.** Rotate dish ½ turn after 7 to 8 minutes. Sprinkle top with nutmeg before serving, if desired.

Makes 6 to 8 servings

Cup Custards: Prepare custard mixture as above except pour into 4 (6-oz.) custard cups. Place in circle on shelf in microwave oven. **Microwave at Low (3) 10 to 12 Minutes,** rearranging after 3 minutes.

Butterscotch Bananas

POWER LEVEL: High (10)
MICROWAVE TIME: 5 to 7 min., total

½ cup brown sugar (packed) **¼ cup rum** **¼ cup butter**	In 1½-qt. casserole stir together brown sugar and rum. Add butter. Cover. **Microwave at High 4 to 5 Minutes,** until sugar is dissolved.
2 large ripe, firm bananas	Cut bananas lengthwise, then crosswise so there are 8 pieces. Add to syrup, stirring to coat each piece. **Microwave at High 1 to 2 Minutes,** until hot. Serve over ice cream.

Makes 4 servings

Chocolate Pudding

POWER LEVEL: High (10) and Medium High (7)
MICROWAVE TIME: 6 to 10 min., total

¾ cup sugar **2 tablespoons cornstarch** **¼ teaspoon salt** **2 cups milk** **2 oz. unsweetened chocolate**	In 1-qt. casserole blend together sugar, cornstarch and salt. Gradually stir in milk, mixing well. **Microwave at High (10) 5 to 7 Minutes,** stirring every 3 minutes, until mixture is smooth, thickened and clear. Add chocolate and stir until melted.
2 egg yolks, slightly beaten, or 1 egg, well beaten	Stir a small amount of hot pudding quickly into egg yolks. Return egg mixture to hot pudding, mixing well. **Microwave at Medium High (7) 1 to 3 Minutes,** stirring after 1 minute, until smooth and thickened.
2 tablespoons butter **1 teaspoon vanilla extract**	Add butter and vanilla. Stir until butter is melted. Pour into serving dishes.

Makes 4 servings

VANILLA PUDDING: Omit chocolate. If desired, add 2 to 3 bananas or 1 cup coconut to this variation as pudding dessert or pie filling.

BUTTERSCOTCH PUDDING: Substitute brown sugar for white sugar. Increase butter to 3 tablespoons.

Favorite old fashioned desserts like bread pudding and rice pudding used to take an hour or more to bake conventionally. Now with microwaving they cook in about ¼ the time.

The special ingredients of bread and rice in these two custard-based desserts actually stabilizes them so they are less likely to overcook or separate than regular custard.

Basic Bread Pudding

POWER LEVEL: High (10) and Medium High (7)
MICROWAVE TIME: 13 to 16 min., total

4 cups bread cubes lightly packed into cup (4 to 5 slices) **½ cup brown sugar (packed)** **½ teaspoon nutmeg** **¼ teaspoon salt** **½ cup raisins (optional)**	Spread bread cubes evenly in 8-in. round dish. Sprinkle evenly with brown sugar, nutmeg, salt, then raisins.
2 cups milk . . . . **¼ cup butter** **2 eggs, beaten**	Measure milk into 1-qt. measuring cup. Add butter. **Microwave at High (10) 4 Minutes,** until butter is melted and milk is warm. Rapidly stir in eggs with a fork and mix well. Pour over bread cubes in dish.

Microwave at Medium High (7) 9 to 12 Minutes. When cooked, center may still be slightly soft but it will set up as pudding cools. Serve warm or chilled.

Makes about 6 servings

Basic Bread Pudding

Old Fashioned Rice Pudding

POWER LEVEL: Medium (5)
MICROWAVE TIME: 13 to 15 min., total

2 cups rice, cooked . . . **1⅓ cups milk** **½ cup brown sugar** **1 tablespoon soft butter** **1 tablespoon vanilla extract** **3 eggs, beaten**	Combine cooked rice, milk, brown sugar, butter, vanilla and eggs in 2½-qt. casserole. **Microwave at Medium (5) for 13 to 15 Minutes,** stirring every 5 minutes. Let stand 10 minutes.
Whipped cream, ... **optional**	Serve warm or cold topped with whipped cream, if desired.

Makes about 6 servings

Cooking Commercial Dry Pudding Mix

Since there is less evaporation in microwaving, microwaved pudding is often creamier in texture, lighter in color and greater in volume than it is conventionally.

POWER LEVEL: High (10)
MICROWAVE TIME: 6 to 8 min., total

1 pkg. (3¾-oz.) . . . . **pudding or pie filling mix, not instant** **½ cup milk**	Empty pudding mix into 1-qt. glass measure. Add ½ cup milk and stir until all mix is moistened and blended.
1½ cups milk	Add 1½ cups more milk and blend well.

Microwave at High (10) 6 to 8 Minutes, stirring thoroughly every 3 minutes. Pour into 4 or 5 serving dishes, or prepared pie crust. Cover top of pudding with wax paper or plastic wrap to prevent "skin" from forming on top. Chill and serve.

Makes 4 to 5 servings

Cream Cheese Pudding: Prepare 1 package of butterscotch commercial pudding or pie filling mix as directed above. Cool until lukewarm. With high speed mixer, whip 1 package (8-oz.) softened cream cheese until light and fluffy. Gradually beat in pudding until smooth. Serve as pudding or pie filling. Garnish with whipped cream, if desired.

Custards and Puddings

Remember that microwaved puddings make good pie fillings, especially if poured into one of the easy to microwave crumb crusts, page 196. However, these fillings are soft and creamy, and they may not hold a very sharp cut unless very well chilled. Since microwaved puddings evaporate less moisture, you may want to reduce the liquid in the recipe by ¼ to ⅓ cup to achieve a firmer pie filling consistency.

Custard and Pudding Dessert Helpful Hints

"What caused my microwaved custard to curdle?"

Too high a power level and over-cooking will cause custards to curdle. When ready to remove from the oven, custard will have a soft center area about the size of a 25¢ piece. Knife plunged in center will have a slight film. Center sets upon standing.

"What utensil is recommended for microwaving puddings and custards?"

For puddings, try using a measuring cup, or microwave safe casserole with handles to make stirring easier. For custards, use microwave safe custard cups or casseroles; using recommended size utensil is important.

"The top of my microwaved custard is watery and foamy. How can I avoid this problem?"

Cooling custards with a paper towel between the cover and rim of the casserole dish will allow the excess moisture to be absorbed by the towel.

Adapting Chart for Puddings and Custards

ITEM	TIME/MIN.	POWER LEVEL	PROCEDURE
Egg Custard, 3 eggs	13 to 16	High (10) and Low (3)	Scald milk at High (10). Cover custard mixture and Microwave at Low (3), rotating dish ½ turn after half of cooking time.
Bread Pudding	13 to 16	High (10) and Medium High (7)	Warm milk at High (10). Microwave pudding mixture at Medium High (7).
Commercial puddings	6 to 8	High (10)	

196 Pies

Just as in conventional cooking, the thickness of a pie crust determines its optimal cooking time. The recipe on opposite page may be rolled out to the traditional ⅛-inch thickness.

Pastries made from pie crust mix, and frozen convenience pastry shells are often somewhat thinner and might require less microwaving time.

Tarts are a new addition to the wide variety of microwave foods. The recipe at right makes about 4 tart shells.

Adapting Basic Pie and Tart Shells

Weigh down pie shells with rice, or dry beans to prevent crust from puffing.

Check for doneness on bottom of crust. It should look opaque and dry. Top will be dry and blistered.

Tart Shells can be shaped over back of custard cups, or inside cupcake pan. Prick dough thoroughly.

Crumb crusts complement creamy fillings. A variety of cookie crumbs can vary flavor. Mix ¼ cup melted butter, 1¼ cups crumbs, 2 tablespoons sugar.
Microwave as in chart below.

Scalloped crusts can be made by pressing cookie crumbs in bottom of pie dish. Stand thin, whole cookies on end around sides of dish before adding filling.

Add chopped nuts to crust mixture for variety. Whole or half nut pieces, or cookie crumbs can be used to garnish pies.

How to Adapt Pies and Tarts

ITEM	TIME/MIN.	POWER LEVEL	COMMENTS
Pie Shells	6 to 7	High (10)	Pastry will not brown. Use food coloring, or suggestions on next page.
Crumb Crust	1 to 2	High (10)	Use a wet knife for neatest cutting.
Crust from a mix	6 to 7	High (10)	Mix and roll out as package directs.
One-crust pie	18 to 22	High (10) and Medium (5)	Microwave shell at High (10). Pour in filling and finish at Medium (5).
Tarts	4 to 5	High (10)	Use basic pastry recipe at right. Loosen cooked pastry immediately after microwaving.

Pies

Plain microwaved pastry looks different from conventionally baked. From top to bottom at right: Conventional, Microwaved, Molasses, Maple Syrup, Chocolate Pastry, Dark Corn Syrup, Vanilla, Egg Yolk Toppings.

Basic Pastry Shell

Add color to microwaved pastry by brushing crust with colorful ingredients as shown at right.

POWER LEVEL: High (10)
MICROWAVE TIME: 6 to 7 min., total

1 cup unsifted all-purpose flour	In small bowl place flour and salt. With pastry blender cut in shortening, until mixture resembles the size of small peas.
1 teaspoon salt	
6 tablespoons shortening	
2 tablespoons cold water	Sprinkle water over flour-shortening mixture. Stir with fork to form ball.

Roll out on floured pastry cloth with rolling pin to ⅛-in. thickness. Let stand a few mintues before shaping. Use to line 9-in. pie plate shaping pastry to the edge of pie plate. Prick pastry with fork. **Microwave at High (10) 6 to 7 Minutes.**

Makes 1 (9-in.) pastry shell

Chocolate Pastry Shell

To flour add only ½ teaspoon salt along with 2 tablespoons cocoa and ⅓ cup sugar.

Quiche Pastry

The butter flavor complements quiche. See quiche recipe page 158.

POWER LEVEL: High (10)
MICROWAVE TIME: 4 to 6 min., total

1 cup unsifted all-purpose flour	In small mixing bowl stir together flour and salt. With pastry blender, cut in shortening until it has the appearance of cornmeal. Cut in butter until particles form the size of peas.
½ teaspoon salt	
3 tablespoons shortening	
3 tablespoons cold butter	
2½ tablespoons cold water	Sprinkle mixture with cold water. Blend lightly with fingers until dough holds together and can be formed into ball. Roll out to fit 9-in quiche dish.
1 egg yolk	Brush pastry with mixture of egg yolk and Worcestershire sauce.
1 teaspoon Worcestershire sauce	

Microwave at High (10) 4 to 6 Minutes.

Makes 1 (9-in.) quiche pastry

Fluffy Marshmallow Fruit Pie

Pie is creamy and soft when served from refrigerator. For firm pieces which hold sharp cut, serve frozen. Frozen pie releases easily from bottom of pie plate if set on a towel dampened with hot water for a few minutes.

POWER LEVEL: High (10)
MICROWAVE TIME: 2 to 3 min., total

Crumb Pie Shell (see page 196)	Microwave Crumb Pie Shell using the flavor of cookie that best complements filling. Cool.
1 pkg. (10-oz.) large marshmallows **½ cup milk**	In 3-qt. casserole place marshmallows and milk. Cover. **Microwave at High (10) 2 to 3 Minutes,** until mixture can be stirred smooth. Chill in refrigerator (about 30 to 40 minutes) or in pan of ice water, until thickened, stirring occasionally.
1 cup whipping cream, whipped **2 cups fresh fruit**	Fold in whipped cream and peeled and sliced fresh peaches, sliced fresh strawberries or fresh whole raspberries. Pour into crust and decorate with reserved crumbs or additional whipped cream, if desired. Refrigerate several hours or overnight.

Makes 1 (9-in) pie

Frozen Chocolate Almond Pie

This pie cuts well straight from the freezer. No thawing is necessary. Use wet knife for sharpest cut. Also see tip with above recipe.

POWER LEVEL: High (10)
MICROWAVE TIME: 3 to 4 min., total

Crumb Pie Shell (see page 196)	Microwave pie shell. Cool.
4 milk chocolate candy bars with almonds (1.15-oz. each) **½ of 10-oz. pkg. large marshmallows (about 20)** **½ cup milk**	In 2-qt. casserole place candy, marshmallows and milk. **Microwave at High (10) 3 to 4 Minutes,** stirring after 2 minutes, until mixture can be stirred smooth. Chill until thickened, stirring occasionally.
1 cup whipping cream whipped	Fold whipped cream into cooled chocolate mixture. Pile into pie shell and freeze until firm.

Makes 1 (9-in.) pie

Apple Graham Pie

POWER LEVEL: High (10) Temp. 199°
MICROWAVE TIME: 10 to 12 min.

½ cup (¼-lb.) butter **¼ cup sugar** **2 cups graham cracker crumbs**	In large glass mixing bowl place butter. **Microwave at High (10) 1 Minute,** until melted. Add sugar and crumbs. Mix well. Press half of mixture firmly and evenly into 9-in. pie plate.
5 cups thinly sliced apples (4 to 6 medium) **½ cup sugar** **1 teaspoon cinnamon**	In large mixing bowl place apple slices; they should be ⅛ to ¼-in. thick. Add sugar and cinnamon, mixing well. Mound and press down into crumb crust.

Cover apples with remaining crumbs to make top crust. Press crumbs down firmly, especially at edges, to prevent boilover.

Insert temperature probe so tip is in center of pie. Cover with wax paper. Attach cable end at receptacle. **Microwave at High (10), Set Temp. Set 199°.** Let stand 10 minutes, then remove paper so topping can crisp. See note at top of page 199.

Makes 1 (9-in.) pie

Pumpkin Pie

POWER LEVEL: High (10) and Medium (5)
MICROWAVE TIME: 37 to 42 min., total

½ cup (¼-lb.) butter	In 10-in. pie plate place butter. **Microwave at High (10) 1 Minute,** until melted.
2 cups vanilla wafer crumbs **2 tablespoons sugar**	Add crumbs and sugar; mix well. Firmly press on bottom and up sides of dish. **Microwave at High (10) 2 Minutes,** rotating dish ½ turn after 1 minute.
1 can (16-oz.) mashed pumpkin **1 cup brown sugar** **1 tablespoon pumpkin pie spice** **1 tablespoon flour** **½ teaspoon salt** **1 can (13-oz.) evaporated milk** **2 eggs, beaten**	In 2-qt. casserole blend together pumpkin, brown sugar, pumpkin pie spice, flour, salt, evaporated milk and eggs. **Microwave at Medium (5) 12 to 14 Minutes,** stirring every 5 minutes, until hot and thickened.

Pour hot filling into prepared pie shell. **Microwave at Medium (5) 22 to 25 Minutes.** Pie is done when edges are set and center is slightly soft. Let stand about 15 to 20 minutes.

Makes 1 (10-in.) pie

Fruit pies like Apple Graham Pie, page 198, require standing time after microwaving. During this time they continue to cook, due to internal heat. Standing time allows fruit to settle and after cooling, the pie is firm and easy to cut. A pie or fruit cobbler with crumb or streusel topping will have firmer top surface (which is more easy to serve) if top is patted down during dessert's standing time.

Pies Microwaving Helpful Hints

"Can two-crust pies be cooked in my microwave oven?"

Since two-crust pies need dry heat to brown and crisp, they should be cooked in a conventional oven. As a variation, try microwaving the Apple Graham pie on page 198.

"How can I avoid overcooking marshmallow pie fillings?"

Remove marshmallows from the oven as soon as they begin to puff. Air heats and expands inside marshmallows causing them to puff before melting.

"What are some suggestions to add color to microwaved meringue topped pies?"

You may add color and beautifully garnish meringue by sprinkling on toasted coconut, grated lemon peel, or chocolate shavings. For vanilla or butterscotch pies, add maple flavoring to meringue for attractive brown color and good taste.

"My tart shells cracked as I removed them from the inverted custard cups. How can I avoid this?"

Using a knife tip, carefully loosen the shells as soon as they are removed from the oven.

Defrosting Frozen Pre-Baked Pies

POWER LEVEL: Defrost (3)

AMOUNT	TIME MINUTES	COMMENTS
Whole Pie (14 to 26-oz.) cream or custard type	3 to 5	Remove from foil container to glass pie plate or platter. Add 3 to 4 minutes for fruit or nut pie.
Piece of Pie cream or custard type (1 or 2 pieces)	½ to 1	Place wedge on microwave safe dessert plate. Add 1 or 2 minutes for fruit or nut pie.

Microwaved Meringue Topping

Meringue sets well in a microwave oven, but top will not brown. See picture above for tips for adding color to top of pies, if desired.

POWER LEVEL: Medium (5)
MICROWAVE TIME: 3 to 4 minutes

3 egg whites .... **½ teaspoon cream of tartar** **6 tablespoons sugar**	In medium size, clean mixer bowl, beat egg whites with cream of tartar until stiff peaks form. Gradually beat in sugar to make glossy meringue. Spread over pie. (Meringue sets best when spread over hot pie filling). **Microwave at Medium (5) for 3 to 4 Minutes.** Makes Topping for 9-inch pie.

200 Cakes

The popularity of microwaved cakes is indicated by the many new utensils being developed for cooking them. Microwaved cakes will not brown, but they are moist, airy, fluffy and have greater volume than when conventionally baked. This is because the air inside a microwave oven is room temperature not hot and dry like a conventional oven. Hot dry air bakes a crust around the edges of cakes, which contains their volume.

Volume and Browning: Microwaved cake at right does not brown or develop a crust but has greater volume than the conventionally baked cake at left. A plastic fluted tube dish allows heat to penetrate all sides.

Omit One Egg in preparing batter for cake mixes. This technique improves texture and controls volume. Do not reduce water.

Adapting Cake Mixes for Microwaving

Cakes requiring the addition of oil microwave best. White cake mixes do not require addition of oil to the batter, but we recommend that ⅓ cup of oil be substituted for an equal amount of water called for on the package.

Some cake manufacturers recommend omitting an egg when preparing batter for microwaving and we agree (see above) that this technique can improve cake results. Other sources recommend eliminating ¼ to ½ cup water for a more level top; but we feel this makes the cake dryer.

DISH SIZE	AMOUNT OF BATTER	POWER LEVEL	TIME/MIN.	COMMENTS
12×8×2-in. glass	3½ cups	Medium High (7)	14 to 16	
8-in. square, or round dish	1-layer size pkg. or ½ pkg. of 2-layer size	Medium High (7)	7½ to 10	
9-in. round	3 cups	Medium High (7)	7½ to 9½	Cake mixes vary in their ability to be microwaved. There may be moist spots on the surface which will evaporate as the cake cools. Cool on a wire rack to avoid soggy bottom. Any left-over batter can be used to make cupcakes.
Tube, 16 cup	1-two layer size	High (10)	14 to 16	
Loaf, 9×5×5×3-in. glass	2-layer size pkg.	Medium High (7)	12 to 14	
13×9×2-in. glass	2-layer size pkg.	High (10)	11½ to 14½	Rotate dish ½ turn every 7 minutes.

Since most cakes are frosted or served with a topping you won't be aware of the difference in appearance but you will appreciate the time saved in baking.

Rich Cake Batters microwave best. Cakes made with oil microwave especially well. See adapting tips with chart below right.

Not recommended. Cakes like chiffon and angel food need dry heat and do not microwave well.

How to Microwave Two Layers at Once

If your oven has a shelf, place it in highest position. Arrange one layer each in center of oven shelf and floor.

Microwave first ½ of time at Medium High (7). After ½ time, remove cake layer on oven floor and place it on shelf; then place cake layer that was on shelf on oven floor. **Microwave second ½ of time at High (10).** Cool on rack.

Because of the density and size of cakes cooked in 12×8×2-in. and 13×9×2-in. dishes, they do not adapt well to shelf cooking of cakes.

ITEM	COOKING TIME/MIN.
8-in. round or square dish, 2-layers	14 to 15
9-in. round, 2-layers	13 to 14

Microwaved Cake (second from left) looks different from conventional cake (below), until frosted or topped.

Whipped Topping with Drizzled Chocolate

Peach Upside Down Cake (page 207)

Adapting Cakes for Microwaving

Fluted Tube Cake: Use plastic microwave-safe tube dish. Cake is done when inserted toothpick comes out clean.

Oblong Cakes adapt well to microwaving. Either 12×8×2-in. or 13×9×2-in. glass dishes may be used.

Stir and Frost Cakes can be microwaved in their own container. Follow package directions.

Cupcakes: Use any left-over batter from cake layers for cupcakes. See chart page 204.

Adapting Your Favorite Cake Recipes

Use times and baking directions shown below for your favorite cake recipes. Heavier cakes (those with added ingredients such as fruit, nuts, vegetables, etc.) will take slightly longer than plainer cakes.

SIZE, SHAPE	POWER LEVEL	COOKING TIME/MIN.	STANDING TIME/MIN.	COMMENTS
12×8×2-in. glass	MH (7)	11 to 15	10	If serving cake from baking pan, grease bottom and sides. If removing to serving plate, line bottom of baking dish with cut-to-size piece of wax paper. Cool on rack after microwaving to settle and dry on top, or cake may fall or crack when removed from pan.
8-in. square or round	MH (7)	7½ to 9	5-10	
9-in. round	MH (7)	7 to 8	5-10	
10-in. tube	High (10)	11 to 13	20	
Cheesecake, 9-in.	MH (7)	21 to 23	Chill	
Loaf	MH (7)	11 to 13	20	*NOTE: For 13×9×2-in. size only, rotate dish ½ turn after 7 minutes.*
13×9×2-in. glass	High (10)	12½ to 14½	20	

How to Microwave Frostings and Toppings

Cream Cheese Frosting: In 2-qt. casserole place 1 lb. pkg. confectioners sugar. Place 1 pkg. (8-oz.) cream cheese, 6 tablespoons butter and 2 teaspoons vanilla extract over top. Microwave at High (10) for 1 minute, just until ingredients can be beaten together.

Confectioners Sugar: In 1½-qt. casserole stir 1-lb. pkg. confectioners sugar, ¼ cup milk, ¼ teaspoon vanilla. Top with ¼ cup sliced butter. Microwave at High (10) 2 minutes. Stir smooth.

Fruit Topped Cake: Prepare dish by buttering sides well. Coat sides with finely ground nuts. Line bottom with circle of wax paper; pour in ½ can pie filling, then gently pour 2 cups prepared cake batter over top. Microwave as in chart (cake mix page 200, recipe cakes page 202). Invert finished cake.

Easy Fudge Frosting: In 1½-qt. casserole stir 1 cup sugar, ¼ cup butter, ¼ cup evaporated milk. Microwave at High (10) 3 to 4 minutes, until bubbly. Blend in 1 cup semi-sweet chocolate bits, 1 cup marshmallow creme and 1 teaspoon vanilla extract.

Chocolate Beauty Cake

POWER LEVEL: High (10)
MICROWAVE TIME: 8 to 10 min., total

1½ cups unsifted all-purpose flour **1 cup brown sugar (packed)** **¼ cup cocoa** **1 teaspoon baking soda** **½ teaspoon salt** **½ cup water**	In mixing bowl stir together flour, sugar, cocoa, soda and salt. Add water and stir to a stiff shiny batter, about 100 strokes.
½ cup water **⅓ cup cooking oil** **1 tablespoon vinegar** **½ teaspoons vanilla extract**	Add additional ½ cup water, oil, vinegar and vanilla. Stir until smooth and well blended.

Pour batter into greased 8-in. round dish. **Microwave at High (10) 8 to 10 Minutes.** Let stand directly on heat-proof counter or wooden board to cool. Finish with favorite frosting, or as desired.

Makes 1 (8-in. round) cake

Basic Butter Cake

POWER LEVEL: High (10)
MICROWAVE TIME: 8 to 10 min., per layer

2 cups unsifted all-purpose flour **2 cups sugar** **3 teaspoons baking powder** **½ teaspoon salt**	In large mixing bowl stir together flour, sugar, baking powder and salt.
1 cup (½-lb.) butter, softened **1 cup milk** **1½ teaspoon vanilla extract** **1 egg**	Add butter, milk, vanilla and 1 egg. Beat 2 minutes at lowest speed of mixer, scraping bowl constantly for first ½ minute.
3 eggs	Stop mixer and add eggs. Continue beating at lowest speed, scraping bowl often, 1 more minute. Batter will look curdled.

Pour batter into 2 paper towel lined 8-in. round dishes; spread evenly. Microwave 1 cake at a time. **Microwave at High (10), 8 to 10 Minutes.** Let stand directly on heat-proof counter or wooden board to cool 15 minutes. Cake may then be turned out on wire rack to complete cooling, if desired.

Makes 2 (8-in. round) cakes

Chocolate Chip Filled Cupcakes.

Chocolate Chip Filled Cupcakes

Batter from 2-layer chocolate cake mix **Chocolate Chip Filling (below)**	To make each cupcake, measure about 1 tablespoon batter into paper liner. Cover with 3 teaspoons filling. Top with 1 more tablespoon of batter.

Microwave cupcakes using chart below. As cupcakes cook, filling will form in center.

Chocolate Chip Filling: Stir together 1 pkg. (8-oz.) softened cream creese, ⅓ cup sugar, 1 egg, ⅛ teaspoon salt, until well mixed. Blend in 1 pkg. (6-oz.) chocolate chips.

Makes 30 cupcakes

Cupcake Cooking Chart
POWER LEVEL: **Medium High (7)**

CUPCAKES	TIME MINUTES	COMMENTS
1	½-¾	Fill paper liners only half full. When cooking several cupcakes, you may notice some will be done before others. If so, remove those that are done and continue cooking the rest a few seconds more.
2	1-1¼	
3	1½-1¾	
4	2	
5	2½-3	
6	3¼-3½	

When looking at the microwaving charts for both cake recipes and mixes you may have noticed that cakes may now be baked in the large oblong dish, 13×9×2-inch size.

That is because of the special way microwaves enter the oven from both bottom and top. If your oven has energy only from the top of the oven, we recommend that you microwave oblong cakes no larger than 12×8×2-inch.

Cake Microwaving Helpful Hints

"My cake came out rubbery and with hard edges. What did I do wrong?"

Try decreasing cooking time. When toothpick inserted in center of cake layer comes out clean, cake is done.

"My cake batter bubbled over the top of the dish onto the oven floor. How much batter should I put in each dish?"

Your baking dish should be filled only two-thirds full. Microwaved cakes rise higher than those baked conventionally. If you are using a cake mix, using one less egg than the package recommends will also help eliminate this problem.

"The top of my cake was still wet after the recommended cooking time. Should I cook it longer?"

Microwaved cakes look slightly glossy right after you remove them from the oven, but they continue cooking during standing time.

Note: The volume of cakes from a mix is influenced by the brand and type of mix used. Mixes vary from brand to brand.

How to Microwave Special Cake Mixes

1. Prepare batter according to package directions.
2. Pour batter into greased 8-in. round dish.
3. Microwave at Medium High (7), according to chart below.
4. Cake is done when toothpick stuck in center comes out clean.
5. Let cake stand directly on heat-proof counter or wooden board to cool.

POWER LEVEL: **Medium High (7)**

CAKE	TIME MIN.	COMMENTS
Boston Cream Pie	5 to 7	Prepare custard filling and frosting as package directs.
Pineapple Upside Down Cake	9 to 12	To prevent spillover, remove ¼ cup batter to make 2 cupcakes.
Snackin' Cake	10 to 12	

Convenience Cake Defrosting Chart

Cakes packaged in foil should be removed from the foil and placed on a plate, or on an all cardboard lid. Frosted layer cakes can be defrosted on the styrofoam base.

Watch icing and frosting closely as they melt easily. Defrosted cakes should be cool and easy to cut. Let cakes stand 2 to 5 minutes before serving.

POWER LEVEL: **Defrost**

ITEM	TIME/MIN.
2 to 3-layer, frosted (17-oz.)	2
1-layer, frosted, filled or topped (12½ to 16-oz.)	2 to 3
Pound Cake (11¼-oz.)	2
Cheesecake, plain or fruit topped (17 to 19-oz.)	5 to 7
Crunch Cakes and Cupcakes (3 or 4)	1 to 2

Popular Carrot Cake

POWER LEVEL: High
MICROWAVE TIME: 15 to 17 min., total

1¼ cups sugar 1 cup cooking oil 1 teaspoon vanilla extract 3 eggs 1½ cups unsifted all-purpose flour ¾ teaspoon salt 1½ teaspoons baking soda	In large mixing bowl blend sugar, oil and vanilla. Add eggs and beat well.
2½ teaspons cinnamon	In small bowl, stir together flour, salt, soda and cinnamon. Add to sugar-egg mixture and mix in.
2¼ cups raw grated carrots ½ cup chopped walnuts	Fold in carrots and walnuts. Pour batter into greased 12×8×2-in. dish.

Microwave at High 13 to 15 Minutes, rotating dish ½ turn after 8 minutes. Let stand directly on heat-proof counter or wooden board to cool. Frost with Cream Cheese Frosting, page 251, if desired.

Makes 1 (12×8×2-in.) cake

Honey Drizzle Cake

This recipe won $5,000 in a microwave recipe contest. The syrup is plentiful, and some people prefer to use only half of it to soak into cake.

POWER LEVEL: High
MICROWAVE TIME: 16 to 18 min., total

5 eggs ¼ cup sugar ⅛ teaspoon salt	Separate eggs. In large mixer bowl beat egg whites until foamy. Gradually beat in ¼ cup sugar and salt until fluffy.
½ cup sugar 1 teaspoon vanilla extract	In small bowl beat egg yolks, ½ cup sugar and vanilla until thick and pale.
1½ cups chopped pecans 1½ cups fine vanilla wafer crumbs 1½ teaspoons baking powder ½ teaspoon cinnamon	Fold yolk mixture into egg whites thoroughly. Blend pecans, wafer crumbs, baking powder and cinnamon; sprinkle over top. Fold all ingredients together well.

Pour into greased 8-in. square dish. **Microwave at High 8 to 10 Minutes.** Remove cake and cook Honey Syrup (below). Carefully pour syrup over cake. Serve in small pieces, warm or cold, with unsweetened whipped cream.

Honey Syrup: In 2-qt. casserole stir together 1½ cups water, 1½ cups sugar and ⅔ cup honey. **Microwave at High 8 Minutes,** stirring after 4 minutes.

Makes 1 (8-in.) square cake

Orange Glazed Fruit Cake

Orange-Glazed Fruit Cake

POWER LEVEL: High (10)
MICROWAVE TIME: 13 to 15 min., total

1 cup (3 to 4-oz.) coconut 1 cup unsifted all-purpose flour 1½ cups confectioners sugar 2 teaspoons baking powder	In mixing bowl stir together coconut, flour, confectioners sugar, and baking powder.
¾ cup butter, melted 3 eggs, beaten ½ cup milk	Add butter, eggs and milk. Mix well.
2 cups chopped candied fruit 1½ cups chopped pecans	Stir in fruit and nuts. Pour batter into greased 16 cup plastic fluted tube dish.

Microwave at High (10) 13 to 15 Minutes. Spoon Orange Glaze over hot cake in pan. Cool 1 hour before inverting onto serving dish.

Orange Glaze: In 1-qt. casserole stir together ½ cup sugar and 1 cup orange juice. Cover. **Microwave at High (10) 3 to 5 Minutes,** until boiling.

Makes 1 (10-in.) cake

Pineapple Upside Down Cake

For variety substitute peaches for pineapple and almond extract for vanilla.

POWER LEVEL: High (10)
MICROWAVE TIME: 11 to 14 min., total

¼ cup butter	In 8-in. round dish place butter. **Microwave at High (10) ½ to 1 Minute,** to melt. Sprinkle sugar over butter. Drain pineapple (save liquid) on paper towels and arrange in dish. Decorate with cherries.
⅓ cup brown sugar (packed)	
1 can (8¼-oz.) pineapple slices	
4 maraschino or candied cherries, cut in half	
1¼ cups unsifted all-purpose flour	In small mixer bowl place flour, sugar, baking powder, salt, shortening, egg, liquid and vanilla. Beat 3 minutes on lowest mixer speed, scraping bowl constantly first ½ minute. Carefully spread batter over fruit in dish.
¾ cup sugar	
2 teaspoons baking powder	
½ teaspoon salt	
⅓ cup soft shortening	
1 egg	
Liquid from pineapple plus milk to total ½ cup	
1 teaspoon vanilla extract	

Microwave at High (10) 10 to 13 Minutes. Some batter may run onto edges of dish, but will not spill. When done, toothpick stuck in cake comes out clean. Invert cake onto plate, let dish stand over cake a few minutes. Serve warm.

Makes 1 (8-in.) round cake

Early American Gingerbread

POWER LEVEL: Medium High (7)
MICROWAVE TIME: 5 to 6 min., total

1½ cups unsifted all-purpose flour	In mixing bowl stir together flour, sugar, baking soda, ginger, cinnamon and salt.
½ cup sugar	
¾ teaspoon baking soda	
½ teaspoon ginger	
½ teaspoon cinnamon	
½ teaspoon salt	
½ cup soft shortening	Add shortening, egg, molasses and water. Beat 2 minutes on medium speed of mixer until well blended.
1 egg	
½ cup light molasses	
½ cup hottest tap water	

Pour batter into greased 8-in. round dish or 9-in. plastic tube dish. **Microwave at Medium High (7) 5 to 6 Minutes.** When cake is done let stand directly on heat-proof counter or wooden board to cool.

Makes 8 servings

Basic Cheesecake

Cheesecake, which is a custard rather than a batter, is especially appropriate for microwaving.

POWER LEVEL: High (10) and Medium (5)
MICROWAVE TIME: 22 to 24 min., total

3 tablespoons butter	In 8-in. round dish place butter. **Microwave at High (10) ¼ to ½ Minute,** to melt. Stir in crumbs and sugar. Press mixture on bottom and sides of dish. **Microwave at High (10) 1½ to 2 Minutes,** rotating dish ½ turn after 1 minute, until set.
1 cup fine crumbs (graham cracker or chocolate cookie)	
2 tablespoons sugar	
4 eggs	In blender container place eggs, sugar, cream cheese, vanilla and salt. Blend on high speed 1 minute until smooth. (If mixed with electric mixer, use large mixer bowl and mix at high speed 3 minutes.) Pour over back of spoon into crust.*
1 cup sugar	
2 pkg. (8-oz. each) cream cheese	
2 teaspoons vanilla extract	
¼ teaspoon salt	

Microwave at Medium (5) 23 to 26 Minutes, until center is almost set. Refrigerate at least 3 hours before serving. Garnish with Whipped Cream Cheese Topping (below) and chocolate curls, if desired.

Makes 1 (8-in.) cheesecake
8 to 12 servings

*Pouring over spoon prevents crust from breaking.

Whipped Cream Cheese Topping: In small mixer bowl place 1 pkg. (3-oz.) softened cream cheese, ½ cup whipping cream and 2 tablespoons sugar. Beat until fluffy. Serve in dollops or spread over top.

Creme de Menthe Cheesecake

Prepare recipe above with Chocolate Cookie Crust. Omit vanilla, add ¼ cup green creme de menthe to filling.

Irish Coffee Cheesecake

Prepare recipe above with Graham Cracker Crust. Omit vanilla, add 1 teaspoon instant coffee powder and ¼ cup Irish mist liqueur to filling.

208　Cookies

Brownies and bar cookies exemplify the best of microwaved baking. Their taste, texture and appearance compare favorably with microwaved baking and they can be ready to serve in 6 to 10 minutes.

Molded cookies microwave with ease using our new directions below. You can keep the dough refrigerated and make just a few at a time for a fresh quick snack. Or, if your oven has a shelf, double the amount for more servings.

Adapting Tips for Microwaving Cookies

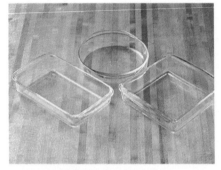

Bar cookies can be microwaved in square or oblong dishes.

Drop dough in four equal mounds in dish. Spread evenly before baking.

Place dish directly on counter top to cool and firm.

Mold individual cookies from firm dough and microwave in 2 or 3 rows (4 to 5 cookies per row) on wax paper covered corrugated cardboard, or use microwave safe plastic baking sheet.

Small cookies can have brown spots below the surface where cooking begins. Watch carefully and do not overcook. Large bar cookies microwave more evenly.

Check bars for doneness on bottom of dish. Bars are done when they are just set. **Molded cookies** will look dry on top when done.

Adapting Chart for Cookies

POWER LEVEL: **High (10)**

ITEM AND COOKING CONTAINER	TIME/MIN.	COMMENTS
Bar cookies, (6×10×2-in.)	9 to 11	Bar cookies are done when set on bottom and glossy on top. Place dish directly on counter top for 15 to 20 minutes to cool and set. If using 6×10×2-in. dish, divide batter equally into two batches.
(8×8×2-in.)	8 to 10	
(12×8×2-in.)	4 to 5	
Molded individual cookies, (microwave safe baking trivet or corrugated cardboard sheet)	3 to 4 per dozen	Cover trivet or cardboard with wax paper. Place cookies 2-in. apart. Rotate ½ turn after ½ time. Microwaved cookies are soft, not crisp.

Chocolate Chip Bars

Chocolate Chip Bars

POWER LEVEL: High (10)
MICROWAVE TIME: 5 to 7 min., total

½ cup (¼-lb.) butter, softened	In small mixer bowl cream together butter and sugar, until fluffy. Add egg, milk, and vanilla. Mix well.
¾ cup brown sugar (packed)	
1 egg	
1 tablespoon milk	
1 teaspoon vanilla extract	

1¼ cups unsifted all-purpose flour	Stir together flour, baking powder and salt. Add to creamed mixture. Blend well. Stir in ½ cup chocolate pieces and nuts. Spread in greased 8-in. square dish. Sprinkle with remaining ½ cup chocolate pieces. **Microwave at High (10) 5 to 7 Minutes,** rotating dish ½ turn after 3 minutes, until done. Cool and cut into bars.
½ teaspoon baking powder	
⅛ teaspoon salt	
1 cup (6-oz.) semi-sweet chocolate pieces, divided	
½ cup chopped nuts (optional)	

Makes about 24 bars

Basic Brownies

You can microwave brownies from a mix using these same directions.

POWER LEVEL: High (10)
MICROWAVE TIME: 6 to 7 min., total

2 eggs	In small bowl at medium speed on mixer, beat together eggs, sugar, salt and vanilla, about 1 minute until light.
1 cup sugar	
½ teaspoon salt	
1 teaspoon vanilla extract	

½ cup (¼-lb.) butter, melted	Add melted butter. Continue beating until thoroughly blended.

¾ cup unsifted all-purpose flour	Mix in flour and cocoa at low speed.
½ cup cocoa	

1 cup chopped nuts	Stir in nuts. Spread evenly in greased 8-in. square dish.

Microwave at High (10) 6 to 7 Minutes, rotating dish ½ turn after 3 minutes. When done, top looks dry and will spring back when lightly touched. Cut when cold.

Makes about 20 brownies

Raspberry Tart Squares

POWER LEVEL: High (10)
MICROWAVE TIME: 8 to 10½ min., total

¾ cup butter	In 12×8×2-in. dish, place butter. **Microwave at High (10) 1 to 1½ Minutes,** until melted. Stir in brown sugar, flour, baking powder, salt, oatmeal and pecans; blend well. Remove half of crumb mixture to bowl or wax paper. Pat remaining crumbs evenly over bottom of dish.
1 cup brown sugar	
1½ cups unsifted all-purpose flour	
1 teaspoon baking powder	
½ teaspoon salt	
1½ cups quick-cooking oatmeal	
1 cup finely chopped pecans	

1 jar (12-oz.) raspberry jam	Cover patted-out crumbs with raspberry jam and sprinkle with remaining crumbs over top.

Microwave at High (10) 7 to 9 Minutes, rotating dish ½ turn after 4 minutes.

Makes about 30 squares

For the first time we have added molded cookies to our microwave cookie collection. Microwave ovens with energy coming from the top and bottom cook these cookies evenly, but it is still important to watch them carefully near the end of the cooking time.

You may have recognized the recipes for molded cookies on this page as being old favorites of yours. These types of cookies may be easily adapted to microwaving because they make fairly thick cookies. If your oven does not have microwave energy from both top and bottom, rotate once or twice during cooking.

Easy Nut Balls variation, Chocolate Surprise Cookies variation, Easy Nut Balls dusted with confectioner's sugar and Peanut Butter Cookies.

Easy Nut Balls

POWER LEVEL: Medium High (7)
MICROWAVE TIME: 3 to 4 min., per 8 to 12

1 cup butter	In large bowl cream butter,
½ cup powdered sugar	powdered sugar and salt together. Add vanilla.
¼ teaspoon salt	Blend in flour ⅓ at a time.
1 teaspoon vanilla	
2¼ cups flour	
⅔ cup chopped	Stir in nuts. Shape into
pecans, walnuts or almonds	1-in. balls and place in rows, 2-in. apart on wax paper covered cardboard sheet or microwave-safe plastic baking tray.

Microwave at Medium High (7) 3 to 4 Minutes. Remove cookies from oven on wax paper and sprinkle tops with additional powdered sugar. Cool.

Makes 36 cookies

Variation: Flatten dough balls with fork dipped in sugar. Top with maraschino cherry half, ⅛ teaspoon jelly or pecan half. Microwave as directed above.

Peanut Butter Cookies

POWER LEVEL: Medium High (7)
MICROWAVE TIME: 2½ to 4 min., per 8 to 12

½ cup butter	Cream together butter,
½ cup brown sugar	sugar and peanut butter.
½ cup granulated sugar	Add egg. Blend in flour, soda, salt and vanilla. Stir
½ cup chunky peanut butter	well. Shape dough into 1-in. balls. Arrange in rows
1 egg, beaten	on wax paper covered
1½ cups flour	cardboard or microwave-
¼ teaspoon soda	safe plastic baking tray.
¼ teaspoon salt	Space balls 2-in. apart.
1 teaspoon vanilla	Flatten with fork dipped in sugar.

Microwave High (10) 2½ to 3 Minutes. Remove on wax paper to cool. Microwave remaining cookies using fresh wax paper for each load.

Makes 36 cookies

Chocolate Surprise Cookies

POWER LEVEL: Medium High (7)
MICROWAVE TIME: 2½ to 3½ min., per 8 to 12

1 cup butter	Cream butter, sugar and
¾ cup sugar	salt together in a large
¼ teaspoon salt	bowl. Stir in chocolate.
2 squares unsweetened chocolate, melted (see tip on page 213)	Add eggs beating until fluffy. Blend in vanilla.
3 egg yolks, beaten	
1 teaspoon vanilla	
2½ cups flour	Add flour ⅓ at a time
30 pecan halves, or well drained maraschino cherries	until blended.

To make each cookie, mold about 1 teaspoon dough around a pecan half or well drained cherry. Arrange 2-in. apart, in rows, onto wax paper covered cardboard sheet or microwave-safe plastic baking tray. **Microwave at Medium High (7), 2½ to 3 Minutes.** Remove on wax paper to cool.

Makes 36 molded balls

Variation: Follow directions above only fill spritz cookie gun with dough and squeeze individual cookies onto baking sheet.

As we discuss below, thin refrigerated and drop cookies do not microwave well because the centers cook much faster than the outside edges.

Helpful Hints for Microwaving Cookies

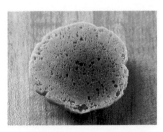

"My microwaved cookies have hard overcooked centers. Why is this?"

Because they are rich, cookies can easily overcook. Cook until just set. Let stand before cutting bar cookies, or removing molded cookies to plate.

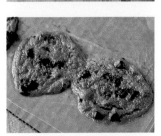

"My bar cookies were not done on the edges and stuck to the bottom of the dish."

Try placing the dish directly on counter top to cool 20 minutes or more. Also, lining the dish with wax paper before pressing in dough will aid in easy removal.

"Can refrigerator cookie rolls be adapted for microwave baking?"

We have tested various brands of individually sliced refrigerator cookies and feel that they do not microwave well. Their concentrated richness causes running and brown spots in the center.

"Can I cook large batches of molded cookies in my microwave?"

Yes, by using your shelf. Place one plastic or cardboard tray of cookies on the shelf and a second one on the oven floor. Switch positions after half of time.

How to Microwave Cookies Mixes

Drop cookies made from mixes do not microwave well and, like drop cookies from scratch, are not recommended for microwaving. However, some varieties of molded peanut butter cookies from a mix may be microwaved like the recipe at the left.

Package cookie mixes adapt quite well in the microwave oven. Select 12-oz. to 16-oz. packages of cookie mix. Prepare mix as directed on package except be sure liquid totals 2 tablespoons. (You may have to increase water measurement called for on the package.)

The technique described below lets you microwave cookie mixes rapidly in the form of bar cookies.

Spread batter in lightly greased 8-in. square dish. **Microwave at High (10) 7 to 9 Minutes,** rotating dish ½ turn after 3 minutes. Do not overcook; when done, top surface will appear set. Cool at least 20 minutes before cutting into bars.

Candies demonstrate many of the advantages of microwaving. Chocolate and caramelized mixtures, which require careful attention and constant stirring by old-fashioned methods, microwave with occasional stirring. Syrups and candies are very hot. Use care in stirring and when transferring mixtures from the microwave oven to your work counter.

How to Microwave Peanut Brittle

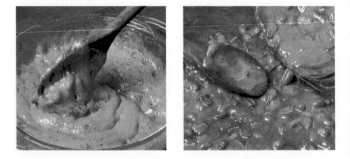

Stir well to combine sugar and corn syrup. Stirring this mixture helps it to microwave evenly. Add peanuts, stirring well. Stir again when adding butter and vanilla.

Stir in baking soda until mixture is light and foamy. Spread out quickly on greased cookie sheet. When cool, flex sheet to remove.

Munching Peanut Brittle

Almond Brittle

Substitute 1 jar (7-oz.) dry roasted almonds for peanuts and 1 teaspoon almond extract for vanilla. Omit butter and add 1 cup (4-oz.) shredded coconut.

Munching Peanut Brittle

This is the same old-fashioned recipe which required constant stirring in a black iron skillet. Stir only 4 times when microwaving.

POWER LEVEL: High (10)
MICROWAVE TIME: 8 to 11 min., total

1 cup sugar	In 1½-qt. casserole stir
½ cup white corn syrup	together sugar and syrup. **Microwave at High (10) 4 Minutes.**
1 cup roasted, salted . . . peanuts	Stir in peanuts. **Microwave at High (10) 3 to 5 Minutes,** until light brown.
1 teaspoon butter . . . . . . **1 teaspoon vanilla extract**	Add butter and vanilla to syrup, blending well. **Microwave at High (10) 1 to 2 Minutes** more. Peanuts will be lightly browned and syrup very hot.
1 teaspoon baking . . . . . . **soda**	Add baking soda and gently stir until light and foamy.

Pour mixture onto lightly greased cookie sheet, or unbuttered non-stick coated cookie sheet. Let cool ½ to 1 hour. When cool, break into small pieces and store in air-tight container.

Makes about 1 pound

Candies

Microwaving easily softens and melts candy ingredients.
Most of the ideas below take less than 6 minutes.

Other Candy Ideas

Caramel Popcorn: In 4-qt. dish place 1-lb. box brown sugar, ½ cup butter, ½ cup light corn syrup, 1 tablespoon water and 1 teaspoon salt. Microwave at High (10) 12 minutes, stirring after 5 minutes. Add 2 teaspoons soda. Pour over 3 quarts popcorn and 1 cup peanuts; toss. Spread on foil to cool or form into balls.

2-Minute Fudge: Stir together 1-lb. box confectioners sugar, ½ cup cocoa, ¼ teaspoon salt, ¼ cup milk and 1 tablespoon vanilla extract until blended in 1½-qt. dish. Top with ½ cup butter. Microwave at High (10) 2 minutes. Stir smooth. Blend in 1 cup chopped nuts. Pour into wax paper lined 8-in. square dish. Chill.

Chocolate Nut Bark: Melt 12-oz. pkg. semi-sweet chocolate bits as shown below. Stir in 1 cup whole toasted almonds. Spread thinly over waxed paper covered cardboard, or cookie sheet. Chill until firm. Break into pieces.

S'Mores: On paper plate or napkin place graham cracker square. Top with square of chocolate bar and 1 marshmallow. Microwave at High (10) 15 to 20 seconds.

Caramel Apples: In 1-pt. measure place half of 14-oz. pkg. unwrapped caramels with 1 tablespoon water. Microwave at High (10) 3 minutes. Stir until smooth. Insert wooden sticks into stem ends of 4 apples for dipping.

Marshmallow Crisp: In 12×8×2-in. dish melt ¼ cup butter at High (10) 1 minute. Add 10-oz. pkg. marshmallows; cover. Microwave at High (10) for 3 minutes. Stir. Add 5 cups crispy rice cereal. Blend and press firmly into pan.

How to Melt Chocolate

Chocolate Bits: Cover dish of bits with plastic wrap and Microwave at Medium (5). For 6-oz. pkg. (1 cup) Microwave 3 minutes until bits are glossy but hold their shape. For 12 oz. pkg., microwave 6 minutes.

Chocolate Squares: Melt in paper wrappers, seam side up. Microwave at Medium (5) 1 minute per square, or until squares feel soft. Chocolate burns easily, so watch carefully.

Other Dessert and Dessert Sauce Ideas

Cherries Jubilee: Into 2-qt. dish drain juice from 2 cans (16-oz. each) dark sweet cherries. Stir in 3 tablespoons cornstarch, 1 tablespoon lemon juice, 1 teaspoon grated lemon peel and ¾ cup sugar. Microwave at High (10) 5 to 7 Minutes, stirring after 3 minutes. Add cherries.

Marshmallow Cream Sauce: In glass or ceramic bowl add 2 tablespoons milk to 2 jars (7-oz. each) marshmallow creme. Microwave at Medium (5) for 2 to 3 minutes. Stir well. Good on chocolate ice cream.

Mint Sauce: Place 1 package (6½-oz.) chocolate-covered mint patties in 1-qt. glass measure with ¼ cup whipping cream. Microwave at Medium (5) for 2 to 3 minutes. Good on mint ice cream or angel food cake.

Dessert Fondue: Prepare Fudge Sauce (below) or Butterscotch (right); thin with brandy, rum or liqueur if desired. Pour into fondue pot. Dip banana slices, maraschino cherries, pineapple chunks and other fruits, or angel food or pound cake pieces.

Pudding Parfait: Make pudding from a mix, page 194, or Chocolate Pudding, page 193. For a special dessert, layer pudding with whipped cream and crushed cookies or toasted coconut or nuts in parfait glass.

Peach Trifle: An elegant English dessert. Split 1-layer yellow cake or half of large pound cake into 2 thin layers. Line 2-qt. bowl or pan with 1 cake layer, cutting to fit. Top with half of 12-oz. jar of peach preserves. Make 2 packages (3-oz. each) vanilla pudding mix page 194. Pour half over preserves. Repeat layers.

Soften Ice Cream and Commercial Sauces: Microwave ice cream at Warm (1) for ½ minute per pint (or 1½ to 2 minutes per half gallon). Remove metal lid from commercial jars of sauce before warming at High (10) ½ minute.

Fudge Sauce: In 3-qt. dish mix 1 cup sugar, ¼ teaspoon salt and 1 can (5.3-oz.) evaporated milk. Microwave at High (10) for 5 to 6 minutes until boiling. Stir in 2 squares (2-oz.) unsweetened chocolate until melted. Add 2 tablespoons butter and 1 teaspooon vanilla extract.

Toasted Coconut: Spread 1 cup coconut (4-oz. can) in thin layer in glass pie plate. Microwave at High (10) for 5 to 7 minutes, stirring every minute. Serve over pie, pudding, or frosted cake.

Dessert Sauces

Delicious, smooth and creamy dessert sauces microwave with exceptional ease and speed.

Scrumptious Butterscotch Sauce

POWER LEVEL: High (10)
MICROWAVE TIME: 3½ to 4½ min., total

1 tablespoon cornstarch . . . . In 1½-qt. casserole stir together cornstarch and brown sugar. Stir in half & half, corn syrup and salt. Add butter. Cover. **Microwave at High (10) 3½ to 4½ Minutes,** stirring after 2 minutes, until thickened and sugar is dissolved.

1¼ cups light brown sugar (packed)

½ cup dairy half & half

2 tablespoons light corn syrup

⅛ teaspoon salt

¼ cup butter

1 teaspoon vanilla extract . . . . . Add vanilla and stir until smooth and well blended. Serve warm or cold.

Makes 1½ cups

Cinnamon Sugar Sauce

POWER LEVEL: High (10)
MICROWAVE TIME: 3 to 4 min., total

½ cup sugar . . . . In 1-qt. casserole stir together sugar, cornstarch, cinnamon and water, until completely smooth. Cover. **Microwave at High (10) 3 to 4 Minutes,** stirring sauce after 1½ minutes.

1½ tablespoons cornstarch

1 teaspoon cinnamon

1 cup hot tap water

2 tablespoons butter . . Stir in butter until well blended. Serve warm.

Makes 1⅓ cups

Lemon Sauce

Prepare recipe for Cinnamon Sugar Sauce, omitting cinnamon. Stir 1 tablespoon lemon juice and 1 to 2 teaspoons finely grated lemon peel into sugar mixture. (Shown over Early American Gingerbread on page 191.)